Politics in Thailand

Politics in Thailand

By David A. Wilson

Assistant Professor of Political Science
University of California, Los Angeles

PUBLISHED UNDER THE AUSPICES
OF THE SOUTHEAST ASIA PROGRAM
CORNELL UNIVERSITY

Cornell University Press
Ithaca, New York

PREFACE

THAILAND is not an important nation in terms of international power. It has a small population (perhaps 25,500,000). It can muster only a small army. It commands no important trade routes. Its economic potential does not appear to be very great and remains little developed even though Thai farmers contribute over 1,000,000 tons of rice to the international market each year. The kingdom's gross geographical product in 1950 has been estimated to have been only about one and a quarter billion dollars, of which 57 per cent originated in agricultural and extractive industry.

From the point of view of the Southeast Asian peninsula, however, Thailand is a nation of importance. Its size and potential are not out of proportion to those of its major neighbors—Burma, Vietnam, and Malaya—and are considerably greater than those of Laos and Cambodia. Given the strategic importance of this area south of China, east of India, and north of Indonesia, the study of Thailand has an extrinsic and immediate interest. As a member of the Southeast Asia Treaty Organization and an avowed adherent of the Western side of the Cold War, Thailand's nature and future are of particular interest to the United States of America and its allies.

As a political phenomenon Thailand also has genuine intrinsic interest. The fact that of all the nations of South Asia,

Thailand was the only one which retained most of the attributes of sovereignty during the century of European imperialism in that part of the globe is the kingdom's most prominent claim to political fame. But while this state of affairs symbolizes certain truths about Thailand and Thai leaders, it has, I think, tended to obscure others. The kingdom has been considered *sui generis*, impenetrably exotic, and inherently inexplicable. Much of the slim library of works on the subject has carried this message.

In fact, Thailand has been relatively neglected by Western scholarship until quite recently. This deficiency is particularly obvious in regard to politics. Most books published on Thailand before World War II were of the nature of general reviews of a variety of aspects of the country and society in which some discussion of politics formed a part. These works were most often the by-product of visits to Thailand for reasons other than deliberately planned research. Notable among such books are Sir John Bowring's *The Kingdom and People of Siam* (1857), Ernest Young's *The Kingdom of the Yellow Robe* (1898), and Cecil Carter's *The Kingdom of Siam* (1904). Probably the most valuable book of this kind is Walter A. Graham's *Siam*, particularly the second edition (1924). None of these early books makes more than a survey of the government, however.

The decade before World War II saw the publication of several more scholarly works touching on the politics of the kingdom, notably Kenneth P. Landon's *Siam in Transition* (1939), the same author's *The Chinese in Thailand* (1941), and Virginia Thompson's *Thailand: The New Siam* (1941). Two books by H. G. Quaritch Wales, *Siamese State Ceremonies* (1931) and *Ancient Siamese Government and Administration* (1934), also gave some insight into the kingdom's traditional forms of government.

In the post-World War II period, particularly the past decade, there have been a number of serious studies made of various aspects of Thai history and society. Most noteworthy among these are James C. Ingram's *Economic Change in Thailand since 1850* (1955), John E. deYoung's *Village Life in Modern Thailand* (1955), G. William Skinner's two studies *Chinese Society in Thailand* (1957) and *Leadership and Power in the Chinese Community of Thailand* (1958), and Walter F. Vella's *Siam under Rama III, 1824–1851* (1957). There have also been several short political studies, including W. D. Reeve's *Public Administration in Siam* (1951), John Coast's *Some Aspects of Siamese Politics* (1953), Walter F. Vella's *The Impact of the West on Government in Thailand* (1955), and James Mosel's essay, "Thai Administrative Behavior" (1957). None of these makes any attempt to analyze more than a few of the elements which make up the Thai political system.

My purpose in writing *Politics in Thailand* has been to analyze the general characteristics of political relationships there. I have sought to present them at a level of generalization appropriate to the fundamental, concrete experiences of Thai politicians and also to show them as a universal human phenomenon. My study is not at least three things which some readers might expect it to be. It is not a political history of Thailand, although all things discussed are given a historical dimension. It is not an exegesis of Thai legal statements as to what the institutions of politics are to be, although legal texts have been considered as evidence of intent and perception. It is not an effort to unravel the details of the incredibly intricate web of personal and clique relationships which are so apparent in Thai politics, although the nature of such relationships is considered as they have meshed and clashed with other forces and influences.

My study isolates and brings into relief those elements of Thai politics which constitute recurrent patterns of institutional behavior. In this sense my work is an examination of Thailand's constitution. I have also tried to bring forward the more prominent dynamic aspects of the structure of institutional behavior. I have emphasized the theme of the interplay of cultural, social, and legal forces which, unforeseen by the participants, has resulted in both gradual and sudden changes.

Throughout, the analysis is focused on the structure of power rather than on the development of policy. In this analysis ideological and policy matters enter as determinants of motive in the relationships of power. Thus adherents to a particular political group or organization may well be moved by the policy of that organization. Policy issues and ideological questions are considered in the following pages not on their merits but in terms of their effectiveness in strengthening power relationships.

Fundamentally, however, issues of politics are moral issues, and power has no ultimate meaning apart from its uses for good or evil. Therefore I would like to disclaim a moral fallacy which is often dangerously implicit in an analysis and description of behavior. It is the notion that what is, is right. This is not true, and no ascription of regularity to social relations is intended to demonstrate that there either cannot be or ought not to be change.

Behind this work lies my hope that it will contribute to a fuller understanding of politics in a certain type of sociocultural situation. I have tried to avoid treating Thailand as a quaint, exotic, and fundamentally irrelevant accident of history. With perhaps a suggestion of paradox, however, I believe the politics of Thailand has several peculiar characteristics which make it useful for comparative study.

First of all, Thailand's society is relatively simple. For example, it is for the most part ethnically homogeneous. It is located in a compact geographical area. It has no complex and rationalized system of castes or classes. Secondly, Thailand's society has been relatively stable. For almost two centuries it has not been disrupted by the intrusion of foreign rulers, wars of liberation, or any of the varieties of civil strife prevalent in the world of the 1950's. Finally, Thailand's politics is prima facie both sophisticated and successful. The government of the kingdom rules a substantial population of high civilization and maintains peace and other conditions conducive to humane livelihood. Moreover, the government has faced in its recent history a number of external challenges which to other peoples have proved overwhelming. These three aspects of Thailand's politics recommend it as a manageable and worth-while object of study.

The study is based on literary sources, personal observation, and systematic investigation. I spent about four years in the country at two different times between 1952 and 1958. During that time I had a variety of experiences including teaching, newspaper work, and scholarly investigation which provided some different viewpoints of Thai life. The interpretation that follows is the result.

I now turn to the gratifying task (though one difficult to express adequately) of acknowledging the help and inspiration of others. This work would not have been possible without the free gift of time by many Thai politicians and officials with whom I talked, some repeatedly and some at great length. I would like to thank them all. I would also like to acknowledge the help received in obtaining information from the National Library, the Čhulalongkǫn University library, the Secretariat of the National Assembly, the Department of the

Interior and the Election Division of the Ministry of the Interior, the Institute of Public Administration, and other offices of the government of Thailand.

Very special acknowledgment is due Mr. Warin Wonghanchao, my assistant while I was in Bangkok, for the endless variety of work he was willing and able to undertake for me. Thanks also go to Miss Rumpha and Miss Sumana, for help in problems of language and translation. The translations, unless an English source is cited, are, however, my responsibility. Others associated with the Cornell Research Center in Bangkok are due grateful acknowledgment.

I would like to express a very special gratitude to George McT. Kahin who, as my friend and mentor, has sustained and encouraged my work to a degree only I can appreciate. I also want to extend special thanks to Professor Lauriston Sharp, director of the Cornell Thailand Project, who has spent many hours reading and criticizing my work and talking about Thailand and Thai politics both in Ithaca and in Bangkok. Professors Knight Biggerstaff, Mario Einaudi, John M. Echols, and Frank H. Golay have all made substantial contributions to my intellectual growth which I would like to acknowledge here.

My thanks are also due to Mr. Herbert P. Phillips, Mr. Herbert Feith, Mr. Reuben Frodin, Mr. Robert B. Textor, Mr. Howard Swearer, Mr. Frank Trager, and Mr. A. M. Halpern, all of whom have read and carefully criticized parts of this work. Professor Fred W. Riggs, Mr. Edgar Shor, Professor William Gedney, Professor L. M. Hanks, Jr., and Mr. Marvin Brown have all given freely of their time in talking over aspects of Thai politics or Thai society, and I am grateful for their help. My thanks also go to Miss Kay Ellis, who typed the final manuscript.

Both the field research and the writing of this study were

made possible by the generous financial help of the Ford Foundation, which granted me a Foreign Area Training Fellowship. The Cornell Research Center in Bangkok also gave certain funds toward special parts of the research.

In the preparation of this book, I have drawn on materials previously presented in *Marxism in Southeast Asia* (1959) edited by Frank Trager and *The Role of the Military in Underdeveloped Countries* (1962) edited by John Johnson. I am indebted to The RAND Corporation and the publishers, Stanford University Press and Princeton University Press, respectively, for permission to utilize these volumes.

Finally, to my wife, Marie, for many contributions, my loving thanks.

It is perhaps fortunate for all the afore-mentioned that I alone am responsible for the weaknesses and mistakes.

D. A. W.

Los Angeles
May 1962

Note on the Transliteration of Thai

THAI names (with certain exceptions), publication titles, and terms have been transcribed according to a phonetic system based on that recommended by the Library of Congress Orientalia Process Committee which in turn is based on the "General System of Phonetic Transcription of Thai Characters into Roman" recommended by the Royal Institute of Thailand and outlined in the *Journal of the Thailand Research Society* of March, 1941. I have not distinguished long and short vowels, and I have changed the transcription of those central unrounded vowels transcribed ú to ü.

Briefly the system is as follows. The voiced unaspirated stops are written *b* and *d*; the voiceless unaspirated stops are written *p*, *t*, *čh*, and *k*; the voiceless aspirated stops are written *ph*, *th*, *ch*, and *kh*. The glottal stop is, in principle, not transcribed but occasionally a hyphen appears in its place between vowels for clarity. The voiceless spirants are written *f*, *s*, and *h*, and the voiced nasals, *m*, *n*, and *ng*. The nine vowels are written thus: front unrounded, *i*, *e*, *ae*; central unrounded, *ü*, *oe*, *a*; back rounded, *u*, *o*, *ǫ*. In the initial position, the voiced semivowels are written *y* and *w*. In the final position, they are respectively written as *i*, and as *o* when following *a* or *ae* or as *w* when following *i*.

CONTENTS

CHARTS AND TABLES

Politics in Thailand

I

HISTORICAL
BACKGROUND

THAI kingdoms in the valley of the Čhao Phraya River have
held sway over great areas of central mainland Southeast Asia
since the fourteenth century.[1] The fertile alluvial plain of the
river basin is superbly suited to the irrigated cultivation of
rice. Therefore it has been able to support the population
and provide the surplus of sustenance needed to maintain a
formidable state.

[1] The terminology used in reference to the Thai and Thailand is a
source of some confusion. The language and culture group (Thai,
T'ai, or Tai) lives in Thailand, Laos, northern Vietnam, southwest
China, and northern Burma. In various places, these people are known
as Thai, Shan, Lao, and, in the case of those living the Čhao Phraya
Valley, Siamese. The present kingdom of Thailand was officially
named Siam (Prathet Sayam) until 1939 as well as from 1946 to 1949.
In 1939 and again in 1949 the name Thailand (Prathet Thai) was
adopted. There is a suggestion of nationalism and even irredentism in
this name.

The most illustrious capital of the Thai kings before the Bangkok period was Ayutthaya (founded in the fourteenth century A.D.), located on the west bank of the river about 50 miles from the present mouth. The dynasties of Ayutthaya fell on evil days in the latter half of the eighteenth century. The last king was overthrown and the city sacked by its traditional Burmese antagonists in 1767. The kingdom then fell into disorder, and several aspirants contended for the throne. The dominions were finally reunited in a number of hard-fought campaigns by King Tak Sin of Thonburi, who reigned until 1782. He was deposed by his senior general, Čhao Phraya Čhakkri, the founder of the present Čhakkri dynasty of Bangkok.

The first three reigns of the Čhakkri dynasty [2] which ended in 1851 constitute a period of reconstruction of the glories of the traditional kingdom and the expansion of the domains of the kingdom. When Rama III died, the dominion extended

---

[2] Čhakkri, the dynastic name, is derived from the title held by the founder before he ascended the throne. The dynasty is also known as Rathanakosin, an honorific for Bangkok, the capital. The kings have elaborate honorifics, but it is convenient to refer to them as Rama followed by a Roman numeral designating the reign. This style was adopted by Rama VI for himself and his predecessors and is, in fact, precisely correct only for the first six reigns. Thai names and titles are a constant matter of confusion. Thai names are usually preceded by a title implying rank. It is convenient to refer to members of the royal family as Prince (e.g., Prince Damrong). Under the absolute monarchy nonroyal officials had one of the following titles, arranged in descending order—Čhao Phraya, Phraya, Phra, Luang, and Khun. Under the constitutional system no further titles of this kind have been conferred, and it has become customary to use either the title Nai, meaning mister, or a military rank. Older men still use their pre-1932 titles, however. Following the title is the given name and then the family name. People are best known by their given names and are customarily addressed by it plus a title. Such usage is generally followed in this book.

over present-day Thailand and in addition made claims in Kedah, Kelantan, Trengganu, and several other small Malay states; in Cambodia; in most of Laos; and in the hill country west of Chiengmai up to the banks of the Salween. The government was in a splendid state of vitality as it faced the power of Western nations which intruded their domination over Southeast Asia in the second half of the nineteenth century. The kingdom remained autonomous within the makeshift structure of empire.

Thailand's successful response to the challenge of Europe is largely a credit to the wit and will of three Čhakkri kings— Rama IV (Mongkut), Rama V (Čhulalongkǫn), and Rama VI (Wachirawut)—the wit to understand the changing place of the kingdom and the will to act accordingly. During the years of their combined reigns (1851–1925) the difficulty which overwhelmed all other public matters was to find the way to maintain the independence of the kingdom. The policy followed by all three was one of yielding the necessary concessions while at the same time reorganizing and consolidating what remained. It was a policy conducted with honor but without false pride and, as the course of events proved, it was a wise and realistic one.

Rama IV came to the throne at the age of 46. Throughout most of his previous adult life he had been a scholarly Buddhist monk, a student of European languages and science as well as of Buddhism and the traditional culture of Thailand. During the late years of the third reign, he was the center of an up-to-date (i.e., receptive to the West) group at court which after his enthronement became the nucleus of his administration.[3] This group appears to have been aware of the perilous meaning of European expansion in Asia and to have

[3] Prince Damrong Rachanuphap, *Prawat bukkhon samkhan* ("Lives of Important People"; Bangkok: Phrae Bhithaya Co., 1953), p. 115.

concluded that the kingdom's survival depended on conciliation of the rising powers.[4]

Two major concessions to the West were made in the fourth
reign (1851–1868). The first of these was the negotiation of
a series of treaties with European powers which opened the
kingdom to international trade by limiting the government's
power to levy duties and trade taxes. Thailand also consented
in these treaties to extend to the nationals of the respective
powers the privilege of extraterritoriality.[5]

These treaties marked the turning point between ancient
and modern Thailand. Both their effects and implications
struck at the traditional system of government. If the kingdom
was to survive, then fundamental fiscal and legal transformations were required. First of all by restricting the power to
levy taxes on trade, the traditional quasi-monopoly of trade
from which the throne had derived much of its cash revenues
was destroyed. Moreover, it could not be replaced by duties
adequate for the needs of the government without an increase
in volume of trade of such magnitude as to change the economy of the country.[6] As Sir John Bowring, the British nego-
tiator of the first of these treaties, remarked, the treaty "involved a total revolution in all the financial machinery of the
government." [7]

The provisions for extraterritoriality, granted in these
treaties, put in doubt the entire legal structure of the kingdom
and implied suspicion of the competence and justice of the

[4] Prince Damrong Rachanuphap, "The Introduction of Western
Culture in Siam," *Journal of Siam Society*, XX (Oct., 1926), 89–100.

[5] James C. Ingram, *Economic Change in Thailand since 1850* (Stanford, Calif.: Stanford University Press, 1955), pp. 33–35.

[6] Walter F. Vella, *The Impact of the West on Government in
Thailand* (Berkeley: University of California Press, 1955), p. 333.

[7] Sir John Bowring, *The Kingdom and People of Siam* (London:
Parker and Sons, 1857), II, 227.

administration. Both of these matters, the limitation on revenues and extraterritoriality, became increasingly difficult for the Thai government to manage in the following decades. Their ramifications were a stimulant to reorganization and reform.

In addition to the economic and legal concessions made in the treaties, Rama IV also was forced to yield a claim over territory. In the early 1860's, France from a base in Cochin China sought to extend its influence into Cambodia, which the king of Thailand claimed as a vassal state. When the French persuaded the king of Cambodia to sign a treaty of protection with them in 1863, the Thai objected strenuously but with little effect. Thailand continued to press its claim of sovereignty, however, and was ultimately able to negotiate a treaty with France by which Thailand relinquished its claim over Cambodia proper in exchange for French recognition of Thailand's sovereignty in the two Cambodian provinces of Battambang and Angkor. This treaty was signed in 1867 and was the first of many concessions of territory Thailand was forced to make to France and Britain before 1909.[8]

Rama IV was fundamentally a man in the spirit of traditional Thailand even though he was appreciative of both the threat and the value of the encroaching Western power. At bottom he was not prepared to comprehend or to accept the political and social implications of Westernization. During his reign few fundamental changes were made within the country, although the king and his immediate group did turn the face of the Thai ruling class westward. His legacy to his son, Rama V, was still largely a traditional Southeast Asian kingdom with its intricate web of feudal and bureaucratic relationships.

The reign of Rama V (1868–1910) was a period of trial

[8] D. G. E. Hall, *A History of South-East Asia* (London: Macmillian and Co., 1955), pp. 561–564.

and of reform. The young king came to the throne under most inauspicious circumstances as a boy of 15. Boy kings until then had been strikingly unsuccessful in the trying business of holding the Thai throne against ambitious rivals. In later years Rama V described his feelings in a famous letter saying:

I was fifteen years and ten days old, without a mother. None of my relatives on the maternal side were particularly able. As for my paternal relatives, that is to say the high princes, they were all under the influence of the Somdec Chao Phya [the regent] and had to look to their personal safety and well being rather than supporting me. . . . As for myself, at that age I knew nothing of statecraft and was so seriously ill that but a few people thought I would survive. At the time of my father's death, therefore, I was like a human trunk, the head of which had just been cut off, propped up merely to serve as a figure head.[9]

His crown was actually maintained by the longest regency in the history of the kingdom, and the kingdom's affairs were managed by the regent who had been a close associate of Rama IV throughout his reign.[10]

In addition to the fact that Rama V reigned as a minor for five years, another extraordinary set of events made it clear that a new era had arrived. During the regency, the king made two trips abroad to observe the manners, customs, and methods of European rule in Asia. In 1870 he visited Singapore, Batavia, and Semarang, and in 1872 he toured major cities of British

[9] *Chumnum phrarachaniphon nai rachakan thi 5, phak pakinyaka, phak 1* ("Collection of Royal Writings in the Fifth Reign, Miscellaneous, Part 1"; Bangkok: Fine Arts Dept., 1950), p. 13; the translation is from *Journal of the Siam Society*, XXXVIII, no. 2 (1951), 92.

[10] Vella, *Impact*, pp. 334–335; Prince Damrong Rachanuphap, *Phrarachaphongsawadan krung rathanakosin rachakan thi 5* ("Royal Chronicles of the Bangkok Dynasty, Fifth Reign"; Bangkok: privately printed by Samosan Sahamit, 1951), pp. 16–27.

India.[11] Such extended voyages outside the realm were un-precedented. Moreover, according to Prince Damrong they made a deep impression on the young king who was to reform his country.[12]

During the reign of Rama V, Thailand passed through the most pressing period of European imperialism. Both Britain and France were pushing out to protect and extend their empires. The British were on the Thai northern and western borders, in Burma, and also on the southern border, in Malaya. The French continued to press westward from Cochin China and Tongking into Laos and Cambodia.

The loss of territory over which the kingdom had claim of dominion took the form of a number of diplomatic dramas in which France, Britain, and Thailand all played important roles. The most dramatic of these were enacted between 1885 and 1896 when France was most insistent upon the territorial extension of its Indochina holdings. In 1888 Thailand was persuaded to yield to France its claim to Sip Sǫng Chu Thai in northern Laos. In the early 1890's France began to claim all territory east of the Mekong as rightfully part of the ancient Vietnamese domain and therefore as part of French Indochina. After a series of border incidents, France lent vigor to its demands by having a gunboat steam up the river to Bangkok. Britain, upon whom the Thai government depended for support, would do no more than suggest that the Thai yield, and they did so in a treaty signed in 1893. This forward policy of France alarmed Britain sufficiently to press for an agreement guaranteeing the neutrality of the Čhao Phraya Valley, and one was signed between the two European powers in 1896.

[11] Prince Damrong Rachanuphap, *Khwam songčham* ("Memoirs"; Bangkok: Klangwitthaya Press, 1951), pp. 366–400.
[12] *Ibid.*, pp. 396–400.

This agreement was the turning point in the struggle for Thailand's independence. In the following year Rama V went on a state visit to Europe, where he was well received. During the period of greatest tension between Thailand and the two European powers, the matter of extraterritoriality caused considerable difficulty. Whereas the treaty rights had originally been accorded to a limited number of foreign nationals, these rights were in the 1880's and 1890's extended, more or less arbitrarily, by the treaty powers to a group of persons designated protégés, i.e., Asians who claimed the protection of the powers. By this process great numbers of foreign Asians— Vietnamese, Cambodians, Chinese, Javanese, etc.—were removed from Thai jurisdiction.[13] Following the Anglo-French Agreement of 1896 and the king's tour of Europe, Thailand embarked on a policy of attempting to regain its legal sovereignty. The policy was pursued in part by bargains over further territorial concessions. Thus in treaties signed in 1904 and 1907 with France, Thailand yielded two Cambodian provinces and the province of Saiburi (west of the Mekong and opposite Luang Prabang) and in return gained jurisdiction over all French protégés. In a treaty with Britain in 1909, Thailand exchanged the four Malay provinces of Kedah, Perlis, Kelantan, and Trengganu for jurisdiction over British Asian protégés. This treaty marked the last concession Thailand made to a European power.

Because of the continuing question of extraterritoriality, the domestic law of the kingdom was a central matter in the relationship with European powers. The effort to end the special legal position of foreigners involved a complete revolution in the administration of justice and the forms of law. In

[13] Luang Nathabanja, *Extra-Territoriality in Siam* (Bangkok: Bangkok Daily Mail, 1924), pp. 247–250.

1897 a commission was appointed to study the problem of revision of the law in order to bring it into conformity with standards acceptable to the powers and thereby end the justification for consular courts. In 1908 the first of a set of new law codes, the criminal code, was issued. The process of revision and the first code served to encourage the British agreement in 1909 by which the eventual yielding of special treaty rights was accepted. The agreement was conditioned on the completion of codes on all subjects.[14]

Rama V died in 1910 at the not very advanced age of 57. He had reigned 42 eventful years. His greatest accomplishment was the preservation of the independence of his kingdom by skillful diplomacy and by hastening to adapt and adopt the methods of the West.

He was succeeded by his vivacious son, Wachirawut (Rama VI), who in turn was succeeded by his younger brother, Prachathipok (Rama VII). During the reigns of these two kings (1910–1935), the reforms and policies began by Rama V were worked out. A national consciousness arose in the governing class, the bureaucracy became infused with a spirit of professionalism, the nation reached a state of complete legal equality in the world, and a constitutional system was established.

Rama VI was the first Thai king to be educated abroad. His reign was a colorful period in which the select of Bangkok society were introduced to many social aspects of the West such as Western dress and cotillions. In addition, the king was in effect the founder of intellectual nationalism among the educated Thai. He wrote a number of articles in the press under various pen names which expounded the subject of

[14] René Guyon, *The Work of Codification in Siam* (Paris: Imprimerie Nationale, 1919), pp. 9–16; Luang Nathabanja, p. 275.

love of nation and also attacked the developing separateness of the Chinese community in the country.[15] From this period onward the immigrant Chinese community became an issue and a problem in Thailand.

The king also addressed himself to the primary problem of regaining full legal autonomy for the nation. He pressed forward the work of legal condification, and this was substantially completed in his reign.[16] World War I, which had effectively ended European imperial expansion, presented an opportunity to demonstrate Thailand's potential role in the world and to bring forward demands for equal treatment. The general sentiments in the country were by no means entirely with the Allied powers since the memory of the recent indignities suffered at the hands of Britain and France was fresh. The king, however, had been educated in England and personally felt close ties of affection with the British. Over strong objection from some of his advisers, he put Thailand into the war on the side of the Allies, and a small expeditionary force including a flying corps was sent to France.

The implications of this act were not left undiscussed at Versailles where the Thai delegation was quietly active. A course of negotiations was set in motion which by 1925 had resulted in the signing of new treaties with all powers. These treaties established a final date for the abandonment of all legal and fiscal limitations on the nation.[17]

Rama VI died in 1925 without a male heir and was succeeded by his younger brother, Prachathipok, who, since he was the youngest son in his line, never expected to come

[15] G. William Skinner, *Chinese Society in Thailand: An Analytical History* (Ithaca, N.Y.: Cornell University Press, 1957), pp. 164–165.
[16] Guyon, p. 16.
[17] Francis B. Sayre, "Siam's Fight for Sovereignty," *Atlantic Monthly*, CXL (Nov., 1927), 674–689.

to the throne. There was a considerable contrast between the reigns of Rama VI and VII which can be explained in part by the personalities of the kings. Rama VI was a strong-minded man with his own ideas and great energy. He believed in absolutism probably as much by temperament as a matter of theory, and he ran the government largely by himself. He did not utilize the training of his royal relatives as fully as either his predecessor or his successor and was not entirely popular with the more powerful among them. With the en-thronement of Rama VII, however, this attitude was reversed, and top positions as well as high policy came almost com-pletely under the control of a small group of high princes working with the king. Where Rama VI had been extravagant and colorful, Rama VII was careful and, apparently, rather shy.[18]

It is generally believed that Rama VII was personally in-terested in granting a constitution to the country as a crown-ing touch to the liberalization and modernization that had been the policy of the dynasty. This plan is said, however, to have met strong resistance among his advisers, and nothing was done before the revolution of 1932.

The Revolution of 1932

In 1932 a group of middle-level officials in the military and civil services organized a *coup d'état* which ended the control of the royal family over the government and established a quasi-parliamentary constitution. The origins of this event lay in three converging trends. First was the diminishing psy-chological power of monarchy. This was a result of demo-

[18] Vella, *Impact*, pp. 351–360.

cratic ideas from the West, the softening of the more
extravagant claims by the dynasty itself, and the diffident
personality of Rama VII. The second trend came from the
increased professional *expertise* among officials—especially
those who had been educated in Europe—which aroused resentment against the growing royal monopoly of power.
Third was the worsening state of finances in which the government found itself as a result of the developing world depression
and previous extravagance.

The so-called "promoters" of the coup were divided into
a variety of groups which over subsequent years divided, re-
formed, and in various ways struggled in the political arena.
The main division in the early years was between older army
officers who provided the prestige and younger military and
civil officials who in large measure provided the fire. Colonel
Phraya Phahon Phonphayuhasena is representative of the older
generation. He had received advanced military education in
Germany and had risen to a position of importance. But he
found himself bumping against the top level dominated by
the royal family. Phraya Phahon, who was the senior military
man of the coup group and subsequently became Prime
Minister, explained in later years that although he felt himself
well qualified in technical matters, the prince in command of
the army did not see fit to consider Phraya Phahon's advice.
This hardened his heart against the royal family and motivated
him to join the coup.[19] The younger revolutionaries, from
among which three men—Field Marshal Phibunsongkhram,
Nai Pridi Phanomyong, and Nai Khuang Aphaiwong [20]—

[19] Kulab Saipradit, *Büanglang kan pathiwat, 2475* ("Behind the
Revolution of 1932"; Bangkok: Čhamlongsan Press, 1947), pp. 110–116.
[20] The names of these three men are rather confused in the literature. Phibunsongkhram was born Plaek Kittisangkha. After he was
commissioned, he was given the royal title Luang Phibun Songkhram.

subsequently became Prime Minister, centered in a group which had studied in France in the 1920's. The group was divided into two segments, the military and the civilians. These younger men were moved both by the same frustrations as the older group and by a certain ideological conviction. In France they had had an opportunity to observe and study the politics of Europe and had absorbed some of the ideals underlying such politics. It is not surprising that the ideological leader of the coup group as a whole was Nai Pridi, a Doctor of Law from the University of Paris.[21]

During the years before the coup, the government suffered from financial difficulties. Inheriting a chaotic state of affairs from the preceding reign, the government of Rama VII found itself faced with a shortage of funds. An effort to effect savings was made by reducing the payroll and also cutting expenses from the royal court on down. This course of action created some uneasiness and dissatisfaction in the services, particularly, it seems, in the army.[22]

On June 24, 1932, at dawn the troops which were under the command of the coup group moved to seize certain key positions in the city of Bangkok and various high officials of the government. The end of the absolute monarchy was proclaimed, and the king was invited to rule under a constitution. Within a few days the matter was settled. The king accepted a provisional constitution. The coup group, organized under

---

Later he changed his name to Plaek Phibunsongkhram but is known as Field Marshal Phibunsongkhram. Pridi Phanomyong was given the royal title Luang Pradit Manutham and is sometimes referred to by that term. Khuang Aphaiwong was given the royal title Luang Kowit Aphaiwong but has not used it since his first term as Prime Minister in 1944.

[21] Düan Bunnak, *Than pridi rathaburut awuso* ("Mr. Pridi, Elder Statesman"; Bangkok: Soemwithaya Banakhan, 1957), pp. 1–18.

[22] Vella, *Impact*, pp. 356–360.

the name People's Party, appointed itself as provisional parliament, and a government acceptable to both the king and the People's Party was formed. This government was to set the pattern for postcoup governments on subsequent occasions. The Prime Minister was a conservative judge who had not participated in the coup but was adequately sympathetic with its more moderate objectives. His cabinet included the key figures in the coup.[23]

Absolutism had served the Thai well for centuries in an age when the form of society was static. With a self-contained, purely peasant culture, affairs of state were simple and the power of the government was limited. It performed the needed ceremonials and fought the inevitable wars and did little more. But from the beginning of the age of international commerce, this simplicity was doomed. So long as the monarchy provided the dynamic leadership for the necessary adjustments, its apparent position seemed strong. But its foundations were weakened, and with the development of a rationally organized and technically expert state structure it lost the effective ability to control the bureaucracy. When the monarchy faltered in its leadership, the internal dynamic of this great bureaucratic organization threw it off.

As a self-proclaimed constitutional government, the new regime needed to provide a constitution. The first of what was to be a long line of permanent and provisional constitutions was promulgated on June 27, 1932. His Majesty King Prachathipok, having announced that he had granted the request of the coup leaders that he remain on the throne as a constitutional monarch, said he was giving the kingdom a provisional constitution.[24] This constitution, apparently hur-

[23] Kenneth P. Landon, *Siam in Transition* (Chicago: University of Chicago Press, 1939), p. 17.
[24] *Bangkok Times Weekly Mail*, June 27, 1932, p. 26, and following issues; July 4, 1932, pp. 2–3, 10–13.

riedly drafted by Pridi Phanomyong after the successful coup,[25] was in force until the promulgation of the first permanent constitution on December 10 of the same year. It is of interest only in comparison with the succeeding version. Such a comparison gives some indication of the compromises necessary to keep the peace between the supporters of the royal house and the coup group.

The first substantive act of the new assembly, appointed by authority of the provisional constitution, was to set up a committee to draft the permanent constitution.[26] The committee returned with a draft on November 16, 1932, which it submitted along with an explanatory statement. The president of the committee announced that debate would necessarily have to be over quickly because the royal astrologers had selected December 10 as a most auspicious day for promulgation of the document and in the meantime it must be copied in three great manuscripts. The assembly thereupon adjourned for 10 days to consider the draft.[27] The assembly met again on November 25, debated morning and afternoon until November 29, and then adopted the final draft on December 2, 1932—in plenty of time for it to be engrossed. Although a few spoilsports wrote letters to the press complaining of unnecessary expenditure of public funds, the constitution was proclaimed to the nation on December 10, 1932, in a great ceremony of national celebration.

The structure of government outlined in this document was the classic parliamentary type with a single legislative house and a royal cabinet responsible to it. All power of in-

[25] Phairot Chaiyanam, *Khamathibai kotmai rathathammanun priap thiap* ("Lectures on Comparative Constitutional Law"; Bangkok: Thammasat University, 1952), II, 32.

[26] *Raingan kan prachum sapha phuthaen ratsadon* ("Reports of the Meetings of the House of People's Representatives"), 1st sess., 2475 (1932), pp. 13-14.

[27] *Ibid.*, pp. 357-368.

dependent action was taken from the king. The constitution contained one unique and crucial provision. It declared that because the country needed a period of tutelage before entering full democracy, half of the parliament would be appointed by the government. This condition was to continue until half the eligible voters had completed four years of school or to continue for 10 years, whichever came first. By this provision, effective executive control of the government was insured, and the pattern of the monarchy continued. This style has persisted to the present. The executive power has been inclined to brook no nonsense from parliament.

Since the *coup d'état* of 1932, internal politics of Thailand has been in large measure a matter of factional in-fighting. The end of the monarchical principle and of the king's domination of the group which controlled government and policy left something of a void. There has been no unanimity of opinion about who shall have power or on the proper method of getting power.

The first five years of the constitutional regime were filled with a number of significant events which amounted to a shaking down of the regime. The first was the *cause célèbre* of Pridi Phanomyong's Economic Plan of 1933. The People's Party at the time of its seizure of power had issued a manifesto which set forth a six-point program:

(1) freedom and equality of the people in politics, law, courts, and business;
(2) internal peace and order;
(3) economic well-being and work for all by means of economic planning;
(4) equality of privileges;
(5) freedom and liberty not conflicting with the foregoing;
(6) education for all.[28]

[28] Vella, *Impact*, p. 371.

Pridi took point three as a mandate to draft a general and rather elaborate economic plan for the nation.[29] The core of this plan was a radical statism which would have nationalized virtually all natural and industrial resources including land. The people, with some minor exceptions, were to become state employees. The plan immediately met strong opposition and was labeled, with perhaps some indelicacy but also with practical justification, as Bolshevism. Discord appeared in the People's Party between Pridi's civilian reformers and the more conservative army group.[30] The compromise premier seized the opportunity to close parliament and rule by decree. A broad law against communism was proclaimed, and Pridi was personally urged to go abroad. It looked briefly as if the People's Party had been shattered. With the settlement of the Communist issue, however, an army group somewhat different from that of 1932 but headed by Phraya Phahon recaptured power and set itself up as the government.

Within a few months the People's Party regime was threatened by a rebellion of provincial army and civil officials led by Prince Bǫwǫradet, a former Minister of Defense. The intentions of the rebels are still somewhat obscure, but it is clear that they threatened the monopoly of power of the People's Party. The rebel army reached the outskirts of the

[29] See Landon, pp. 29–31 and pp. 260–323, for a translation of the plan and related documents. For the original text of the plan and King Prachathipok's criticisms see Pridi Phanomyong, *Khao khrong kan sethakit khǫng luang pradit manutham lae phraborom rachawinit chai* ("The Economic Plan of Luang Pradit Manutham and the Royal Criticism"; Bangkok: Samnak phim S. Silapanon, 1956).

[30] There are various stories about the details of the rifts among different personalities on this occasion as on subsequent similar moments of tension. It seems to me impossible to arrive at historically valid conclusions about such details. The significant aspect of such personal antagonisms is that they can be relied upon to provide dynamic impulse to the life cycle of ruling groups. See the discussion in Chapter IX.

capital where it was then defeated and dispersed by the firm resistance of the government troops and the failure of expected treachery among armed units in the city. Although the king denounced this rebellion while it was going on and afterward, he was seriously compromised in the minds of the People's Party leaders. After the rebellion the place of royalty sank to its lowest in Thailand. Many high princes were in exile, and many of their supporters were in prison. Within two years of the failure of the Bọwọradet rebellion, Rama VII had gone into exile in Britain and abdicated the throne. The People's Party leaders presented the crown to King Čhulalongkọn's 16-year-old grandson, Prince Ananda Mahidon, who was in school in Switzerland.

In international affairs, Thailand's long struggle for complete autonomy was finally achieved by 1938, after Pridi, recalled and officially cleared of charges of communism, negotiated new treaties with all powers. These new treaties fulfilled the promises of the treaties of 1925 giving Thailand control over all legal and fiscal aspects of its administration. But by this time the world situation had changed. Thailand was bound up now with the fatal struggle impending in East Asia between Japan on the one hand and Britain and the United States on the other. The objectives of foreign policy were the same—continued independence—but the problem to be faced was new

The period of rising international tension coincided with the emergence of the figure of Colonel (later Field Marshal) Phibunsongkhram as the dominant personality in Thai politics. This man, coming from rather obscure origins and rising in the army by a combination of ambition and ability, a promoter of the coup in 1932, the officer who suppressed the rebellion of Prince Bọwọradet, had through various vicissitudes come to personal control of the army. He had been Minister of

Defense since 1934, and in 1938, when Phraya Phahon chose to retire, Phibun became Prime Minister.

While the general tone of the People's Party had been moderately nationalistic from 1932, the first Phibun era from 1938 to 1943 was one of extreme nationalism on the lines made popular in Italy, Germany, and Japan. In the years before the beginning of the Far Eastern war, Phibun and Pridi worked closely and enthusiastically in a policy which aimed to glorify the Thai nation first at the expense of the Chinese minority within the country [31] and subsequently at the expense of France in Indochina.[32] With characteristic acceptance and adaptation of foreign models, the government issued a series of acts, decrees, and pronouncements which produced many of the trappings if not the substance of fascism in the Thai setting.[33]

The approaching war in the Far East began to have its direct effect in Thailand with the expansion of Japan's interest south from China.[34] Japan's relations with Thailand were characterized by a cordiality cultivated on both sides.

But the Thai government was as surprised at the speed and vigor of the Japanese attack throughout the Pacific as were the British and Americans. At dawn on December 8, 1941, Japanese troops landed at a number of points on the Gulf of Siam without forewarning, and the Japanese ambassador in Bangkok presented the cabinet with the alternative of permitting passage of the troops on their way to Burma and Malaya or of fighting. The situation was complex. The idea of Asia for the Asiatics and a Japanese-led Asian co-

[31] Skinner, *Chinese Society*, pp. 261–272.

[32] Luang Vichitr Vadakarn, *Thailand's Case* (Bangkok: Thammasat University, 1941), *passim*.

[33] Vella, *Impact*, pp. 382–386.

[34] John L. Christian and Nobutaka Ike, "Thailand in Japan's Foreign Relations," *Pacific Affairs*, XV (1942), 195–221.

prosperity sphere was not without its supporters in Thailand as in the rest of Asia. At the same time the immediate prospect on December 8 was cooperation or the martyrdom of independence which had been preserved through the worst European imperialism. Although the impulse to resist was clearly present, the wherewithal was deficient. It was decided to accept the best terms possible from Japan and preserve some freedom of movement.[35]

Japanese troops were stationed in Thailand not as an occupation force but as friendly allies. Thailand signed a treaty of friendship and cooperation with Japan and subsequently declared war on Japan's enemies, Great Britain and the United States. Such a status permitted the government considerable control of affairs within its borders. From the very beginning various leaders were probing and exploiting all opportunities. The broad policy line of the nation was well summarized in a remark Field Marshal Phibunsongkhram is said to have made to his chief of staff in 1942: "Which side do you think will be defeated in this war? That side is our enemy." [36]

Pridi Phanomyong, the second most prominent man in the kingdom, left the cabinet to become regent immediately after the Japanese invasion. During the war he became the focus of the anti-Japanese underground which was in contact with China, the United States, and Britain. Phibunsongkhram also made some effort toward underground contacts late in the war, but it was his role to play the villain for the Allies in

[35] Nicol Smith and Blake Clark, *Into Siam* (New York: Bobbs-Merrill Co., 1946), pp. 261–266; Čharun Kuwanon, *Chiwit kan tọsu khọng čhomphon p. phibunsongkhram* ("The Life and Struggle of Field Marshal P. Phibunsongkhram"; Bangkok: Aksọn Charoen That Press, 1952), pp. 149–220.

[36] Net Khemayothin, *Ngan tai din khọng phan-ek yothi* ("The Underground Work of Colonel Yothi"; Bangkok: Thanakan, 1957), p. 1.

the postwar years. The effect of this development of a two-pronged approach toward the war situation was to resound in postwar politics. While the details have not been revealed, it is clear that the war broke up the unity of purpose of the People's Party, a breach that never healed.[37]

By 1944 it had become sufficiently clear to a number of politicians that Phibunsongkhram would have to go. He was, of course, completely unacceptable to the Allied powers which, it was apparent, would drive Japan out of Southeast Asia. At the same time he had also lost the confidence of the Japanese through his schemes of duplicity. Because of the deprivation and hardship which had resulted from the general breakdown of the economy of Southeast Asia, Phibun's popularity in the country had ebbed. Pridi was able to engineer in parliament the overthrow of the government, and Phibun was replaced by Khuang Aphaiwong, who was well known in the country and was generally uncommitted abroad. Khuang held the office of Prime Minister until the defeat of Japan.[38]

Thailand was better prepared for Japan's defeat than for its initial victories. The kingdom's major problem was to avoid treatment as a defeated enemy. The Free Thai underground was the national ace in the hole. Thailand's ambassador to the United States, Seni Pramoj, had from the very beginning of the war declared his Free Thai status and had built good relations with the United States government. Pridi also had contacts through the Office of Strategic Services organization with which he had been cooperating in the last years of the war. The United States government was inclined to be lenient. Seni Pramoj rushed back to the country after Japan's defeat

[37] *Ibid.*, p. 45; Khuang Aphaiwong, *Kan tọsu khọng khaphačhao* ("My Struggle"; Bangkok: Pramuansan, 1958), pp. 67–79.
[38] Khuang, pp. 83 ff.

to take over as Prime Minister under the aegis of Pridi. Seni
took charge of negotiating a postwar settlement. By the beginning of 1946 he had signed a treaty with the less sympathetic British, and Thailand was accepted again in international
society

Postwar Thailand

The war shattered the People's Party. In getting the nation
out of the conflict it was necessary to drop Phibunsongkhram
and also to allow the reentry of royalist sympathizers on the
political scene. Postwar politics was largely a matter of
struggle among three groups for dominance. One was the
military group, personified in Field Marshal Phibunsongkhram
and based of course mainly in the army. The second group, at
first centering on the figure of Pridi Phanomyong, was rooted
in parliament and the civil service. The third group, considerably smaller but having much prestige, was traditionalist
and royalist in character. Khuang Aphaiwong and Seni Pramoj
were its public leaders.

Because of the overthrow of the Phibun dictatorship and
the extrication of Thailand from its position of international
embarrassment at the war's end, Pridi Phanomyong was, in
1946, in a position of great prestige and, for the moment, unchallenged dominance. His prospects, however, were not
enviable. He faced a turbulent political situation with not
only the parliament but also the military and civil services
which were divided by wartime sentiments and ambitions for
the future. The economic situation was precarious as well.
Inflation was under way, and the country's major exportable
commodity—rice—was tied up by agreements with Great

Britain.[39] Perhaps most serious of all problems was the growth of widespread corruption of the government aggravated by a breakdown of morale and discipline in the services and new opportunities available in the chaotic conditions of the postwar years.[40]

On the international scene, Pridi also faced a number of problems. Although Thailand had avoided for the most part being treated as an enemy by the Allied powers, there remained the necessity to rebuild its prestige in the world, to settle relations with neighboring lands which were in a turbulent state, and to seek admittance to the organization of the United Nations.[41]

Early in 1946, the parliamentary situation was crystallized by a general election and the promulgation of a new constitution. The drafting of this document was done in a number of committees in consultation with Pridi, the Prime Ministers, and the House of People's Representatives during the last half of 1945 and the early months of 1946. The new version of the constitution was promulgated in May, 1946.[42] Parliament was changed from a single house with half the members appointed by the government to a bicameral form. The upper house (Senate) was elected by the popularly elected lower house.

For the first time parties began to play a role. Two groups (Constitution Front and Cooperation Party) which combined to make a substantial majority supported Pridi and packed the Senate with his followers. The opposition formed around

[39] Alec Peterson, "Britain and Siam: The Latest Phase," *Pacific Affairs*, XIX (Dec., 1946), 364-372.

[40] W. D. Reeve, *Public Administration in Siam* (London and New York: Royal Institute of International Affairs, 1951), pp. 69-77.

[41] Russell H. Fifield, *The Diplomacy of Southeast Asia, 1945-1958* (New York: Harper and Brothers, 1958), pp. 237-243.

[42] Phairot Chaiyanam, pp. 70-76.

Khuang Aphaiwong and the Democrat Party. The complexities of the situation also forced Pridi to come down from his
position of eminence as regent and elder statesman to accept
the prime ministership himself. In this exposed position he
was vulnerable to the vigorous attack of the nation's highly
skilled slanderers and rumor mongers as well as to more restrained critics.

Whether or not Pridi might have weathered the perils of
this office under more or less normal conditions will never
be known. His first two months of office were occupied by
the promulgation of the new constitution and the election
of the upper house which took place on May 24, 1946. On
June 9 the young king Ananda Mahidon, who had returned
to the country after spending the war period in school in
Switzerland, was found shot in bed. The circumstances sur-
rounding this unfortunate event were obscure and mysterious;
and the government was unable or unwilling to make a con-
clusive and credible explanation of the shooting. Thereafter
the burden of criticism against Pridi turned from corruption
and partisanship to regicide. Within two months Pridi had
voluntarily resigned the Prime Minister's office in favor of his
own choice, Luang Thamrong Nawasawat, a fairly conservative and independent follower.

The general decline of the prestige and power of the Pridi-
dominated Thamrong government continued, as a result of
corruption and economic difficulties as well as the king's death
case, and caused its enemies to take heart. One aspect of the
overthrow of Phibunsongkhram in 1944 had been the dis-
mantling of his control clique within the army and a strong
attempt to prevent the development of any new group of army
politicians. Such an effort was widely resented among the
officers, however. In the autumn of 1947 a broad conspiracy
of troop commanders was organized around the figures of

two retired high officers. In this conspiracy Field Marshal Phibunsongkhram, living in semiretirement, was no doubt indirectly instrumental, and the memory of his services to the army was a persuasive tool. On the night of November 8, 1947, the group moved to seize power completely and set aside the constitution. Pridi fled the country, and Luang Thamrong and other Pridi followers went into hiding to avoid arrest.

Fearing difficulty both internally and in diplomatic relations if they were overly bold, the leaders of the *coup d'état* asked Khuang Aphaiwong, head of the Democrat Party, to form a caretaker government until a new election could be held in January, 1948. Following the election he was able to form a government on the basis of an unstable majority in parliament.

The status of the government having been regularized by the election and, soon thereafter, by foreign recognition, Khuang settled down to solve some of the immediate problems of the country. But the Coup d'Etat Group (Khana Rathaprahan), as the organization behind the coup was called, was impatient to show its hand, and on April 6, 1948, less than two months after the formation of the government, Khuang was forced out at gunpoint. Field Marshal Phibunsongkhram succeeded him as Prime Minister

The period from 1948 to the end of 1951 was one of extraordinary instability even for Thailand. In the light of subsequent developments it is clear that a variety of groups and cliques were maneuvering for advantage. The supporters of the fugitive Pridi were driven out of politics. The conservative Democrat Party group, under Khuang, had been given some substance and reputation by the governments between November, 1947, and April, 1948. This group was strongly represented in parliament and was rather peevish about the ouster of their leader by force. Within the military also there was no unity. The navy and marines were not in sympathy with the Coup Group. Top naval leaders were intimates both of Luang Thamrong, the last Prime Minister before the coup, and of Khuang. On the whole, the navy was antagonistic to Field Marshal Phibun and other army men. Within the army, younger professionals were not easily persuaded that the old officers who had been discredited in wartime should reestablish their hold. The Coup Group was divided within itself in the effort to take complete charge of the army and other government organizations. Field Marshal Phibun played his own game, gathering around him supporters from the wartime period, and other leaders began fighting among themselves.

The period was marked by several serious showdowns. On October 1, 1948, a group of army general staff officers was arrested, tried, and convicted of revolt. They were the most aggressive leaders of the anti-Coup Group faction in the army. In February, 1949, a revolt broke out in the middle of Bangkok in which it is understood the marines were supporting a comeback by Pridi. The revolt failed and was followed by a purge, the equal of which had never been seen in Thailand. A number of officials and politicians were shot under mysterious circumstances.

During 1950, one of the two senior Coup Group leaders was forced into exile under vague charges of rebellion. In June, 1951, the navy and marines showed their hand again by kidnaping Field Marshal Phibun and going into revolt. This was suppressed by the army and air force after three days of heavy fighting.[43] At this point two younger men had emerged as dominant powers. They were General Phao Siyanon, an intimate associate of Phibun since 1933 and the son-in-law of the remaining senior Coup Group leader, and General Sarit Thanarat, a junior Coup Group leader and

[43] John Coast, *Some Aspects of Siamese Politics* (New York: Institute of Pacific Relations, 1953), pp. 52–54, 57–58.

professional army man. General Phao was director-general of police and General Sarit commander of the Bangkok army at this time. Field Marshal Phibun, still Prime Minister, was a captive of the situation in which he stood as chief between the two.

In the same period the parliamentary situation had gone through some radical changes. At the time of the coup the constitution of 1946 was set aside in favor of a provisional constitution. One of the important acts of the Khuang government was to appoint an assembly of members of parliament and experts to draft a new permanent constitution. Their work was finished at the end of 1948, and a new form of parliament was established which added to the troubles of the military. It was a bicameral assembly of which the lower house was elected by universal adult franchise. The new provision for an upper house was a departure from the long effort to exclude the throne from politics and marked the beginning of a resurgence of royal authority. Members of the upper house were appointed by the king upon the countersignature of the president of his Privy Council, whom he appointed with the countersignature of the president of the lower house of parliament. For the first time in the experience of the military, the selection of parliament was completely free of direct control by the government. The military leaders were thrown into a position of dependence upon elected members of parliament. The constitution put other irritating limitations upon the military as well.

The constitution lasted three years, from January, 1949, to November, 1951. During that time Khuang's Democrat Party held a majority of seats in both houses. Although the Democrats never attempted to exert their parliamentary power, presumably recognizing the ultimate futility of such an effort, they were a potential threat. At the end of 1951, after the emergence of the Phao-Sarit combination, the military moved to eliminate this irritant. On the night of November 29 the national radio broadcast an announcement signed by a group of military and police officers that suspended the constitution and reestablished the constitution of December 10, 1932. This action was justified by the assertion that the "present world situation has fallen into a generally critical condition due to the danger of the Communist aggressive threat." [44]

The legal situation was somewhat complicated by the fact that King Phumiphon was at that moment on his way back to Thailand from Switzerland after completing his education. It may be surmised that he was not altogether pleased with the abrupt change of the rules, but there was little that he could do. Soon after his arrival in the capital, a royal proclamation was issued (December 6, 1951) announcing the reestablishment of the 1932 constitution but also revealing that it was necessary to amend certain sections. The appointed category of members of the House of People's Representatives provided for in this constitution was charged with the task of amendment. The House set up a drafting committee whose report was adopted on February 26, 1952, without substantial debate or opposition.[45] The list of 123 appointed members included only a tiny sprinkling of nonmilitary men.

The Coup Group government adopted anticommunism as a keystone of its policy both domestically and abroad. Within the country the policy was directed against the Chinese community and also against opposition politicians. The anti-Communist drive culminated at the end of 1952 in a wide roundup of suspects in what was reputed to be a Communist

[44] "Thalaengkan" ("Announcement"), *Royal Thai Government Gazette* (*from the Thai Version*), Special Edition, vol. LXVIII, pt. 71, Nov. 30, 1951.

[45] Phairot Chaiyanam, pp. 151–155.

plot. Those arrested and later tried included writers, intellectuals, young military officers, and Chinese who were associated with leftist thought. At the same time an anti-Communist act was rushed through parliament which granted broad powers to convict on charges of Communist conspiracy.

It is a temptation to say that the breakup of the Phibun-Phao-Sarit group was inevitable. The triangular structure in which Phibun had to balance the remaining two against each other was inherently unstable. The elements were unequal and difficulties evidently too great. Phao and Sarit, both about the same age, were in natural competition for the succession to Phibun. It is not possible to say whether this competition was personal, but in the course of events both Phao and Sarit became the heads of separate clique structures based in different institutions, the fates of which were bound to the success of their leaders. Phao as director of police and secretary-general of the government's parliamentary organization led a complex group which was free of and opposed to the dominance of the army under Sarit. These factors were the basis of the tension which led to the coup of September 16, 1957.

The dramatic turning point seems to have been the tour of the United States and Great Britain by Field Marshal Phibun in 1955. Upon his return it was announced that a new era of democracy had arrived. Several royal acts were passed to give emphasis to this idea. An act for the registration of political parties, the first in Thai history, and an act for decentralization of power to local governments were particularly important. At the same time the Prime Minister set up two institutions of public information which developed rapidly. They were the regular press conference of the Prime Minister and the so-called "Hyde Park." The Hyde Park scheme gave opportunity to politicians to discuss politics publicly in the central park of Bangkok.

The motive behind this sudden lifting of repression in the

realm of politics is difficult to know clearly. Apparently Phibun was impressed during his visit in the United States and Britain by the relatively untroubled position of power enjoyed by popularly elected leaders such as President Eisenhower and Winston Churchill. Being himself in a difficult, not to say shaky, position between two strong men, he may well have thought of this as a way out. Anticipating the general election scheduled for early 1957, he may have decided to build himself a base of power in the general public. It is also possible to imagine that, having been impressed by the general strength and wealth of democratic countries, he made a simple equation in his mind. It is fully consistent with his conception of himself as the founder of the modern Thai nation that he might have decided to leave full democracy as the crowning achievement of his long career.

In any event, the establishment of democracy in 1955 opened the way to one of the most colorful and active periods in Thai politics. A number of political parties were registered, and the elements in the coming struggle began to shape up quickly. The parties, of which ultimately there were more than 25, can be sorted into four groups. The first and pivotal group was actually only one party, the massive official government party, Seri Manangkhasila, with the government's parliamentary supporters as its core. General Phao was its secretary-general and organizing genius. The second group included a number of parties which supported individuals in the government but not the government as such. The most interesting of these were the Thammathipat, which supported Phibun, and the National Democratic Party, which supported Sarit. In the course of events neither of these came to anything. The next group was also one party, the Democrats, with Khuang Aphaiwong as head. This group of conservatives made up the only party of any continuity of tradition. The final group comprised a number of leftist parties. The two most important of these, the Free Democrat and the Economist, were built around members of parliament from northeast Thailand. This group, which subsequently united with smaller parties to form the Socialist Front, led the fight against the government's foreign policy

The second and perhaps more important aspect of the period was the sudden and almost violent outburst of public discussion. After years of repression the public of Bangkok was given carte blanche to discuss politics. This "great debate" was led, one might almost say monopolized, by the press and the Hyde Park speakers who vied with each other in the violence and audacity with which they attacked the government and what it stood for. All in all, the government leaders found it difficult to get a hearing for their views, and one might suspect that the public was somewhat skeptical about their democratic tendencies.

As the election campaign developed, it became apparent that Phibun and Phao were going all out for popular support while Sarit stayed in the background. Phao poured everything available into the Seri Manangkhasila Party. It was reported that at least 20,000,000 baht (1 baht = U.S. $0.05) was spent by the party, 10 times as much as any other organization.[46] The civil service was dragooned into party work. While no other party succeeded in putting candidates up for all 160 seats, the Seri Manangkhasila endorsed no less than 230 candidates.[47] Phibun, who was head of the party, chose to lead a slate of candidates in the Bangkok district against the most popular opposition leader, Khuang Aphaiwong.

Tension was high on election day. The results of the polling were a moral defeat for Seri Manangkhasila. Accusations of

[46] *Bangkok World,* Feb. 25, 1957.   [47] *Ibid.,* Feb. 26, 1957.

corruption of the polls actually began the day before election when a follower of Field Marshal Sarit demanded an explanation for falsified ballot papers which he claimed to have discovered marked with Seri Manangkhasila numbers. From then on the press and the streets of Bangkok were clamorous with readily accepted stories of ballot-box stuffing, double voting, intimidation, and falsification of returns. Against such a background the fact that Seri Manangkhasila had returned a bare majority of the elected members and that at least half their incumbent members had been defeated was adequate to shatter any popular triumph or prestige.

The election opened a brief period of political instability for the country comparable to 1932–1935 and 1947–1951. Public dissatisfaction with the conduct of the election in February, 1957, which was vigorously expressed in the press and among students, caused the government to declare a national emergency. Sarit, who had successfully disassociated himself from the Seri Manangkhasila Party, was appointed commander in chief of all the forces. In public statements he proclaimed the elections to have been "filthy" on all sides and assumed responsibility for cleaning up the mess. In spite of his dominant position, Sarit made no immediate move against the Phao faction. His administration of the emergency served to dissipate public outrage but did little to revive public respect for General Phao or the Seri Manangkhasila.

Phibunsongkhram was able to form a government in March following considerable difficulty in conciliating the various factions in the party and military groups. Although General Phao received the powerful Ministry of the Interior, Sarit and his followers together held the stronger cabinet position. After a series of events in parliament and the cabinet, Sarit broke openly with Phibun and Phao. On September 16 a *coup d'état* by a military group under Sarit's leadership took place. Tanks rolled, the constitution was suspended, and parliament was dissolved. Phibun fled the country, and a few days later Phao was permitted to go into exile.

New elections, administered by a caretaker government appointed by the military group, were conducted in December. They were carried out in a quiet atmosphere, and public interest was focused on their manner rather than on political issues. The dominance of the military was a foregone conclusion. A new Unionist Party, which had appeared before the 1957 coup with the tacit support of Sarit, ran against the Democrats and the Socialist Front. After the election Sarit announced the formation of a new combine, to be called the National Socialist Party, which was intended to amalgamate the Unionists, appointed members of parliament, and any others who would support the new government. General Thanǫm Kittikhačhǫn, Sarit's immediate deputy in the army, took over the office of Prime Minister. Sarit, who was in a precarious state of health, left the country almost immediately for extended medical treatment in the United States.

Thanǫm's government was faced with a number of difficulties which weakened its grip on power. The more fundamental of these were fiscal (a result of falling revenues which presented obstacles to the drafting of a budget satisfactory to the bureaucracy) and political (a result of the disparate elements in the government's military and parliamentary support). The conflicting claims and demands of these elements, exacerbated by opposition politicians and newspapers, prevented the government from taking any decisive action toward possible solutions. The situation moved from one minor crisis to another until October, 1958, when Field Marshal Sarit suddenly returned to the country and, in another bloodless coup, overthrew the entire system and established himself temporarily as a military dictator. A number of the loudest parliamentary and journalistic opponents of the government were jailed, and political parties were outlawed.

In January, 1959, a new interim constitution was decreed.[48] It provided for an appointed assembly with the dual function of legislative body and constitutional commission. The government was given broad discretionary powers. The field marshal took the Prime Minister's office himself. A very tough line was proclaimed against dissident elements and corruption. The new army group under Field Marshal Sarit again established tight control over the machinery of government in the pattern of 1947 and 1951.

Field Marshal Sarit, calling himself the leader of a revolution, directed the attention and energies of his government to two areas of difficulty—national peril and national development. Difficulties in both Laos and Cambodia, on the kingdom's eastern frontier, provided manifest threats to Thailand's international position, and the field marshal justified his short-run constitutional powers by these exigencies.

The government's adoption of a national economic development plan and a national educational development plan in 1960 served as a longer-run basis for political legitimation.[49] In 1961 Field Marshal Sarit declared to the constitutional assembly that he saw the education system and the economy as the foundation for democracy. He told the prospective draftsmen of a new constitution that they could depend upon him to devote his energies to these problems while they concerned themselves with the "appropriate" institutional forms for Thailand.[50]

[48] *Ibid.*, Jan. 29, 1959. See Appendix B.
[49] *Royal Thai Government Gazette (from the Thai Version)*, Oct. 28 and Nov. 7, 1960.
[50] *Rathasapha San* ("Journal of the National Assembly"), Nov., 1961, pp. 75–82.

II

ECONOMIC AND SOCIAL SETTING

THAILAND is a rich country, and national wealth makes a difference in national politics. The country's wealth must be judged in comparison with the number of people, which is not large, and their enterprise, which is not negligible. Food and raw materials provide the basis for simple and fairly comfortable rural and urban life. Tin and wolfram ores are mined in the isthmus and western hills and exported in ore form. The forests of the north produce quantities of valuable timber, the most important of which is teak. In the south Thailand joins the rubber-producing area of Malaya, and many small holders grow rubber for export in crude form. Although these products are important in international trade and contribute substantially to foreign exchange, revenues, and the total national product, the industries and people engaged in them are not many, perhaps 1 or 2 per cent of the population.

The cultivation of rice occupies more than three-fourths of

the working people of the nation; [1] perhaps 95 per cent of the cultivated land is planted to rice,[2] and the rice product is the most valuable item of the economy as well as of foreign trade. There are, of course, other crops cultivated either for commerce (such as coconuts, peanuts, cotton, tobacco, sugar cane, and rubber) or for consumption (such as fruits and vegetables), but their cultivation is either a narrow specialty or a side line.[3] In other words, Thailand is a wet rice cultivation society par excellence with a surplus of more than 1,000,000 tons of grain a year.

The kingdom has an area of about 200,000 square miles in central mainland Southeast Asia and a population of about 25,500,000. The climate is warm, moist, and monsoonal. Within the country there are four distinct regions. The northeastern plateau is a semidesert drained by sluggish rivers into the great Mekong River. The Chao Phraya River watershed, almost entirely in Thailand, consists of two regions—the northern highlands, which are drained by the Ping, Wang, Yom, and Nan rivers, the major tributaries of the Chao Phraya, and the central region, a broad alluvial plain and delta. The southern isthmus, essentially north-south mountain ridges drained by short rivers into the Gulf of Siam and the Indian Ocean, connects the mainland of Asia with the Malay Peninsula. Thailand borders Cambodia on the east, Laos on the east and north, Burma on the north and west, and Malaya on the south. It has 1,650 miles of coast on the Gulf of Siam and the Indian Ocean.

Bangkok is the only city in the country. More precisely,

---

[1] Thailand, National Economic Council, *Statistical Yearbook of Thailand*, 1952, pp. 336–342.

[2] James C. Ingram, *Economic Change in Thailand since 1850* (Stanford, Calif.: Stanford University Press, 1955), p. 50.

[3] *Ibid.*, p. 51.

the city is the Bangkok-Thonburi metropolitan area with a population of over 1,000,000. After Bangkok, there is nothing more urban than several large towns of some regional importance. The extraordinary manner in which Bangkok dominates Thailand may be best understood in geopolitical terms. Located astride the Čhao Phraya River near its mouth, the capital is in a position to control the prime gateway to international trade. This natural drainage through the city has been paralleled and elaborated by railways from all regions. The development of commerce in the past century and the government's strategic control over it in the capital city also simplify the problem of revenues. Much of the cost of government to the country at large is collected in a painless slice off the top of trade and commerce centered in the port and city.[4] In its strategic location controlling access to the country, the government has been able to moderate the impact of the commercial revolution on the agricultural population and to inhibit social upheaval.

The Economy

Thailand has always had plenty of land available to accomplish the economic objectives and maintain the standard of living of an increasing population. At the same time, although the economy appears to have changed considerably, the fact is that such change has been generally a matter of quantity rather than kind. On balance the economic system remains today much as it was a century ago.

During this past century the economy of Thailand as a whole has changed from a system of largely self-sufficient

[4] *Ibid.*, pp. 182–188.

production to a system of international trade based on rice-grain surplus, supplemented by forest products, rubber, and tin. In the middle of the nineteenth century, the government of Thailand yielded to the pressure of events and ended the policy of restricted commercial intercourse with the rest of the world. In 1855 the first of a number of commercial treaties with Western powers was signed by Thailand and Great Britain. This event is a convenient mark for the opening of the Thai economy to the world. For two reasons the course of change has been and continues to be most gradual. First, the government of the kingdom by means of a consistently conservative economic policy has been reasonably successful in mitigating the impact of new economic forces. Secondly, the abundance of land has permitted both the absorption of increased population and the realization of increased production without doing violence to social relations. Therefore severe pressure of population on the land and the related problems of peasant indebtedness, landlord-tenant conflict, and impoverishment of the rural population have occurred rarely in Thailand. At the same time, because of the very small scale of industrial development, the working-class proletariat is small. The economic development of the country has not produced that kind of economically depressed group—a desperate peasantry or an oppressed and depersonalized worker group—to which revolutionary programs might offer an appeal.

There have been three principal changes in the Thai economy in the past century.[5] These are the development of a partial money economy, the change from largely subsistence production to specialization and exchange in parts of the economy, and the appearance of an ethnic aspect to the division of labor. The first two changes have affected only part

[5] *Ibid.*, p. 216. The following discussion of Thailand's economic history is largely based on Ingram.

of the nation even today. The third developed as a result of Chinese immigrants' filling the new demand for free labor and for merchants in an exchange economy. The social effects of economic change and development have not been radical, and the social system of the greater part of the population has not been seriously disrupted. Ingram summarizes the history of economic change in this way:

The Thai population has largely remained in agriculture, and has neither improved techniques nor increased the proportion of capital to labor. Moreover, most changes in the economy as a whole have been in volume rather than in kind. New methods have not been used, new products have not been developed. No product of any importance (besides rubber) is exported today which was not exported in 1850.[6]

It would appear that this rather striking fact about the development of the Thai economy in certainly one of the most dynamic, not to say revolutionary, centuries of human history reveals a great deal about the Thailand of today. When it is kept in mind that almost 85 per cent of the population of the kingdom continues to find its livelihood in agriculture and when it appears that the way of life of the cultivator has been changed little in a century, it is to be expected that the overwhelming proportion of the population would be little affected by economic motives for political activity.

Subsistence is still the basis of rural household economy after 100 years of commercial revolution. The primary crop of the representative farmer is rice, which is at the same time the staple of his family's diet. But as the kingdom's economy became monetized and participant in the world market, rice, as the main cash crop, was produced in vastly greater quantities.[7] The relative importance of cash in the household economy

[6] *Ibid.*, p. 209.   [7] *Ibid.*, pp. 43–52.

varies with the amount of surplus rice available for sale.[8] The tendency in areas of substantial rice surplus, particularly in the central region, is for the household to live on its own rice supplemented by fish and vegetables gathered from the lush countryside. Any other goods, such as cloth, meat, tools, animals, and luxuries, are bought with cash from the proceeds of the sale of surplus rice.[9] The proportion of bought goods in contrast to those produced at home may be reduced to nothing in more remote regions, and it is certain that many families in the nation are still virtually self-contained economic units. Luxury is not the proper term to use when describing rural life in Thailand, but it is a land of sturdy and wholesome peasantry. Suffering and fear do not dominate any significant part of the population, although hardship is not unknown or even, in some regions, unfamiliar.

This comparatively happy situation is a result of natural blessing to a great extent, of the plentiful rich land in proportion to its population, and the climate and geography are such that fish abound in the streams and canals and many fruits and vegetables grow without care. But the policies of a government whose interest lay in stability have contributed to this security of the rural populations. While the state has been extremely conservative economically in order to forestall internal unrest and external intervention, its policies have not been inflexible. On the one hand, the state has prevented any rapacious commercial exploitation of the land to the fundamental detriment of subsistence. On the other hand, the state has increased its police services to the end of greater domestic peace and also pursued an enlightened land policy which has

[8] *Ibid.*, p. 250.
[9] Kamol Odd Janlekha, *A Study of the Economy of a Rice Growing Village in Central Thailand* (Bangkok: Ministry of Agriculture, 1955), p. 132.

in fact strengthened the cultivator's title and secured his status.[10]

The lure of cash is a most potent force for social change in a subsistence economy, but some areas of the country, particularly in the northeast region, still have little contact with the world market. The average distance of farms in that region from a highway open six months or more is over 8.5 miles and from a railway over 50 miles. The national average for the same distances are over 6 and 42 miles, respectively.[11] These figures merely illustrate the still-incomplete penetration of the world into the Thai countryside. The large number of farms far from transport are operated almost completely in a self-sufficient manner producing their own food, fuel, housing, and tools.[12]

Nevertheless, the commercial market does touch much of the country. The farm survey of 1953 revealed that the average cash expenditures of farm families for living expenses in the kingdom was 2,877 baht (U.S. $140 approx.) while it was 3,983 baht in the central plain, the most commercialized rice farming area.[13] The national average for farm operating expenses was 664 baht, and the central plain's average 1,335.[14]

Coupled with the large element of subsistence farming in the economy is the small freeholder pattern of farm tenure. Both the agricultural census of 1950 and the Economic Farm Survey of 1953 agree that over 85 per cent of the cultivated land is operated by the owner.[15] The small percentage of land operated on a rental basis is for the most part held on a fixed rent tenure, either cash or kind, so that the evils of share-

[10] Ingram, pp. 75–87.

[11] John C. Kassebaum, *Economic Farm Survey, 1953* (Bangkok: Ministry of Agriculture, 1955), p. 80.

[12] Ingram, p. 208.   [13] Kassebaum, p. 38.   [14] *Ibid.*, p. 32.

[15] *Ibid.*, pp. 62–63.

cropping are generally absent from the Thai agricultural scene.[16]

As might be expected in the light of the pattern of an independent peasantry operating in a quasi-subsistence manner, the problem of rural indebtedness is slight. The Economic Survey drew the conclusion, as a matter of fact, that in view of the total value of assets in the hands of farmers the percentage of debt (1.79 per cent) was exceptionally low in comparison to total farm valuation and that use of the sound credit standing of the Thai farmers for productive investment is an unexploited possibility.[17]

These data indicate in a rough manner the economic status of the rural population of Thailand. They are in sound, solvent condition and, in spite of increased commercialization, they continue to follow a way of life rooted in tradition, to a great extent self-sufficient although on a low standard of living. They are insulated from many of the blows and disruptions of market instability. It is reasonable to conclude from this evidence that any expansive thrust of political or economic demand is for the moment negligible. The Thai peasantry must be considered a fundamentally conservative element in Thai society. When the relative size of this group in proportion to any or all other socioeconomic groups is considered, the conservative course of Thai history is not surprising.

Nonagricultural industry has its own socioeconomic peculiarities. In general, it may be said that nonagricultural industry is organized in two ways—either as government or government-aided industry or as private investment by aliens, primarily Chinese. This division has come about historically as a result of the reluctance of the Thai to enter into occupations—other than government service—on a purely cash basis. There are several explanations for this situation. For example,

[16] *Ibid.*, pp. 70–73.   [17] *Ibid.*, p. 251.

agriculture as a source of livelihood has historically been sufficiently secure so that it retained a comparative advantage, both psychological and financial, over the wage or profit incentives of labor or business.[18] The same sufficient security is characteristic of government service. In addition, it is highly esteemed and influential. Because trade lacked traditional support and market exchange relationships might have strained traditional social bonds, the Thai evidently found this field unattractive and left such opportunities to aliens.

The pattern of industrial organization is also a matter of social significance. Private investment in nonagricultural as well as in agricultural enterprise is organized as small family business. The home workshop, the home store employing largely family labor or a few wageworkers integrated into the family pattern, is the dominant form of business activity. The World Bank estimated that in 1958 there were only about 300, or about 2 per cent, of a total of 16,000 industrial establishments in the country which employed over 50 workers. This figure included at least 40 government-operated or government-aided establishments. The estimated employment of all these establishments, large and small, was 316,000 workers.[19] The bulk of urban workers are probably employed in small shops mostly with less than 10 workers.[20] This type of quasi-family organization, while implying poor standards of hygiene and safety, involves an intimate pattern of interper-

[18] Ingram, pp. 210–211.
[19] International Bank for Reconstruction and Development, *A Public Development Program for Thailand* (Baltimore: Johns Hopkins Press, 1959), pp. 89–90.
[20] *Final Report of the Demographic and Economic Survey, 1954* (Bangkok: Central Statistical Office, Office of the National Economic Development Board, 1959), vol. I, Table 22-1, p. 457; Lauriston Sharp, ed., *Thailand* (New Haven: Human Relations Area Files, Inc., 1956), pp. 431–435.

sonal relations between employer and worker and probably includes a higher degree of social integration than is characteristic of large factories.[21] Since the boss and workers are approximate social equals in a small shop, this pattern does not stimulate working-class solidarity or working-class political activity.

The role of the state in the economy is a traditional one. In the premodern period, foreign trade from the capital was a monopoly of the king and probably one of the primary sources of royal income.[22] This monopoly was abandoned with the opening of the country to European traders, and liberal principles took a leading position in the commercial sector until the end of World War II. In the postwar period the government has played an important part directly and indirectly in the marketing of rice abroad with related control of collection and export.[23]

Such activities as irrigation, railway construction, electricity production, and water supply have been the exclusive domain of the state. The government also entered early into manufacturing. The first government factory was built during World War I, and in subsequent decades the state has entered the sugar, distilling, and tobacco business.[24] The state also plays a part of undetermined but substantial importance in the private sector of the economy. There are a number of public organizations which have monopolistic powers in certain industries such as trucking, forestry, and many others. Such powers, while not used to end the participation of private capital, give the state immense influence over industry. Moreover, the government or its agencies own shares in private corporations and on occasion have guaranteed the financial standing of privileged firms.

[21] International Bank, *Public Development Program*, p. 88.
[22] Ingram, pp. 26–29.   [23] *Ibid.*, pp. 87–92.   [24] *Ibid.*, pp. 139–144.

In those few industries where there are comparatively large organizations, the state plays an important role. For example, the State Railways of Thailand is the largest single employer among economic enterprises.[25] The largest manufacturing organization in the kingdom is the State Tobacco Monopoly.[26] Other government enterprises—sugar refineries, liquor distilleries, textile and paper mills—are among the few large-scale industrial establishments. This creates the peculiar situation that in an economy based on liberal principles a large segment of the nation's industrial laborers consists of state employees.

But the society of Thailand is still preponderantly preindustrial in its organization, patterns of living, patterns of production, and technology. In general, it has been insulated from the revolutionary changes of the past century both because of the accidents of geography and history and because of the conscious efforts of its leaders.

The Society

The late John Embree said in his discussion of Thailand's social system:

The first characteristic of Thai culture to strike an observer from the West, or from Japan or Vietnam, is the individualistic behavior of the people. The longer one resides in Thailand the more one is struck by the almost determined lack of regularity, disciplined and regimentation. In contrast to Japan, Thailand lacks neatness and discipline; in contrast to Americans, the Thai lack respect for administrative regularity and have no industrial time sense.[27]

[25] Thailand, *Statistical Yearbook*, 1952, p. 340.   [26] Ingram, p. 142.
[27] John F. Embree, "Thailand—A Loosely Structured Social System," *American Anthropologist*, LII (1950), 182.

Embree summed up this characteristic of Thai social life with the felicitous bit of jargon, "loosely structured." By this phrase he meant to underscore the degree of independent action and the importance of the individual will among the Thai. He was comparing his observation of Thailand with his views of the Vietnamese and Japanese, but the characterization etches one of the most striking qualities of Thai society. The Thai seems determinedly autonomous. He carries the burden of social responsibility lightly. Within a structure of social obligation and rights, he is able to move and respond to his personal and individual inclinations without suffering a mortal social wound.

This characteristic personal avoidance of regimentation by the Thai is supported by at least two fundamental social factors. Hinayana Buddhism, the religious tradition from which Thai Buddhism springs, has as its central tenet salvation through individual accumulation of merit. The making of merit and progress along the eightfold path to enlightenment are viewed as lonely and individual tasks in which, generally speaking, one may not look to others for assistance.

> By oneself is evil done;
> By oneself one suffers;
> By oneself evil is left undone;
> By oneself one is purified.
> —Dhamapada [28]

This conception of the cosmic role of the individual certainly reinforces the flexibility of permitted behavior and mitigates feelings of social obligation. The significance of any relationship between this cosmic outlook and social behavior is neither easily measured nor demonstrated. Nevertheless, the

[28] Dr. Luang Suriyabongse, *Buddhism in Thailand* (Bangkok: Phrae Bhithaya Co., n.d.), p. 20.

persuasive case made by Max Weber for the interdependence of cosmic view, religious interest, and social behavior makes analogues wherever observed worthy of note.

The second factor of importance in strengthening Thai "individualism" has been the very substantial luxury of resources in which Thai society has developed. Economic satisfactions resulting from this situation have been discussed above. At this point it is sufficient to point out the relationship between material plenitude and individualism. Since their arrival in the valley of the Čhao Phraya River in the thirteenth century, the Thai people have had a surplus of land resources, the fundamental form of economic wealth. To this day population density in heavily cultivated areas of Thailand is below comparable areas in China, Japan, Vietnam, or Java. This surplus had encouraged something of the pioneering spirit and economic self-reliance among the Thai. Land surplus and low population density are correlated with loosely organized villages and geographic mobility.[29]

Observers agree that the communities of rural Thailand are loosely organized in comparison with their counterparts in other Asian areas. Patterns of village allegiance or community solidarity are weak. The institutions defining a village are quite likely to be not concerned with the corporate entity of the village itself, which may be quite incidental. For example, in the central plains village of Bang Chan, the Bang Chan temple and government school define the village by their clientele. Thus the community, insofar as there is one, exists to support or receive the services of these institutions.[30] Although the situation may be somewhat extreme in Bang Chan because it is a settlement of recent origin, the character

[29] Ingram, pp. 43–44.
[30] Lauriston Sharp *et al., Siamese Rice Village* (Bangkok: Cornell Research Center, 1953), pp. 16–18.

of a village as a clientele is consonant with the traditional social organization of the kingdom. The nature of the co-operative effort of villagers is another aspect of the loose and individualistic character of rural social organization. Such work, which is not uncommon particularly at harvest time, is structured on the basis of personal reciprocity of the individual members of fairly stable groups. It is not conceived as duty to community, village, or any other corporate body.[31] Moreover, the villages have no status as legal persons and apparently hold no community property.

The fluidity of social status characteristic of both traditional and modern Thailand appears to be a natural correlative of the individualistic type of personality. Both social mobility and geographic mobility are clear aspects of the society. Mobility and its relationship with individualism contribute to the weakness of group and community institutions. Geographic mobility takes two forms, urbanization and rural migration. The population of Bangkok, the only genuine metropolitan center of the country, has increased substantially in the past 30 years.[32] The increase is statistically large enough

[31] Embree, p. 188; Sharp *et al.*, *Rice Village*, pp. 153–155. Some evidence exists that in older villages in the northeastern part of the country there may be greater elements of cooperation. But observers in the area have also noted the free and open nature of the settlements. Cf. Charles Madge, *Village Communities in Northeast Thailand* (New York: UNTAA, 1956).

[32] The population of Phra Nakhon (Bangkok) Province increased at a rate of 37.62 per cent in the period 1919–1929 and 29.86 per cent in the period 1937–1947, against a national rate of 24.97 and 20.59 for the same periods. It should be noted that the 1937–1947 period includes the war years, which temporarily arrested the urban flow (Thailand, *Statistical Yearbook*, 1952, p. 8). A population survey of Bangkok Municipality in 1954 showed that about 38 per cent of the population had migrated to the city within the previous seven years. Of these about 96 per cent were from other areas of Thailand (*Demographic and Economic Survey, 1954,* vol. I, Table 7–14, p. 123).

to indicate considerable movement from the country into the city. This evidence is supported by impressions received in the city. Many people of all classes who were born and raised in provincial areas have come to the city for education or to seek their fortunes. This situation would not appear to be a development of recent years only. The ambitious individual has always gone to the capital to improve his lot.[33] In addition to country-city migration, however, there has apparently been at various times movement around the country. Although documentation is difficult to provide, it is evident that the opening of new lands which has taken place in the past century involved substantial movements of people.[34]

Geographical mobility goes hand in hand with an idealized tradition of mobility up and down the scale of social status. Old Thai society was made up of a system of social grades. At the bottom were slaves of two types (redeemable and unredeemable).[35] The remainder of the cultivators were free men. Upon this foundation of cultivators and laborers was a complex structure of grades and offices which comprised the ruling group. This group was divided broadly into royalty and nonroyalty, each sector being subdivided into a large number of ranks. The ranks of nonroyalty were in fact non-hereditary commissions from the king or high officials and

[33] Kumut Chandruang, *My Boyhood in Siam* (New York: John Day Co., 1940), pp. 13-27.

[34] The village of Bang Chan which has been under study by the Cornell Thailand Project is known to have been first settled about 80 years ago. Migration into the village, however, has been going on continually. How widespread this situation is, of course, remains open to question. Cf. Sharp *et al.*, *Rice Village*, pp. 23-24; Janlekha, p. 30, Table 5.

[35] Horace G. Quaritch Wales, *Ancient Siamese Government and Administration* (London: Bernard Quaritch, Ltd., 1934), p. 59; W. A. Graham, *Siam* (2d ed.; London: Alexander Moring, Ltd., 1924), I, 237-238.

were more like civil service offices than European noble ranks. A man might well hold several ranks durings his life and his son hold none. Royal status was obtained hereditarily, but there was in theory no continuity of status from father to son. Rather the passage of royal status from generation to generation was governed by a rule of declining descent so that in five generations a family out of the line of royal succession returned to common status.[36]

Although the significance of the correlation of land surplus and the characteristic Thai Buddhist ethic with this condition of rural mobility and community looseness may be questioned, it is sufficient for the present purpose to cite these facts as aspects of Thai individualism and self-reliance, as well as fluidity of status. In the face of this fluid system, any analysis of Thai society in terms of class structure is most problematical. On the one hand, social status was and still is graded to an extraordinary degree, while, on the other, it is difficult to see any rigid lines of class division. Social gradation has been given substance in both law and language.[37]

The traditional law of social organization in Thailand was designed to structure society as a monolith integrated to serve the state, or more precisely the king. The guiding principle was the Thai *sakdi na* system. Each man was allotted thereby a degree of dignity and privilege measured quantitatively. Free men obliged to the king or some royal department of the

[36] Mary Rosamond Haas, "The Declining Descent Rule for Rank in Thailand: A Correction," *American Anthropologist*, XXIII (Oct.-Dec., 1951), 585-587.

[37] A characteristic of the Thai language is the fact that it is extremely difficult, if not impossible, to avoid the expression of relative social status of speakers. That is to say that all terms of personal reference —pronouns, titles, and the like—carry with them definite connotations of social status. The linguistic function of social status in Thai is comparable to that of gender in English.

court were registered and received the *sakdi na* number 25.
With this as a base each official or prince was allotted his
sakdi na grade up the scale. This system was part and parcel
of the patron-client relationship by which Thai society was
traditionally integrated. Each freeman was supposed to be
under the protection of a certain royal official and obliged
to his department for *corvée*. These departments were social
as well as administrative organizations of the state. Within
each there was a structure of officials and freemen.[38]

Traditional Thai social structure thus emphasized a consciousness of status rather than class. It can be seen that insofar
as institutions made up of legal and nonhereditary relationships of right and obligation and vertically organized social
groups had a genuine vitality, they worked against the development of class consciousness. It would be easy to over-
estimate the vitality of traditional institutions, of course, but
on the other hand it would be a facile projection to read a
dogma of class consciousness into traditional Thai society.
There are little data available on the day-to-day conditions
of a century or more ago, but there is no evidence of the kind
of social unrest which would indicate class conflict. Social
grades shaded delicately from one to another, and the Thai
view of society was up and down within groups rather than
over any impenetrable wall of class distinction. If aspiration
to rise in society moved a man, the next higher grade was never
beyond the hope of attainment.

Status among the Thai was, and as a matter of fact continues
to be, conceived as a personal attribute. A man's social position is a consequence of his merit, in either the Buddhist or
civil service sense of the word. As merit of men is capable

[38] Wales, *Siamese Government*, pp. 35, 49–50; M. R. Khükrit Pramoj,
"The Social Order of Ancient Thailand (II)," *Thought and Word*,
I (March, 1955), 17–18; Graham, I, 234–237.

of delicate gradation, so is social status. As merit is something that can be acquired rather than an accident of birth, so is social status.

It is not surprising that the social system of present-day Thailand, as an outgrowth of this tradition, is similarly fluid. Although the *sakdi na* system and other aspects of the intricately structured legal forms of the old social system have been abolished,[39] social mobility and fluidity of social groupings are, if anything, a greater reality than formerly.

The primary social division of Thailand is between country and city. The two are largely self-contained but tangential. Rural society in Thailand is remarkably homogeneous throughout the country in terms of economic status and occupational role. There are, of course, certain specialties other than the fundamental work of farming and fishing, but these are for the most part services for the producers. Significant in such social homogeneity is the conspicuous lack of any group of rural landlord gentry.[40] The representative rural type is the small freeholder operating his farm on a more or less commercialized basis. The stability and security of rural life in Thailand are factors essential to the make-up of the nation's present situation and underlie certain characteristics of government and politics as they are now known.

The more complex urban, primarily Bangkok, society is

[39] The *sakdi na* as part of the civil service organization was replaced in 1928 by a civil service law. As a mode of structuring society it disappeared with the reorganization of the interior and military administrations and the abolition of slavery and *corvée* in the reign of Rama V (1868–1910). See below, Chapter III.

[40] A likely explanation for the lack of a class of landlord gentry in rural Thailand is that until recently, at least, there has been much more arable land available than labor to till it. Since the authority to muster labor derived from royal authority, persons on the rise along the scale of power gravitated to the court.

related only marginally to the rural society. It is here that the mobility and finely graded social status which characterize Thailand are most clear. At least five criteria of status have been noted: economic standing, political power and connections, education, outlook on life, and family background.[41] In various permutations and combinations they determine social status. Urban society may then be analyzed into five social status groups or classes: old elite, new elite, upper middle class, lower middle class, and lower class.[42] In regard to this analysis, however, it is particularly necessary to exercise caution. As Herbert Phillips has said:

The term [class] must be understood not in the sense of restrictive and exclusive classes but rather in the sense of a group of discrete individuals who by virtue of various implied and arbitrary criteria have a common prestige status. . . . [M]embers of a particular class do not have a strong sense of kinship with other members of their own class. Indeed, this general lack of class consciousness, of common class interests, prohibits Bangkok society from being viewed as having a true class system. . . . Bangkok society is in no way marked off into static social compartments, out of which people never move. Present urban society is characterized by an extraordinary amount of status (or class) mobility, both up and down the ladder: people are constantly changing jobs, changing their statuses, moving in and out of the city, and the like. As a result of this frequent movement, class lines tend to become blurred and unclear.[43]

The same caution applies to an analysis of Thai society into self-conscious economic classes or occupation groups. Any generalized feeling of belonging to the working class or

[41] Sharp, ed., *Thailand*, p. 165.
[42] G. William Skinner, *Leadership and Power in the Chinese Community of Thailand* (Ithaca, N.Y.: Cornell University Press, 1958), pp. 18–19.
[43] In Sharp, ed., *Thailand*, pp. 162–164.

peasant class or ruling class is at most incipient. The common attitude, which is consonant with the general Thai attitude of personal orientation, is the more personal "I am a farmer," "I am a taxi driver," "I am a government official." Opportunities for change and for advancement, as well as the ties of many with the countryside and families on the farm, work to dissolve the feeling among urban people. Among farmers the strong tradition of the independent freeholder involved in that pattern of personal relationships which made up his entire life role has inhibited the development of a feeling of class membership.

Another factor which retards the growth of class feeling is the rather strong nationalistic feeling toward the large Chinese minority. This group, whose members may be either native or China born, constitutes around 10 per cent of the population of the kingdom. The Chinese as a social minority evoke an attitude of ethnic solidarity within their group and against it as well and at the same time cut across certain socially significant occupational groups such as free wage laborers and merchants, both large and small.

Overseas Chinese are the most important minority in the country socially, economically, and politically. They are distinct culturally and linguistically from the Thai and have been immigrating to Thailand for centuries from the regions of Southeast China. The total number of ethnic Chinese was estimated in 1959 by Skinner to be about 2,600,000 out of a total population of about 20,800,000.[44] The great flood of

[44] G. William Skinner, "Overseas Chinese in Southeast Asia," *Annals of the American Academy of Political and Social Science*, CXXI (Jan., 1959), 137. Although Skinner's total population estimate is smaller than the International Bank estimate (*Public Development Program*, p. 3n), it may be assumed that the percentage of ethnic Chinese broadly defined is more than 10 per cent of the total population.

immigration took place in the first three decades of the twentieth century.[45]

Chinese in Southeast Asia are well known for their powerful commercial position, and those in Thailand are no exception. Encouraged to come first as wage labor in such construction as canal and railway building, the enterprising and mobile Chinese proletarian was quick to appreciate the trading possibilities in a developing commercial economy. As the quantity of rice which was entering the world market increased at an explosive rate, the opportunity for middlemen and milling expanded accordingly. While the Thai peasant population directed its enterprise into expanding production and the Thai upper class was absorbed with increasing administrative and political work, the potentials of rice processing were left to Chinese energies for development.[46]

Initially Chinese immigration was almost entirely male, and those who chose to settle in Thailand were apparently assimilated into the Thai population with little difficulty. Around 1910, however, Chinese women began coming in great numbers, and the basis was laid for the growth of a distinct social community. Chinese education was begun, and Chinese community organizations were founded to provide social and welfare services to the Chinese. The Thai elite became quickly aware of this new development, and as early as 1914 the "Chinese problem" was proclaimed, more or less officially. Since the 1932 revolution, some control of the Chinese economic and political position has been a common policy of all governments.[47] The political side of the problem

[45] G. William Skinner, *Chinese Society in Thailand* (Ithaca, N.Y.: Cornell University Press, 1957), pp. 63 and 175.

[46] Ingram, pp. 71–74.

[47] Cf. the statement of Phraya Song quoted in Kenneth P. Landon, *Siam in Transition* (Chicago: University of Chicago Press, 1939), p. 312.

has been from time to time exacerbated by domestic Chinese politics as well. During the Japanese attempt to conquer China, the Chinese in Thailand were openly anti-Japanese and the Thai government for both domestic and international reasons embarked on a virulent campaign to cut off immigration, break the Chinese domination of internal commerce, and end Chinese education. In the late 1940's a similar campaign coincided with the vicissitudes of the Chinese revolution. In the most recent years a somewhat intimidated Chinese community, split within itself over the political situation in China, has been seeking a *modus vivendi* with Thai political leaders.[48]

The four most important economic or occupational groups in Thailand are: (1) the rural agrarian-fishing class, the basic producers of the country; (2) the laboring class, primarily but not exclusively urban since it includes miners, forest workers, and construction and transport workers; (3) the governing group, including civil and military officials, politicians, and princes and the like, primarily urban but in touch with the countryside; and finally (4) the commercial class, ranging from large import-export merchants to peddlers with a carrying pole, another connecting link between country and town, nation and world. The comparative sizes of these groups are suggested by their respective percentages of the total labor force: the rural producers constitute about 84 per cent of the total; the laboring group, excluding rural labor, is about 3 per cent; the governing group comprises about 3 per cent; and the commercial group is about 6 per cent.[49] The fact that economic group lines in some cases coincide with ethnic

[48] G. William Skinner, "Chinese Assimilation and Thai Politics," *Journal of Asian Studies*, XVI (Feb., 1957), 237–250; Skinner, *Leadership and Power*, pp. 302–319.

[49] Thailand, *Statistical Yearbook*, 1952, pp. 336–342. The remainder are in unclassified occupations.

group divisions is an important aspect of the society of Thailand. For example, the rural producers and governing groups are almost exclusively Thai; the commercial group is dominated by Chinese and other non-Thai nationalities although the Thai, particularly in recent years, are by no means completely excluded. Historically, free labor was largely Chinese because much labor was recruited by the government from China in the last century in preference to paying the high wages necessary to attract Thai off the farms.[50] In recent years, it would appear on the basis of impressionistic observation that this situation is breaking down, both because of assimilation over a generation of Chinese workers into the Thai ethos and because the incentive of wages is becoming more compelling for the Thai in certain rural areas. Therefore the labor group, which might be expected to develop some approximation of class consciousness, is splintered into various ethnic groups.[51]

Groups and Their Attitudes

In the society of Thailand there is a clear distinction between those who are involved in politics and those who are not. The overwhelming majority of the adult population is not. The basis for this distinction lies in the view of the world and society as a system of statuses of differing rights and powers which results in a "we and they" psychology of politics. For the greater number of people in the country,

[50] Ingram, pp. 56–57.
[51] Sharp, ed., *Thailand*, pp. 431–435; Skinner, *Leadership and Power*, p. 19.

politics is viewed as properly the affair of politicians or, more broadly, of the ruling class. Because all statuses are associated with degrees of moral excellence, they tend to be considered responsible only to themselves or to higher powers for the proper attributed behavior. Representation or delegation upward associated with downward responsibility is not part of Thai political psychology.

The peasantry as the basic productive force constitutes more than 80 per cent of the population and is the foundation of the social structure. But its inarticulate acquiesence to the central government and indifference to national politics are fundamental to the political system. A tolerable economic situation which provides a stable subsistence without encouraging any great hope for quick improvement is no doubt the background of this political inaction. In the foreground is a real freedom from political and social pressures. Relatively secure in his property rights and usually safe from bandits and plunderers, the Thai farmer may go about his vital activities in security. Although he may fear the intimidation of maverick policemen or his son may get caught in the draft and spend two hard years in military service, usually if the farmer looks to the government for anything, and this he rarely does, it is for assistance. It should provide, and often has done so, a school for his children. If there is a road to town, the government has built it. If his canal is deepened, the government will help. If there is hardship, the government may well provide emergency rice. Because government revenues are for the most part levied indirectly, all this does not seem to cost much.[52] The peasant is free to pursue the activities that are important to him—the cultivation of his

[52] An important source of revenue for the government has been an export tax on rice which, of course, is indirectly a production tax on the farmer.

fields, the promotion of his religion, and the enjoyment of leisure.

Observers agree that the effect of religion and piety in the Thai countryside is very great. The principal activity of its adherents is to support monastic life for men who seek enlightenment, i.e., control over their desires and escape from the endless round of birth and death—or, more simply, the gaining of personal merit. The temple or monastery is generally the principal institution of a village, and its support is an important responsibility of the villagers. The abbot and other venerable monks of the temple are often community leaders whose influence is usually directed for peace and harmony. The government's attitude toward religion is one of benign support which is coupled with a loose control. It is both law and tradition that monks have no place in politics, and the clergy is excluded from a role as an organized national political force.[53]

Urban workers are, like the peasants of the nation, but a latent political force. In numbers they are still relatively few, but, more importantly, labor organizations are undeveloped. The ethnic division between Chinese and Thai workers has retarded the growth of a labor movement because of politically inspired competitiveness and because of great differences in organizing skill between the two groups. The Chinese come from a society in which the tradition of private social organization is strong. They have for years tended to band together in speech groups, benevolent societies, and secret societies for their own welfare and to the exclusion of the Thai. Thai society has no tradition of private organizations, however, and only in recent years has the beginning of a trade union movement appeared. At present trade unions of various degrees of strength do exist in large industrial establishments such as

[53] Sharp, ed., *Thailand*, pp. 338–375.

oil company installations, the State Railways, and the State Tobacco Monopoly. These unions have been in turn grouped loosely in politically inspired labor federations which have little function other than observation and propaganda. But because the bulk of urban workers are employed in small shops, organization is difficult if not impossible.[54]

The ruling class in Thailand may be divided into a three-tiered pyramid. The top section includes perhaps 10 to 15 persons who do or could dominate the ruling class and the country as a whole by manipulating the various political forces. This group includes senior military commanders, a few leaders of great reputation gained in the revolution of 1932 or in the interplay of politics since, and perhaps two or three men around the throne. At any given time there have never been more than six or eight such men in power.[55] The second level of the pyramid is made up of perhaps 1,000 persons including military officers mostly of general officer rank, special-grade civil servants, prominent members of parliament, some princes, and some particularly powerful businessmen. Although the top group dominates, it is only through their manipulation and control of the second group that they gain, hold, and use power. The base of the ruling-class struc-

[54] *Ibid.*, pp. 431–435.

[55] See Chapter IX for a discussion of the nature of the ruling group and its organizations which comprise the upper levels of the ruling class from another point of view. In the last years of the Phibun regime (1954–1957), the true men of power would include Field Marshal Phibunsongkhram, Field Marshal Sarit Thanarat, Police General Phao Siyanon, Field Marshal Phin Chunhawan, Fleet Admiral Yuthasat Koson, Air Marshal Fün Roniphakat, Worakan Bancha, General Thanọm Kittikhačhọn, and Lieutenant General Praphat Charusathian. Their countergroup would include Khuang Aphaiwong, M. R. Seni Pramoj, Prince Dhani Niwat, and perhaps some other intimates of the king.

ture is what may be called the political public. It is made up of educated and articulate citizens in Bangkok and the provincial towns who interest themselves in the details of political activity, and they are for the most part high school and university graduates. They are largely in the bureaucracy but also include those schoolteachers and professional people not employed by the government, journalists and other writers, and Thai members of the commercial white-collar group. It may be estimated that the ruling class as described is between 1 and 2 per cent of the total adult population of the country.

In Thailand the ruling class is distinguished from the general population most clearly by the level of education. As is peculiarly characteristic of bureaucratic societies such at Thailand, education, at least in the procedures of bureaucracy, is a universal trait of the dominant group. Their ability to dominate depends in some measure upon superior know-how in the forms and methods of government and upon a monopoly of this kind of know-how. Up to the present, the educational system of Thailand has been admirably suited to that end. There has been a great change in the system in recent years, as in so many other aspects of Thai society. It is now the primary recruiting agency for the elite. Recent broadening of the educational system [56] throughout reflects new complexities of government and a process of enlarging the ruling class. At the same time, because the educational system touches virtually every Thai, it serves both as an outlet for ambition and as a mode of screening candidates for important posts.

The educational qualification for the upper levels of the ruling class is a university degree or its equivalent. Responsible

[56] Manich Jumsai, *Compulsory Education in Thailand* (UNESCO Studies in Compulsory Education, VIII; Paris: UNESCO, 1951), pp. 56–61.

civil service positions [57] and commissions in the armed services and police are open only to university or military academy graduates. From this it is possible to infer two things about the middle-level group. First, the total number of university or equivalent graduates of all ages is certainly no more than 25,000. This figure would include all aspirant and retired high-level persons. Second, this educational qualification means that Thailand's ruling class is characterized by a certain degree of Westernization. The educational system has been adapted from European and American models, and the curriculum reflects the source. At secondary level and above a substantial part of the curriculum is devoted to the study of a foreign language—generally English. Apart from the actual curriculum, the ideal behavior of Thai students is an amalgam of Western and traditional Thai characteristics. Until World War II, the best secondary schools were administered by Europeans, and university deans were often Europeans. In the decade since the war Europeans and Americans have again taken a considerable, although subordinate, place in upper secondary and university education. Their former leadership has been assumed by Thai educators schooled in Europe or America. At Čhulalongkǫn University well over three-quarters of the faculty have had considerable education abroad. The same is true to some extent of the other universities. This pattern is continued in superior teacher-training schools and among responsible officials in the Ministry of Education. The educated group is thus a tiny group trained in an atmosphere of Western knowledge, spirit, and values, albeit still Thai.

A social fact of supreme importance in the history of mod-

[57] Kasem Udyanin and Rufus D. Smith, *The Public Service in Thailand* (Brussels: International Institute of Administrative Sciences, 1954), p. 41.

ern Thailand is that there, unlike other Asian countries, particularly former colonial lands, no frustrated, unemployed educated class has developed. The traditional occupation of the educated is government, and this field has remained open to the Thai. The number of openings at the top of society has certainly increased in modern times and has permitted the absorption into leadership positions of elements which might have become discontented. At the same time control over the education system, the primary upward pathway and recruiting agency for new members of the elite, has maintained an approximate balance between jobs and qualified applicants for positions of responsibility. The gradual introduction of popular education coupled with the development of a larger bureaucracy and the opening of top jobs to nonroyalty was a substantial result of the establishment of the constitutional monarchy in 1932. Thus the enlargement of the armed services and the police, the increasing need for schoolteachers as a result of the gradual expansion of the educational system, and the general enlargement of the civil service which has been consequent upon the new complexities of the role of modern government—jobs in the management of the economy, the improvement of agriculture, the construction of public works, and the variety of social welfare operations now assumed by the government—have for the most part absorbed the educated into positions of responsibility and prestige, if not wealth.

Because this is the case, the Thai educated group as a whole has a distinctive quality. Most educated Thai officials are faced daily with the stubborn facts of life. They are not, therefore, given to flights of imagination. They fit comfortably into an established structure of social organization. Idleness and failure do not stimulate an examination of the fundamentals of that structure or the ultimate values upon which it is based. In a very real sense, the educated group is a class with a vested interest. Consequently they are conservative and pragmatic rather than radical and speculative.

At present there are five institutions which grant degrees in the country—Čhulalongkǫn, Thammasat, and the Agriculture, Medical, and Fine Arts universities. The last three are training schools of professional level exclusively. The first two, Čhulalongkǫn and Thammasat, are more general and academic in their organization, but neither offers a course in philosophy or religion. At present the system of self-contained faculties effectively limits education to more or less specific professional and career courses. Thus, for example, Čhulalongkǫn has faculties of science (which includes premedicine as well as general science), commerce and accountancy, engineering, architecture, arts, education, and political science. On the whole, training in these faculties is specific, practical, and applied. Two universities for monks are the exception to this practical orientation. The graduates of these institutions, however, are expected to become religious leaders in the Buddhist hierarchy.

As already indicated, another opportunity for education is open to a minority of university-level students, namely, education abroad in Europe or America. These opportunities are in the form of government scholarships for postgraduate study. Scholarships are generally awarded for further professional training and carry with them an obligation for a term of government service upon return. This procedure channels a potentially explosive group into the present social structure and quickly provides them with an interest in its maintenance. Although it is true that Western-trained Thai tend to suffer frustration in trying to implement new techniques in their work, they have few economic or social frustrations to stimulate politically significant discontents.

It must not be overlooked that there is a very small group

of intellectuals among the educated people in the country. This group, which has little inner organization, is composed on the one hand of journalists and writers and on the other of educators and a few leisurely and aristocratic full-time intellectuals. The field of journalism is made up of a core of a few hundred newspapermen, a good many of whom have some education, and they are surrounded by a large number of part-time writers. Journalism is not a particularly esteemed or stable profession, and newspapers and magazines proliferate, prosper, and die at a rapid rate. As a consequence this group of writers is a potential flaw in the conservative structure of the educated class. Many of its members are university students who failed to complete their work toward a degree. Perhaps the combination of low prestige, frustration, and control of a large part of the national stock of literature has made this group the rather querulous and irresponsible critic of government that it has been.[58] The other segment of the intellectual group is made up of university professors and a few full-time writers, most of whom are of royal families or former officials. University professors are actually government officials and as such in no position to exercise academic freedom. At the same time they are few in number and burdened with heavy labors.

In sum, the educated leadership of the nation is a career group. Their place in society is made. They have opportunities for useful, responsible, and satisfying work for which their training is designed to prepare them. Such a group, having a substantial stake in society as it is presently arranged, would understandably be conservative insofar as fundamental social change is concerned.

Except for a general enlargement of the group made easy

[58] See, for example, *USIS Press Section Summary of Editorials and Special Articles from the Thai Language Daily Newspapers* (Bangkok), Nov. 21, Dec. 21, 1956, and other issues.

by a social structure which permits mobility and also the internal power shifts involved in displacing royalty with commoners of the bureaucratic class, the leadership of Thailand has been essentially the same for centuries. This leadership is not faced with the necessity of legitimizing its position, a situation which will continue so long as the masses of people are not sufficiently moved to reject traditional claims of right by the bureaucratic group. That kind of movement ought not to develop while the bureaucratic group remains sufficiently satisfied and therefore cohesive. A mass movement for radical change would require a leadership drawn from the ruling class, and such a leadership would of necessity have lost its stake in the present structure. For the time being traditional claims of the right to rule will provide support for the leadership. It is impossible to predict at what moment or by whom the population will be aroused and demand a new structuring of the rights of ruling.

Moreover, the religious ethic of Buddhism unites the national ruling group with the masses, as has been suggested above. The emphasis upon the virtues of benevolence and something like *noblesse oblige* is not entirely a fiction in the society. It would be less than accurate to give the impression that Thailand is free of exploitation and oppression of the weak by the strong; but the broad consensus on the legitimate differences of rights and obligations existing in a sympathetic natural and economic environment appears to mitigate the extremes of brutality. A successfully integrated social system sustains the Thai leadership. Although quite Westernized, it has not been torn loose from its following, nor has it been intellectually dislocated from its faith and place in a system of values and statuses.

Concretely, Westernization of leadership, while it has gone forward rapidly since the reign of King Rama V (1868–1910), has not created a miniature and imperfect replica of any European nation. Rama V was sensitive to the peril of permitting the state or its leadership to fall under the influence of any particular nation. His policy was to take Western influence from various nations, and this policy has been continued to the present. Students sent abroad have gone to virtually every nation of Western Europe and North America. The advisers employed by the government at various times since the end of the nineteenth century have also been from different Western nations. At the same time the normally short stay of the Thai students abroad, the close supervision given them by Thai diplomatic officials, and the fact that the students visited different nations apparently shattered any ideological coherence among the members of this small group of intellectuals educated in the West.

Westernization has been important among educated Thai. Yet it is Westernization with a difference, resulting from design and from milieu. Westernization was consciously chosen by Thai leaders, not thrust upon them by a politically dominant power. Westernization was taken selectively in terms of both elements and sources. The result has been a peculiarly Thai form of Westernization which today many Thai do not recognize as such. It is in fact a Thai way of life.

In spite of the fundamental homogeneity of the educated, ruling class, this group constitutes several differentiated political forces each with a role to play in the political life of the state. The basis of the differences is first of all institutional. The broadly bureaucratic character of the educated group which connects it with preexisting patterns of organized social life gives that life a pragmatic quality which dilutes ideological tendencies. Such tendencies can be largely explained by the role of the structuring institutions. These institutions are, in approximate order of importance, the military (army, police, air force, and navy), the parliament, the throne, the civil service, and the business community.

The military establishment, since 1932 and more particularly since 1947, has taken upon itself the mission of political mentor of the nation. By means of successful coups, it has staked a claim to political dominance, and this it has enhanced by giving to the Ministry of Defense large budget appropriations which are allocated and audited within the ministry and are generally free of control from outside. The services maintain their own educational institutions in the military academies. Administrative officials within the ministry are officers under discipline, and political control has as always been in the hands of a military officer of high rank. The final and perhaps most important element in the organization of the military for political purposes is the fact that a substantial portion of the armed forces is based in the capital, where they are readily available at times of coups and elections.[59]

Parliament has become the institutional base for provincial politicians. Because of the dominating hand of the executive supported by the military and civil service, elected members of parliament have developed a certain *esprit* of their own. Members who depend on their election skills and position in their constituencies have a common outlook which contrasts with the professional bureaucrats. They seek to further their common interests even though they are divided into voting groups and political parties. These parties have little or no extraparliamentary organization. In general, each member must get elected through his own efforts in his own province. Party labels are incidental. Parties have never represented substantial social forces but only cliques and individuals within the top level of the ruling class. Because the governing group must bargain for parliamentary support while members of

[59] See below, Chapter VI, for a detailed discussion of the military.

parliament must compete with military and civil bureaucrats for position and influence, parliament has tended to take on the character of a separate political force and institution within the political process.[60]

The position of the throne and the use of its prestige in politics are rather obscure. Until 1932 the king and his close advisers were the dominant political force, and the revolution was aimed at the throne's power. Although it was maintained as a symbol of national unity, the royal power sank to almost nothing with abdication of Rama VII in 1935. Since the breakup of the revolutionary group during World War II, however, it is clear that the throne is gaining in power and prestige. Since 1950 the throne has been occupied by an adult who is able to exert, if cautiously, a growing influence.

The civil service as a whole is docile in conflicts for power. Organized on functional lines in the 60-odd departments and 12 ministries of the government, it lacks the unity and hierarchy of the military services which would be necessary for it to take a dynamic part in politics as a single organization. Within the civil service sphere, it is possible for a man to rise to a position of prominence and power from which he may be drawn into the top level. At the same time, because the cooperation of the civil service is vital to the ruling group, it is the most important element of the political public. If the ruling clique decides to press any novel course of action, it is necessary that the groundwork be laid in the civil service.

The Bangkok and national business community, like business communities everywhere, deals in politics on the level of influence. Because of the general conception of the businessmen as alien, i.e., Chinese or European, the community enters politics at something of a psychological disadvantage. For the European this is to a large extent offset by diplomatic support,

[60] See Chapters VII and VIII for elaboration of these points.

but for the overseas Chinese it is necessary to work out an accommodation. From the point of view of the Thai political
leadership, the problem is one of regulation with a double
motivation. On the one hand, since the state revenues rest
substantially on commercial activity—customs, premiums on
exports, and business taxes—careful regulation is vital to the
state's stability. At the same time, the need of the businessman,
particularly the Chinese, for some protection in the face of
heavy regulation makes political influence an important qualification for business management. Thai political leaders have
become increasingly aware of the value of this influence, and
opportunities of enrichment for political and personal uses
have not been overlooked.[61] As the prime source of ready
cash, the business community is a political factor of substance,
but its relative weakness, having neither guns nor votes, makes
it docile.

Public opinion is a political force of some consequence.
While it is true that a large part of the adult population of the
country is politically indifferent or inarticulate, nevertheless
the communication process within the restricted political public and the opinion of this public serves as a dynamic element
in politics. Although there are few studies of communication
or opinion in the country, several apparent characteristics can
be noted.

The heavy concentration of educated and politically interested persons (e.g., university students, civil servants, and
business people) in the city of Bangkok inflates the effect of
informal means of communication and opinion formation.
Rumor and gossip are credible and influential in such a social
situation. Their informal lines of communication keep up a
constant dialogue with the active and colorful city press,
which is manifested in a variety of daily papers and weekly

[61] Skinner, *Leadership and Power*, pp. 191–194, 305–308.

magazines. These publications, which comprise a stable core surrounded by those more ephemeral, are characterized by much comment and few facts. The press is exceedingly political and partisan, and each day and week the public is assaulted by hundreds of thousands of words of opinion. Unfortunately the general level of journalistic ethics is, with a few exceptions, low, and the pervasiveness of venality and open corruption of newspapers is proverbial.[62] Radio and television broadcasting is also important in Bangkok, but in general these facilities stay clear of the struggles of the ruling class. It is not surprising that in such a social situation there are no organizations which are designed to formulate and articulate opinions on special interests or issues. In addition, the communication media and modes of opinion formation are, in terms of policy interest, diffuse and unspecialized.

The opinion of the political public which results from this elementary but involuted network of formal and informal unspecialized communications has the following characteristics. It is interested in and acquainted with great, if not accurate, detail on the lives of prominent people. Judgments are formed on the interpretation of these lives. Opinion of a less personal kind is focused on emotional reaction to slogans. Opinion affects political matters at moments of tension between cliques when apparent popularity, as manifested in the press and other forms, may encourage or confuse the leaders in making their decisions for vigorous action.[63]

[62] Albert G. Pickerell, "The Press of Thailand," *Journalism Quarterly*, XXXVII, no. 1 (Winter, 1960), 89–92.
[63] See below, Chapter IX.

III

AUTHORITY
AND KINGSHIP

THE politics of a people is played out within the limits of their view of the world. In some political systems differences of world view or ideology lie at the root of intractable political divisions and continuing crises. But the people of Thailand share a common outlook, and this is a significant condition of the political life of the nation.[1] While this outlook may vary

[1] It is appropriate to interpose here a caution and disclaimer. It is dangerous if not foolish to attempt to characterize the mental life of a group of people, particularly a large and alien one. On the other hand, an explanation of the political life of a people inevitably forces the line of argument into this problem. The interpretation that follows is impressionistic and necessarily tentative. It is based most of all on several years of teaching in Thai schools and universities, associating with Thai men and women, and reading Thai writings. To this experience are added the insights gained from the following sources: Prince Dhani Niwat, "The Old Siamese Conception of the Monarchy," in *The Siam Society Fiftieth Anniversary Commemorative Publication* (Bangkok: Siam Society, 1954), II, 160–175; Robert Heine-Geldern,

in individual cases by degrees of skepticism about certain traditional symbols, its fundamental principle underlies the attitudes of all groups toward their lives and toward the society in which those lives run their course. Since this work is concerned with politics, it is not the place to present a complete analysis of the Thai world view. Nevertheless, it will be useful to sketch its more important social and political implications here.

According to this characteristic view, the world is a moral continuum. All elements of the cosmos are related to each other in terms of power determined by virtue and moral value. It is the moral value of things which is their true nature and which determines their place in the universe. Moral value is the degree of good attached to the element. The degree of good is a result of acts of will, and thus the universe is understood to be governed by will.

As has been suggested in Chapter II, one result of this view of the world, the importance of which is difficult to exagger-

---

Conceptions of State and Kingship in Southeast Asia (Southeast Asia Program, Cornell University, Data Paper no. 18; Ithaca, N.Y., 1956); Horace G. Quaritch Wales, *Siamese State Ceremonies* (London: Bernard Quaritch, Ltd., 1931); Lucien M. Hanks, Jr., "The Cosmic View of Bang Chan Villagers" (paper presented to the Pacific Science Conference, Bangkok, Dec., 1957); Lucien M. Hanks, Jr., and Herbert P. Phillips, "A Young Thai from the Countryside," in B. Kaplan, ed., *Studying Personality Crossculturally* (Evanston, Ill.: Row, Peterson and Co., 1961); James Mosel, "Thai Administrative Behavior," in William Siffen, *Toward the Comparative Study of Public Administration* (Bloomington, Ind.: Indiana University, Department of Government, 1957); unpublished work by Lucien M. Hanks, Jr., on Bang Chan society, Herbert P. Phillips on Thai personality and values, and Robert B. Textor on Thai magico-religious beliefs and self-image. A convenient summary of some of the concepts involved is to be found in Charoen Chaiyachana, *Sangkhom Süksa* ("Social Studies"; Bangkok: Thai Wathana Phanit, 1952), a textbook of ethics and civics for senior high school students.

ate in the Thai situation, is the idea that in the human universe
one's place is a result of one's own will and that one is therefore ultimately responsible for one's own position in society.
The human world is but one of the worlds in the universe.
There are also the worlds of beasts and things as well as the
higher worlds of celestial beings. These are all locked together
in one systematic universe.

The position of a being, human or otherwise, in this universe may be measured by the degree to which he is subject
to the will and power of others and the sway of his will and
power over others. This conception is the one which must be
referred to throughout this discussion of Thai politics, i.e.,
the necessary and just unity of virtue and power. Those who
have power are good and deserve power. Those who gain
power are good and deserve their good fortune. Power justifies
itself. This idea is not to be understood in a cynical sense which
would lead to the view that might is right. It is rather a magico-
religious view that right is might.

Any world view requires some philosophical rationalization
to make it comprehensible and communicable. The Thai com-
prehension of the cosmos is informed and supported by several
analytically distinct, more or less systematic theoretical
schemes. The most sophisticated of these theories is the system of Buddhist thought. Buddhism of the austere Hinayana
or Theravada school is the professed belief of the overwhelming majority of the Thai people. It carries with it much of the
vast Hindu-Brahmanic system of thought with its subtle dia-
lectic of subjection to life's inevitable suffering and escape
through "right" behavior. A discussion of the intricacies of
this tradition would be out of place here. It must serve as
sufficient to say that the principles of the world view under
scrutiny find their place in this tradition. In general, Thai
Buddhism, as it is practiced, has tended to emphasize the social

rather than the metaphysical implications of the Hindu-Buddhist tradition, leaving undeveloped that aspect of the thought of the Lord Buddha which directed itself to the escape from the suffering of this world. In view of the fact that the amount of worldly suffering laid upon the backs of the Thai appears to be, and probably always has been, less burdensome than is the case in India itself, perhaps this worldly emphasis is more congenial and to be expected.

The principles of magic provide a second set of theoretical explanations related to the Thai *Weltanschauung*. There are, of course, a great variety of magical practices, but they tend to center around the general principle of the manipulation of some sort of formula—material, verbal, or ceremonial—with the purpose of bringing about some desired effect. Now these formulae derive their power from their association with beings high on the moral continuum of the universe. For example, the king's annual ceremonial plowing is efficacious, when properly conducted, because of the high position of the king's role. By this means he expresses his powerful will over the universe. But the formula may also be separated from any particular being and may become an esoteric bit of knowledge of use to anyone who can gain it and manipulate it properly. At the root of this kind of practice is the belief that the world is subject to will properly expressed and thus is open to manipulation.

The pseudo-sciences, such as astrology, palmistry, numerology, and the like, provide another theoretical framework for understanding the world as a moral continuum. These are to be distinguished from magical formulae in that they do not, at least in their pure form, purport to provide power to intervene directly in the workings of the world. Rather they give an understanding of the universe, much as science does, so that those living in it can live as safely and well as possible. But they are distinguished from science by the fact that they are structured around the view of the world as a moral unity. Therefore they claim to distinguish by objective methods not only the true from the false but also the good from the bad.

Finally, concomitant with these rather sophisticated ideas is a vast array of personalized spirits and methods of propitiating them. The ancient animistic belief that the universe is peopled with spirits attendant upon a variety of persons, places, and things remains vital in much of the population of Thailand today. These spirits provide an explanation of the world because it is understood that they are powerful and their wills may cause events. The spirits are related to the other systems of thought. The gods of the Hindu-Buddhist pantheon partake of the nature of spirits. Spirits have the powers of divination and foreknowledge as well as that of intervention in the course of events. The important aspect of spirit beliefs is that these beings are subject to propitiation and thereby can be manipulated in such a way as to improve the situation of the propitiator. By this means the lowly may manipulate the powerful and gain desired ends.

The fact that the observable practices associated with these four ways of thought are a part of the everyday life of a large portion of the Thai nation, without great distinction of social class or even level of education, is adduced here to support the main contention, that the world view of the Thai is an elaboration of the idea that the cosmos is a moral unity. Moreover, a remarkable aspect of the Thai view of the world is its ability to add layers of ideas one on the other. The capacity to entertain an extraordinary mixture of ideas at the same time is quite striking. Such additions may be either contradictory or supplemental. Thus a world traveler about to embark on the latest forms of mechanical transportation may consult his astrologer for the auspicious time for departure. A Buddhist temple will have at the corner of the compound a house for the spirit of the place. A village doctor may say a magic formula, call upon a spirit, and give an injection of antibiotic. Such a capacity for entertaining a variety of logically uncongenial ideas is not limited to the people of Thailand. But there it has been useful in absorbing a number of new concepts and techniques, including many of the most sophisticated scientific ones, and integrating them in a cumulative manner without upsetting the whole.

There is a characteristic set of ethics associated with this cosmic view. The fundamental principle from which the ethical system is derived is that the fates of human beings (as of all others) are ruled by the moral law that good behavior causes good results. It is a common-sense corollary that wise and prudent men will behave well in order to bring themselves good fortune. According to at least one source,[2] the results most desired by men are four in number—fame (*sanrasoen*), fortune (*lap*), high rank (*yot*), and happiness (*suk*). Another source would subsume these values, along with others, under the generalized value of "freedom from subjection to the will of the rulers and of natural forces." [3] That is to say, as a person gains in virtue (merit), he rises first in human society and then in the hierarchy of the universe. As he rises, he becomes subject to the rule of fewer and fewer beings and bound by fewer and fewer rules. Hanks has suggested that the symbolism of mythical beings who are able to change their shape, fly, be in two places at the same time, and live forever is a demonstration of this kind of progressive freedom. Within this world, however, the attainment of the four worldly aims may suffice.

The ideal analysis distinguishes four types of ethically good behavior which bring merit to a person and improve his status

[2] Charoen Chaiyachana, p. 44.   [3] Hanks, "Cosmic View," p. 3.

in the world. These are benevolence (*metta*), sympathy (*karuna*), freedom from envy (*mutthita*), and noninvolvement (*ubekkha*). *Metta* is very similar in content to the Christian virtue of charity. It involves the love of mankind for the sake of their humanity as well as a generalized willingness to be kind and helpful. But *metta* has its personal rewards in the form of 11 beneficial results,[4] namely, (1) peaceful sleep, (2) peaceful waking, (3) absence of bad dreams, (4) love from mankind, (5) love from the nonhuman world, (6) protection by the celestial beings, (7) immunity to fire, poison, and arms, (8) determination, (9) a pure face, (10) continuation of the same status when one dies, (11) a rebirth in heaven if one has not already attained a state of holiness. *Metta* is the supreme virtue which seems to underlie all others.

Karuna is sympathy or pity for those who have suffering. It also involves the desire to help those who have fallen on bad days and the willingness to sacrifice one's own advantage or happiness for others. *Karuna* is characteristically the proper virtue for the powerful in their dealings with the weak and may be expected to manifest itself in generosity. *Mutthita* is the complement of *karuna*. It is the capacity to rejoice in the good fortune of others or at least to remain free from envy in the face of others' good fortune.

Finally, *ubekkha* is the capacity to avoid involvement in other people's disasters in such a way as to make them worse. It means remaining neutral in disputes and at times when *metta* and *karuna* are not appropriate. For example, one should not be concerned for the fate of condemned criminals.

All these virtues have to do with the dominant concern of Thai ethical thinking—social relations. *Metta*, the most generalized of them, while it emphasizes disinterest, is presented in the texts as a means to accumulate personal powers in the

[4] Charoen Chaiyachana, p. 49.

relationships with the beings of the universe. The second and third, *karuna* and *mutthita*, are closely linked to the problem of the relationships between persons of different statuses and emphasize conciliation between potential antagonists. The final virtue, *ubekkha*, is an abstract statement of the much-admired Thai rule of behavior, that of noninvolvement. In popular language, *choei*, meaning to be still, is a vital element in the Thai reaction to situations of social stress. When faced with a trying or embarrassing experience, the Thai is very likely to react by not reacting. He endures, he sits still, he avoids the appearance of being involved.

These generalized virtues manifest themselves in the social behavior of the Thai by their adherence to the belief that the proper manner of ordering specific social relations is by expression of respect. Symbols and gestures of respect from lower to higher status are the very stuff of the actual relationships between persons. Even in the language, as has been mentioned, differences of status and the respectful aspect of those differences are an integral part of the vocabulary. This aspect of language ranges from the elaborate special vocabulary used in addressing the king to the everyday forms of personal address. All pronouns or pronominal forms are status laden so that those Thai who would aspire to modern egalitarianism often borrow pronouns from Chinese or English.

According to the rules of respect, there are certain categories of persons, both general and special, which one is obliged to respect. First among these are one's parents and teachers. Monks, who because of their piety are of the highest earthly status and in a sense outside of the social system, are due special respect. In addition, one is obliged to respect those with power over one because of either birth, age, or degree of virtue.

Respectful behavior may be seen as an analogue of propitation in the world of spirits, of incantation in the world of magic, or of ceremony in the world of kings and celestial beings. Thus the political and social world is open to manipulation by quasi-magical or propitiatory methods. By respectful behavior one propitiates one's superiors in the hope, even the expectation, of resulting benefits. This is such a well-established attitude that the author of the cited textbook of ethics says, "Respect is generally an important instrument in bringing our affairs to beneficial completion." [5] Besides respect there are other forms of propitiation, such as bribes, which are not uncommonly found in Thai politics.

In sum, the world, as the Thai see it, is a hierarchy of statuses and powers, ranging from this life and world through all lives and worlds. The continuum of the Thai cosmos is not that of space and time but that of virtue and power. In the ideal this cosmos is a just one and ruled by an unbreakable law of cause and effect, i.e., right behavior leads to advancement in the hierarchy. The course of events in this cosmos is the result of the interplay of the wills of the multitudes of beings. When this ideal world is combined or infused with ideas of magic and spirit propitiation, the possibility of manipulation of powers is opened. By means of magical formulae, the effective propitiation of spirits, or the correct respectful behavior toward superiors, one can gain intervention on one's behalf in the course of events.

Growing out of this world view are certain characteristics of Thai political life. One of these characteristics is a strong tendency toward ceremonial correctness in political relationships and political activities. Thus there has appeared to be greater satisfaction in elections properly conducted than in those which, although approximating a struggle for political power, are rather rough-and-tumble. A second characteristic

[5] *Ibid.*, p. 68.

is the extraordinary willfulness of Thai political life. Sudden changes of regime, the promulgation of broad decrees affecting the personal lives of the people, and the personal expenditure of government funds are all common phenomena.

In the political world these characteristics have a profound effect on the fundamental attitude toward law and institutions. Although scrupulous attention is given to the formalities of procedure, there appears to be little faith in the necessary regularity of the workings of law and institutions. Intervention by persons of power in the application of law appears to be accepted without disturbance. In such an attitude toward law lies some explanation of the easy recourse to periodic *coups d'état* for the modification of political structures and for adjustment of constitutions.

Political Ideas

Overlaying both the deeper consistency of political outlook and the institutional structure of the Thai ruling class there are a variety of more or less alien ideological symbols useful in the power struggle. Four slogans or catchwords in common use in the Thai political vocabulary sum up the basic attitudes. They are king, religion, nation, and democracy.

The king or the monarchy is a symbol of the nation as a unified entity and of political conservatism. The Thai ruling class takes pride in its bloodless revolution which preserved king and national unity. Its members take satisfaction from the fact that the government form was brought "up to date" without affecting their position or disturbing the long and venerable traditions of good government.

Religion is a symbol of cultural conservatism and unity.

It binds the highest and lowest in what is seen as a just and natural scale of status and right. Bound up with religion is the fundamental ethic of doing good for the sake of one's fate and also of seeking after one's own good fate before all else. It reinforces the social virtues upon which society rests. It encourages a certain love of enjoyment, coolness in the face of trouble, and indifference to disappointment, which make life easier and suffering bearable. These concepts, all of which are a part of Thai social and religious attitudes, are vital in the ruling class. But more importantly they are vital in the nation as a whole and serve to unify the classes in outlook.

While monarchy and religion are symbols of universal meaning among all Thai, nationalism is most vital in the ruling class. Several decades of national education and widespread military service, however, have made symbols and slogans of nationalism current at all social levels. Thai nationalism is for the most part unmilitant. Its historical background is the long diplomatic struggle to maintain independence. Thailand succeeded in this struggle through a process of adapting itself to the ways of the imperialist powers and de-emphasizing its dissimilarities. Because of this history, Thai nationalism is different from other Southeast Asian nationalisms. Culturally, it is not nativist but assimilative. Politically, it is not revolutionary but conservative, often taking the form of appeals for peace and tranquility for the sake of the nation. An important theme of this nationalism is the idea that Thailand is one of the "civilized" nations, is "up to date," has the ability to handle its own affairs, and is the equal of any nation, to which is added a strong element of anti-Chinese sentiment.

Democracy is also a slogan generally accepted by the ruling class. It symbolizes a combination of a sense of duty, of *noblesse oblige*, on the one hand and the end of special legal privileges on the other. When reduced to specifics, the democratic ideal is found to mean a fully elected parliament controlling the government, the purposes of which are the people's happiness and prosperity. These ends are an ancient objective of Thai government. They appear in inscriptions of the thirteenth century. The late Čhakkri kings adopted them as their objectives and rationale; the constitutional government has taken them over as their own. These objectives are congruent with the Buddhist virtue of benevolence which conditions the popular attitude toward government. The ordinary Thai ideally expects benevolence from his superiors, and government is understood as a network of superiors. But in seeking benefit from the government, he does not approach it as an institution with procedures practicable for him. His approach is more likely to be to an individual of power with whom he can establish a personal relationship of obligation. Such a relationship may be family, friendship, or, more likely, a matter of "reasonable" financial persuasion. One developing trend is the use of the vote as a method of obligating the successful candidate to his constituent.

Democracy also carries the meaning of freedom. The Thai of all classes resist regimentation, systematization, and routine. Although the social system requires respect for authority, it also permits room to move. Religion ordains that a man's fate is his own responsibility, and his position is a matter of his personal relationships with other individuals. Any broad legal restraints on individual autonomy are resented and evaded. For the love of this kind of freedom, democracy is a useful symbol.

These symbol-slogans are widely respected, but the ruling class is divided on the matter of emphasis. There are three ideological groupings. The first, which is made up mostly of members of the older, more traditional elements of the ruling class, emphasizes respect for the king and religion but at the same time, because its members have been at a political disadvantage since 1932, also stresses legal, political, and economic freedom.

The second group, in the main the military, is strongly nationalist. Its members claim precedence for national defense, with resultant increases in military budgets and privilege for soldiers. This group also has a fondness for appointing members to parliament for the sake of national stability.

The third group, largely civilian politicians and elected members of parliament, tends to put heavy emphasis upon free elections, strong parliamentary control, and more economic benefits for the voters. Members of this group like to characterize themselves as socialists.

Finally, a word must be said about an attitude of the Thai toward all activities which gives a characteristic quality to their outlook on life in general and politics in particular. This is an assumption that life should be enjoyed. It is summed up in a broadly conceived quality called *sanuk*, which may be translated as enjoyment. The Thai are renowned as a lighthearted people, and this reputation is not undeserved. They appear to believe that all activities should be enjoyable, regardless of how serious they may be in the end. Not only games and recreation should have this quality but also politics, religion, and work. Merit making in the temple should be enjoyable. Temple fairs, elections, travel, and *coups d'état* should be enjoyable. This seeking of enjoyment in all things is fundamental in Thai behavior, and for the Thai it may be said that what cannot be enjoyed is thereby depreciated.

Kingship

Phumiphon Adunyadet, king of Thailand, is the ninth reigning monarch of the house of Čhakkri and the heir of a Thai throne which consciously traces its history to the kingdom of Sukhothai founded in A.D. 1238. Such a lengthy and in many respects splendid tradition, of which reigning Thai monarchs have been aware, can hardly have been without its effects upon the modern state of Thailand. This is especially true because Thailand, having escaped extended foreign domination, has been able to utilize its traditions in the process of transforming the state.

In avoiding subjection to colonial rule, the Thai leadership has necessarily been responsive to alien influence without being overwhelmed by it. The Thai political tradition has, therefore, retained a decided quality of insularity. This insularity may be attributed mainly to the fact that the Thai language remains the only national language and therefore the main vehicle of the great tradition.

Influences from other nations, the importance of which should not be minimized, have been integrated with an already-vital stock of thought and history. The process of change that Thai society is passing through at present seems to be within the tradition or at least to have been given traditional sanction. For example, in a lecture delivered in 1927 and often reprinted, Prince Damrong offered three attributes of national character as explanations of the ability of the Thai nation to dominate central mainland Southeast Asia for 700 years. One of these he translated as the "power of assimilation," which more literally is the "absorption of benefits" (*kan prasan prayot*).[6] The most striking examples of this "power of assimilation," before the advent of European culture, were the absorption of the Mon-Buddhist legal tradition and the Cambodian system of administration.[7]

But regardless of the nation's skill in assimilating persons and ideas from alien cultures, the fact remains that the Thai people look to their own history as a source of inspiration. The models of behavior and culture heroes are Thai kings and personages of note. It is for this reason that the traditions of government constitute a large element of the political ideology or furniture of the minds of living Thai. The sources of Thai history are in themselves slim and rather dubious—a few inscriptions, some court chronicles, and the like. But for present purposes a scrupulously critical history of the Thai nation is not precisely relevant. Here the concern is with the conception of their history and their traditions which contemporary Thai have. It is this conception which molds the behavior and understanding that are part of today's political system.

Kingship was unquestionably the most important element of the traditional system of government. The throne is the most important element of the old system which manifestly exists in this day. The Thai kingship as an ideal conception includes a variety of aspects which, though not entirely consistent in their logic, are sufficiently complementary or analogous

[6] Prince Damrong Rachanuphap, "Laksana kan pokkhrọng prathet sayam dae boran" ("Ancient Forms of Government in Siam"), *Chumnum phraniphon (bang rüang) khọng somdet krom phraya damrongrachanuphap* ("Collections of the Writings (Some Selections) of Prince Damrong Rachanuphap"; Bangkok: Government Lottery, 1957), pp. 4–5.

[7] *Ibid.*, p. 6.

to be able to exist with each other. Since the kingship appears to have been formed historically by means of a process of accretion without ever having been subjected to heavy intellectual attack or criticism, the coexistence of a variety of kingship theories is not cause for surprise.

For purposes of examination, the kingship may be analyzed into the following aspects: (1) father of the people or *phǫ khun;* (2) the wheel-rolling king, emperor, or *čhakraphat;* (3) the god-king or *deva raja;* and (4) a splendid and majestic being of great power or *čhao phaen din.*

The aspect of the kingship which depicts the monarch as the father of the people is considered by Thai historians to be the most ancient and most purely Thai of all conceptions. It has been greatly emphasized in the transformation of the monarchy in recent decades. Prince Damrong has described this conception of the monarchy by saying:

As for the Thai method of government, it respects the king as if he were the father of all the people. The method of government takes the form of government of the family as its ideal. For example, it holds that the father is the ruler of the household. . . . Several households combine as a village under the rule of the "father of the village [*phǫ ban*]," and the persons under his rule are called "children of the village [*luk ban*]." Several villages combine to make a town. If it was a dependent town, it was under the rule of "a father of the town [*phǫ müang*]"; if it was an independent town, the ruler was a "chief [*khun*]." Several towns combined to make a state under the rule of a king, but in ancient times he was called "father-chief [*phǫ khun*]," and officials of various positions had the title "children of the chiefs [*luk khun*]." Thus it can be seen that the Thai method of government was like the father ruling his children . . . such as is used as a principle of government in Siam today.[8]

[8] *Ibid.,* pp. 7–8.

As father of the people, the king was the leader in war and the wise counselor and judge in peace. One particular function of the king, that of the judge of final appeal and source of redress for a grievance, is much emphasized. According to an inscription from the Sukhothai period, the king placed a gong in front of his palace. If any of the people felt aggrieved, he was free to come to the palace and sound the gong, whereupon the king would come out to hear the appeal for redress.[9] This custom is said to have survived throughout the history of the monarchy, and it is known that it was revived in modified form in the later reigns of Čhakkri.[10]

The wheel-rolling king or *čhakraphat* is a Hindu-Hinayana Buddhist conception which came to the Thai from the Mon. This conception justifies kingship not socially as the father of the people but morally as a righteous king. It is associated with the Pali *Dhammasattha* (*Thammasat*), the ancient Hindu-Buddhist law code.[11] The prescription for the monarch is that he

abides steadfast in the ten kingly virtues, constantly upholding the five common precepts and on holy days the set of eight precepts, living in kindness and goodwill to all beings. He takes pains to study the *Thammasat* and to keep the four principles of justice, namely: to assess the right and wrong of all service or disservice rendered to him, to uphold the righteous and truthful, to acquire riches through none but just means, and to maintain the prosperity of his state through none but just means.[12]

The image of the wheel seems to combine a number of ideas. Most important of all is the combination of the symbols for the law of life, the principle of righteousness, and the idea of

[9] *Ibid.*, p. 8; Dhani "Old Siamese Conception," p. 163.
[10] Dhani, "Old Siamese Conception," p. 162.
[11] *Ibid.*, pp. 163–166.   [12] *Ibid.*, p. 163.

power.[13] In this combination lies that important concept of Thai political thought, i.e., the integration and necessary connection between power and righteousness. The conception of the king as a wheel-rolling monarch maintains that by virtue of his adherence to the principles of the law, the norm, and the right (*Thamma*) he gains universal power.

The conception of the wheel-rolling monarch blends closely with that of the *deva raja* or king as divine incarnation or Buddha. This tradition, which is Hindu and Mahayana Buddhist in origin, appears to have come to the Thai from Cambodian sources,[14] although the idea was as widespread in Southeast Asia as Indian influences were.[15] According to the conception of *deva raja*, the king was an earthly incarnation of one of the gods of the Hindu pantheon and as such the proper object of a cult to be conducted by royal Brahmans. Such a cult included a structure of cosmological symbols which in effect transformed the kingdom into the universe and the king into the lord of the universe. To what extent the cult of the *deva raja* was a major part of the theory of Thai kingship at any specific time is not known, although Quaritch Wales suggests that it was of first importance during the Ayutthaya period.[16] There is no question that during the Bangkok period it was less important than the analogous *čhakraphat* concept.

Beyond these specific theories of kingship, what is significant from the Thai view of their traditions, and the tradition of the kingship especially, is the fact that regardless of specific content there was a generalized conception of the king as a special order of being located somewhere in the realm between

[13] *Ibid.;* George Bradley McFarland, *Thai-English Dictionary* (1st American ed.; Stanford, Calif.: Stanford University Press, 1944), p. 237.
[14] Damrong, "Laksana," p. 7.   [15] Heine-Geldern, pp. 6–7.
[16] Wales, *Siamese State Ceremonies,* p. 60.

the natural and the supernatural. Furthermore, it is important to make clear that within the cosmological view of the Thai Hindu-Buddhist tradition, in contrast to the monotheistic Judeo-Christian-Islamic tradition, there is not a sharp dividing line between the natural and supernatural realms. Because of this, there is perhaps an inherent ambivalence on the question of whether or not the king was divine or earthly or both.

The aspect of the kingship which will be considered finally is here designated by one of the various general terms used in Thai for the king, i.e., *čhao phaen din* or lord of the land. This designation is meant to distinguish the generalized appearance and behavior of the monarchy from the point of view of the subjects, regardless of the specific notions listed above.

Splendor and majesty were the primary qualities of the Thai throne in this sense. Without an appreciation of these qualities, it is impossible to understand the working of the monarchy and the system of government. Ordered by and serving to manifest the magical and religious character of the throne, the pomp and ceremony that filled the life of this distant and superhuman king comforted the popular mind with faith, awe, and wonder. There was no tradition of sweeping philosophical inquiry, and the basis for this splendor was spared that destructive intellectual criticism which European monarchs suffered. It was not until European political and social ideas penetrated Thailand in the wake of imperialist merchants and soldiers that the kings of Thailand were required to modify the extremes of their position. As it happened, these European ideas reached the throne first, rather than the subjects. The monarchy by a process of self-modification was able to forestall for a number of years the possibility of public disillusionment.

In premodern Thailand, the king's glittering palace was in the center of the city and surrounded by high white walls. These walls and the soaring spires of bright colors were almost all the public knew of the king. He rarely ventured out. When he did, it was in stately progress by land or water, and he was surrounded and protected by swarms of soldiers and officials. He met only his highest officials, his pages, and his wives, and these meetings were ordered by ceremony. The royal styles (titles) by which he was known and the language by which he was addressed were rich with elaborate terminology borrowed in great measure from the Cambodian and Indian languages.[17] These words were sonorous to the ear but unintelligible to the mind of the ordinary man. Consider the following title of King Čhulalongkǫn (Rama V), who reigned until 1910:

Most excellent royal foot which is a glorious decoration for our hair; King wearing the great crown of the celestial being; royal descendant of the sun who shines like the finest jewel, most excellent of lineage; monarch as supreme as the greatest emperor of the worlds; greatest sovereign of righteousness, supreme King of men, King Čhom Klao the second, Lord of Siam including the north, the south, and all the lands nearby which are Lao, Malaya, Kareni, and many others.[18]

Splendid, mysterious, partaking of the supernormal and the superhuman, final arbiter of life and property, the king was the nexus of society. With some extravagance, which is understandable on the part of a descendant of kings, Prince Dhani has said:

The Siamese political creed was one in which individuals were bound together by their loyalty to the sovereign. Neither patriotism nor communal loyalty in the modern sense had yet arisen to any extent at the time of the fall of Ayudhaya. With the sover-

[17] *Ibid.*, pp. 104–105.
[18] "Prakat tang tamnaeng senabodi" ("Announcement of Appointments to Positions of *Senabodi*"), April 1, 1892, in Sathian Lailak *et al.*, compilers, *Prachum kotmai pračham sok* ("Collection of the Law Arranged by Year"; Bangkok: Daily Mail Press,), XIII, pt. 2, 93–98. This law collection will hereafter be referred to as *PKPS*.

eign in captivity, the political nucleus was gone and the conception of an ordered state just ceased. The whole administration
broke down and with it the social frame of the state and the
not inconsiderable culture of the Ayudhayan Siam was practically
obliterated.[19]

Traditional Bureaucracy

The view of the king as the link of society turns attention
to the second major element of traditional Thai government
which persists in modern Thailand. That is the bureaucracy.
The official organization of the state in the traditional Thai
kingdom was complex and highly differentiated and appears
to have corresponded in a high degree to the social structure
of the society. Insofar as this was true, it unquestionably
limited the ostensibly absolute power of the king. The king
was surrounded and encased in his bureaucracy while at the
same time the bureaucrats derived their authority from the
king. Neither could well continue without the other. The
dependence of the officials upon the king was, of course, a
matter which was explicitly stated again and again. As far as
the throne's dependence on the officials is concerned, there
was a customary practice by which the royal princes and
high officials elected the king. Candidates were limited to a
very few high princes, presumably since the principle of
heredity was also involved.[20]

[19] Prince Dhani Nivat, "The Reconstruction of Rama I of the
Čhakkri Dynasty," in *Rüang phrabat somdet phraphuttha yotfa
čhulalok song fünfu wathanatham* ("On the Cultural Reconstruction
of Rama I"; Bangkok: printed by Sanan Bunyasiriphan, 1957), p. 2.

[20] Dhani, "Old Siamese Conception," p. 169; Prince Damrong
Rachanuphap, *Prawat bukkhon samkhan* ("Biographies of Important
People"; Bangkok: Phrae Bhithaya Co., 1953), pp. 84–86.

A persistent attempt to impersonalize the positions comprising the bureaucratic structure is a striking feature of the traditional Thai system. The throne itself was an institution which transformed the man who held it into the higher being described above. The bureaucracy was a structure of positions, prescribed by law and derived from some view of the cosmos. Like the throne, but to a lesser degree, these positions transformed the incumbents. Each position had a set of titles, regalia, and other perquisites, including a name for the incumbent.[21] To a large extent the personal qualities of the man, his background, were supposedly of secondary importance. These associated symbols helped to standardize and stabilize the positions. In view of the fact that personal loyalty and personal relationships are known to be of great importance in the politics of modern Thailand, however, there is no reason to think that they were not so in traditional times. In any such small group as the traditional Thai bureaucracy, nepotism and other effects of personal relationships were surely important. Prince Damrong reports, in fact, that position and status tended to be hereditary, not because of blood lines but because of educational opportunity. Each son learned the profession of his father so that sons of high officials were trained in the methods of high officialdom, sons of lower officials in lower officialdom, sons of farmers in farming, and so on.[22] The effort to impersonalize the bureaucracy may be interpreted, at least in part, as an institutional antidote to the perils of nepotism and cliques. In the traditional system there was also the institution of the royal harem which was designed to utilize personal ties, i.e., marriage, in order to bind nonroyal and non-Thai families to the Thai throne.[23]

[21] Damrong, "Laksana," pp. 17–18.   [22] *Ibid.*, p. 16.

[23] To what extent abandonment of the institution of the harem was critical in the ultimate weakening of the throne's power is difficult to

According to the traditional view of the government, its purpose was to serve the king. The term still used today for official business is *rachakan,* which is literally the affairs of the king, and the term for civil servants is *kharachakan* or slaves of the king's affairs. The government's business was to maintain and protect the throne because the king was the *sine qua non* of the state, which was in turn his property.[24] Land rights were the king's to grant. Trade was a royal prerogative. No distinction was known between public and private treasure. The church was under his patronage, although his powers over the priesthood appear to have been limited. In general, all rights and obligations drew their authority from the king. It is this structure of rights which most sharply distinguished the traditional heritage of Thailand from European monarchy. In Europe the barons and burgesses held certain rights absolute and independent of the throne and could therefore more effectively resist or limit royal power. But the Thai nobility was dependent upon and more subject to the sway of royal authority.[25]

judge. It cannot be ignored, however, since the function of this institution was to weaken rebellious tendencies in the population. In the words of M. R. Seni Pramoj, "Whenever a prince or noble was suspected of intriguing against the Throne all that the King had to do was to take one of the suspect's daughters to wife. That would have the desired effect. . . . The reason was quite obvious then. It was simply not 'cricket' to rebel against one's in-laws" ("King Mongkut as a Legislator," *Journal of the Siam Society,* XXXVII, no. 1 [Jan., 1950], 46).

[24] Wales, *Siamese State Ceremonies,* pp. 88–89.

[25] As late as the sixth reign of the Bangkok dynasty the king wrote, under the nom de plume Asawaphahu, "As for those who have been royally appointed to government service in various positions—what is the true meaning of this? It is to be servant of the throne. . . . Officials who have power to do something—where is the power understood to come from? Who assigns the power? Or do they shape it themselves? Not at all! Any power there is, is part of the royal power" ("Khwam khaočhai phit" ["A Misunderstanding"; a letter, 1915]).

The most important officials of the Thai government were the two senior ministers and the four ordinary ministers. The symbolic significances of the ministerial positions were evidently rather complex and had by the Bangkok period become confused and perhaps not fully understood. Each office, however, had administrative responsibilities which appear to be quite clear. The two senior ministers had administrative control over the north and south, respectively. They were charged with keeping the peace, administering justice, raising taxes, conscripting labor and soldiers, and in respect to conscription keeping the registration lists of the people.[26] The present Ministries of Interior (*mahatthai*) and Defense (*kalahom*) retain the same names as the two traditional senior ministers.

The second level of the traditional government was made up of the four ministers of the City (*müang*), Palace (*wang*), Fields (*na*), and Treasury (*phraklang*). The Minister of the City was in charge of the administration of the capital and the area under the direct rule of the capital. The Minister of the Palace was the administrator of the palace and its not inconsiderable population and was also in charge of the general administration of justice in the kingdom by virtue of the royal power as a judge. The Minister of the Fields was in charge of farm-land registration, the administration of the king's lands, and the collection of the king's rice. As for the Minister of the Treasury, he was in charge of collecting various kinds of revenues and conducting the royal trade monopolies. The Minister of the Treasury was also the person who dealt with foreign traders in Siam and became thereby the Minister of

[26] Čhulalongkǫn, *Phrarachadamrat nai phrabat somdet phračhulačhomklao čhaoyuhua song thalaeng phraboromrachathibai kaekhai kanpokkhrǫng phaen din* ("Royal Address of His Majesty King Čhulačhomklao Explaining Changes in the Government"; Bangkok: Fine Arts Dept., 1950), pp. 2–3; Damrong, "Laksana," pp. 22–23.

Foreign Affairs.[27] The king's administration also included a number of administrative, judicial, military, and ceremonial departments with a variety of duties connected with the government's business.

Administration of the kingdom beyond the direct control of the capital was carried on by provincial governors. There were three groups of provinces: those of the interior, which were administered under the authority of the ministers and departments of the capital; those of the exterior; and dependent states. In contrast to the interior provinces, the provinces of the exterior were apparently quite autonomous. The governor, appointed by the king, re-created in his provincial capital a small-scale central administration.[28] There were also from time to time dependent states, such as Cambodia, Wiangčhan (Vientian), and various Malayan states, which recognized a tributary relationship to the Thai throne as it, in turn, paid tribute to the emperor of China. These dependent states administered their own affairs.

The bureaucracy ruled the people, who were then, as now, rice farmers. Although a large number of ordinary people were slaves, the distinction was largely a matter of obligations rather than a way of life. Siamese slaves (who might become so as prisoners of war, debtors, or offspring of persons in slavery) were generally not in a worse socioeconomic situation than freemen. Thai society traditionally, as well as at present, is hierarchical in conception and involves strong obligations on the part of the lower to the higher. A freeman's principal obligation to the government was generally in the form of labor, although there was provision for the subsitution of cash payment. This labor obligation could be, and apparently was, often onerous. Each freeman was attached to a department of the bureaucracy and was under the pa-

[27] Damrong, "Laksana," pp. 19–22.   [28] *Ibid.*, pp. 12–13.

tronage of the department's head.[29] The patron's function was to maintain peace among his clients, to protect their interests legally, and to organize and muster them for their *corvée* obligations. He was expected to manage his department in such a way as to provide himself a living as well as to meet royal demands. Officials received no salaries.[30]

Transformations

During the 80 years between 1851 and 1932, the traditional mode of government was fully transformed in such a way that the *coup d'état* in 1932, which ended absolute royal power, seemed a natural step and little more than a minor social disturbance. During this period, the kingdom was under pressure from European influences—economic, technical, intellectual, and armed—which overwhelmed the neighboring kingdoms of Burma, Cambodia, and Vietnam. The great question of policy during these years was, as mentioned before, the maintenance of independence. Thailand narrowly escaped subjection in large part by luck and geography. But credit must be given to the statecraft of the reigning kings of the period. Although there were no radical changes in government during the reign of Rama IV (1851–1868), the personality of this monarch turned the kingdom in the direction of change and innovation. He was himself a scholar and moralist with the wit and industry to investigate and appreciate the challenge and perils of the expanding Europeans.[31]

[29] *Ibid.*, pp. 13–16.   [30] *Ibid.*, p. 17.
[31] For further reading on Rama IV see Abbot Low Moffat, *Mongkut, the King of Siam* (Ithaca, N.Y.: Cornell University Press, 1961), and A. B. Griswold, *King Mongkut of Siam* (New York: Asia Society, 1961).

It was during the 42-year reign of Rama V (1868–1910) that the great transformation took place. The length of the reign was itself part of the luck which assisted the transition of his kingdom from its traditional mode of life and government to a new form better adapted to the needs of the time. The continuity of the monarch lay in the background of the extraordinary changes in institutions and spirit of government and society in this period.

In an earlier time it is unlikely that Rama V would have come to the throne, at least at the time he did, for his father died when he was not yet 16. The throne seems to have been untenable for boy kings in traditional Thailand when it was not unusual for the crown to descend out of the direct line. But in the case of Rama V, regularity was demanded. His dying father entrusted the task of safeguarding the heir and conducting the affairs of the kingdom during his remaining youth to a regent in the person of Somdet Čhao Phraya Si Suriyawong. This man had been associated with Rama IV for many years, both before and during his reign. The Somdet Čhao Phraya was in sympathy with the king's policy of adaptation to the new world in which Thailand found itself in the 1860's.[32]

Rama V had received careful training from his father in the traditions of the kingdom, the affairs of state, and understanding of the world. As a youth he had performed all the necessary ceremonies of his position. He had also been tutored by English and American teachers in the English language.[33] As was mentioned above, he took educational voyages to Java, Malaya, and India in his first years on the throne. These unusual elements of the beginning of his reign set the throne for a period of great change.

[32] Damrong, *Prawat*, p. 115.   [33] *Ibid.*, pp. 1–51.

The changes of the fifth reign may be grouped into three interrelated categories. The first is that group of changes which transformed the king from a mysterious magical being into an exalted and powerful administrative president. The second group included those which reorganized the administration of the kingdom and transformed it from an ancient set of more or less autonomous traditional offices into a system of rationalized and centralized ministries with carefully prescribed duties of a functional character. The third group of changes were those which transformed the rights and obligations of the subjects from personal and direct clientship to impersonal and universal citizenship.

On the occasion of the coronation which marked his accession to full powers in 1872, Rama V issued a proclamation which announced the spirit and rationale of all subsequent changes. He said:

Since we have ascended the throne, we have set our heart on the maintenance of the kingdom and on bringing happiness and prosperity to the royal family, the officials great and small, the Brahmans, and all segments of the population. Anything which is a form of oppression among us and which causes difficulty or trouble it is our intention to permit no longer. It is our impression that in various countries which are great states to the east and the west in Asia—to the east there are China, Vietnam, and Japan and to the west India, countries which practiced oppression by having lesser persons crouch, crawl, and prostrate themselves before princes and persons of high rank, as is the rule in Siam—in these days all these countries have changed and ended this rule. The purpose of the abolishing of crouching, crawling, and prostration is to let be seen the goodness of not having oppression in those countries from now on. Any country or city which has ended customs that are oppressive among themselves—in those countries and cities we see only prosperity coming to them generally. As for Siam, rules of the country of many kinds which are oppressive and are not necessary for justice still remain. We must plan to reduce them.

As for changing those rules, it cannot be done all at one time. We plan to make changes gradually in accordance with the proper time and the time when changes can be made. The country will then gain more perfect prosperity.

As for this rule of crouching, crawling, and prostration in Siam, we see it as a heavy oppression. Lesser persons who must crouch and crawl are fatigued and troubled in order to give honor to those of you who are important. We cannot see that giving honor by crawling and crouching and prostration is of any benefit to the country whatsoever. The lesser persons who must come and crouch and prostrate themselves to give you important persons honor must endure trouble until the end of their time, and then they will escape from you. We look at this practice as an example of all the varieties of oppression. Therefore, we in Siam must forsake the old customs which assert that crouching, crawling, and prostration are respectful. It is our merciful intention to have you all be happy and not have to endure the difficulty of crouching and crawling as before.

Let it be that the rule of crawling and crouching is changed to standing and walking, that the rule of prostration is changed to bowing. . . .

Perhaps you of high rank who like the rule of crouching, crawling, and prostration, who think it is good, are doubtful about how changing the rule will bring prosperity to the country. Well, it is necessary that you know that the changing of the rule of crouching and crawling to that of standing and walking is due to our will to make it perfectly clear that we will not have unjust oppression from now on. Any country where the big people do not oppress the little people will certainly have prosperity.

Let it be so enacted.[34]

[34] "Prakat plian thamniam mai" ("Announcement of a Change of Customs"), *PKPS*, VIII, 114–117.

The earnest desire for improvement, the sense of Thailand's having fallen behind the rest of the world, the determination to learn from the rest of the world while there was still time, all of which Rama V expressed implicitly in this statement made 90 years ago, persist to the present day. The king spoke most explicitly of what he wanted to do very shortly after the above speech when he said:

We have set our heart on protecting the state and having the royal family, the officials, and the people progress. So we have with effort crossed the sea to visit foreign lands in order to see the various countries and customs which will be well suited as models for Siam in future.[35]

Thus without embarrassment the king looked abroad for his inspiration.[36]

In conjunction with the abolition of the most extreme practices of making obeisance to power, the king early in the reign began, perhaps without this precise intention, to bring into question the right of absolute power. He set about establishing formal councils to advise the king on affairs of state. Two councils, known in Thai by the transliterated English names Council of State and Privy Council, were obvious borrowings from Western inspiration. While his first explanation of the need for such councils was that many heads are better than one, before long in the face of doubts he went on to state the idea that the king might commit injustice. The council, he said, "must have the power to delay the king, for example, in matters in which the king has a plan which is not just." [37]

[35] "Prakat wa duay tang khaosin lae phrarachabanyat" ("Announcement about Establishing a Council and an Act"), *PKPS*, VIII, 115.

[36] Prince Damrong Rachanuphap, *Thesaphiban* ("Administration"; Bangkok: Klang Witthaya Press, 1952), p. 7.

[37] "Prakat kan nai thi prüksa rachakan phaen din" ("Announcement on Affairs of Advising the Government"), *PKPS*, VIII, 169–170.

Rama V did not abandon the idea of some specification of royal power. At the height of his reign in a speech discussing the need to reorganize the government completely he said:

There is no law which specifies the royal power in Siam because it is believed that that power is beyond law and that there is no rule, thing, or person which can regulate or prevent it. But in truth any act of the king must be appropriate and just. For this reason we have no objection to a law which specifies the royal power.[38]

Rama V had no intention of encouraging any very stringent limitation of royal power, of course. He considered himself the leader in the efforts to improve the administration of the kingdom. Moreover, he specifically discouraged any idea of a parliament which, he said, would be powerless against him while he held the love of the people and would serve only to terrify the population.[39]

Furthermore, there is no evidence that during the fifth reign there was any serious thought of weakening the royal power. The king was evidently popular with all segments of the population, with the possible exception of some of the older officials. Even in their case, it appears that the king was careful to preserve their dignity and prerogatives while the way of life they knew was being destroyed. During the fifth reign, the king was able to make extended trips to Europe and leave the kingdom in the hands of the government without any difficulties. No doubt the inhospitable nature of the world in which Thailand found itself during the fifth reign— the all-too-clear threat of Britain and France, which had colo-

[38] Čhulalongkǫn, *Phraboromarachathibai kaekhai kanpokkhrǫng phaen din*, pp. 56–57.
[39] *Ibid.*

nized strong neighbors on all sides—was a contribution to the solidarity of the Thai ruling class and their loyalty to their king.

Nevertheless, the process of humanizing the throne, of transforming the king into the president of the administration, and the talk of limiting the royal power and of parliaments served to sow the seeds to be reaped by a less-commanding figure in a less-demanding time.

The fifth reign was marked by vast institutional and administrative changes as well as a change in spirit. The most notable of the institutional changes were the reorganization of the central government, the establishment of uniform provincial administration, and the beginning of general legal reform and codification. The traditional administration was unsuited to the task of modifying the government in the direction desired by the king. The extreme autonomy of the various ministries, departments, and provincial officers made it difficult for the throne to have any very dynamic influence. As long as the throne sought only to support itself in its traditional manner, the system was adequate. But the capacity of the traditional system for obstruction and its propensity for sheer inertia must have been awe-inspiring.

Changes were imperative, however, and Rama V appears to have been dauntless in his efforts to gather the lines of power into his hands. In 1873 the king struck to the root of the problem by beginning a process of reorganizing the collection and disbursement of revenues. He sought, evidently with some success, to end the virtual fiscal autonomy of the various parts of the administration and to establish centralized budgeting, accounting, and auditing procedures. No effort seems to have been made initially to increase actual collections. Rather energy went into developing the skills necessary to manage effective procedures. It was not until 1887 that a broad act was announced which reorganized the process of collection.[40] It has been estimated that revenues more than doubled in the following decade or so without the imposition of any new taxes.[41] By gaining fiscal power, the king was laying the foundation for his further reforms.

The second phase of administrative reform involved both the establishment of new departments and ministries with specific duties of a functional nature, such as the post and telegraph, and the redistribution of traditional duties among the various older ministries. This phase came to a climax in 1892 with the establishment of a cabinet of 12 ministers of equal rank, each in charge of a functional administrative organization.[42] This development had been in preparation for several years, during which time the officials who were affected met in committee regularly with the king to work out the details.[43]

Reorganization introduced some striking changes in the form of government of Thailand. First of all, the division of work according to function rather than territory centralized control in the Council of Ministers, which was dominated by the king serving as president. Secondly, though control was now centralized, the establishment of a regularly meeting cabinet diminished to some extent the role of the king as final arbiter. Potentially the cabinet had become the center of power rather than the throne.[44] Rama V was not concerned with this problem during his reign because the greatest threat to his

[40] Detchard Vongkomolshet, "The Administrative, Judicial and Financial Reforms of King Chulalongkorn, 1868–1910" (M.A. thesis, Cornell University, 1958), pp. 184 ff.

[41] James C. Ingram, *Economic Change in Thailand since 1850* (Stanford, Calif.: Stanford University Press, 1955), p. 177.

[42] "Prakat tang tamnaeng senabodi," *PKPS*, XIII, pt. 2, 93–98.

[43] Damrong, *Thesaphiban*, pp. 6–9.

[44] For further discussion see below, Chapter V.

policy within the country was unquestionably the old order of officials whose independent powers were being rapidly diminished.

Along with this process of rationalization of the central administration, the king undertook to establish a more uniform system of provincial government. Although traditionally the provinces were under the control of the royal court, it would appear that in fact the governors were free to conduct the affairs of their provinces as they pleased so long as they delivered certain revenues to the treasury. Aside from the deliverance of these revenues, their responsibility was to suppress banditry and disturbance.[45] The governor was expected to support himself and his administration through his own efforts, a practice which was hardly likely to produce gentle or benevolent administration.

Rama V sought to bring some order to this confused situation. He began by sending trusted viceroys into the most troublesome areas with authority to regulate the governors.[46] Following the establishment of the new cabinet in 1892, he began to bring the responsibility of all provinces under the Ministry of the Interior. Its minister continued the use of viceroys as the principal means of establishing his control over governors. He grouped into circles provinces among which communication was feasible. Over each circle he put a viceroy. This officer, who was carefully selected for his loyalty and efficiency, undertook, in cooperation with the minister, to set up the new system within the circle. The work progressed slowly. It appears that the establishment of a new circle had to wait upon the recruiting of a viceroy who was willing, loyal, and capable to undertake the work. The new system was also

[45] Damrong, *Thesaphiban*, pp. 53–54.
[46] Reginald Stuart LeMay, *An Asian Arcady* (Cambridge, Eng.: W. Heffer and Sons, Ltd., 1926), pp. 123–129.

dependent upon the expenditure of increased money, and the process of extension was delayed by shortage of funds as well.[47]

These three related phases of reform—fiscal, central, and provincial administration—greatly increased the power of the center. Whereas previously the power of the throne had been glorified as absolute and without limits, its capacity for dynamic action was probably slight. The bureaucracy was firmly entrenched, and the various high offices were protected by their autonomy. The king could, of course, remove any official and replace him with a more honest or loyal one. But even here it is doubtful that a complete change would have been feasible. With the leverage of foreign pressure and the model of foreign governments, Rama V was gradually able to gather authority to himself.

Another group of reforms during the fifth reign struck at the very personal nature of social and political relationships of traditional Thailand. From the early years of the reign, Rama V announced his determination to end slavery in the kingdom as quickly as possible, consistent with the protection of the welfare of the slaveowners. His first act was to provide that no person born in his reign should be a slave. Those children born into slavery were to be freed at the age of 21. A later act provided that slaves were to be credited with a specified monthly wage to be applied against their purchase price until they were free. Finally, the criminal code of 1908 imposed stiff penalties upon trading in slaves.[48]

Certainly as significant for the society as a whole was the gradual abolition of *corvée* labor. This process had actually been going on for many years. Ingram reports that from the

---

[47] Damrong, *Thesaphiban*, pp. 79–91; Detchard, pp. 106–144.
[48] Detchard, pp. 56–58; "Phrarachabanyat that" ("Slavery Act"), *PKPS*, XX, 24–26.

time of Ayutthaya the government had been urging the acceptance of cash payment in lieu of work obligations, and this practice had apparently been extended during the early reigns of Bangkok.[49] With the extension of the uniform administration of the provinces, however, it was possible to bring some regularity into the multitude of customary obligations to the king and provincial officials. In 1900, it was enacted that thenceforth any labor drafted from the population was to be paid,[50] and in 1901 it was enacted that industrious persons were to be exempted from drafted labor.[51] The responsibility for the administration of drafting labor was transferred from the traditional chiefs to the new provincial officials. In the same year (1901), virtually all personal obligations to the state were transformed into a head tax on all men from the age of 18 to 60.[52]

This process of transformation did not initially include the obligation for military service which remained to every man at any time during his adult life. By 1905, however, the traditional haphazard methods of drafting military recruits had become an obstacle to the training of soldiers. Obligations for military service were then transformed from a lifetime obligation to serve whenever called into a system of universal conscription for two years of military training.[53]

Rama V died in 1910 in the forty-second year of his reign.

[49] Ingram, pp. 59–60.

[50] "Phrarachabanyat laksana ken čhang, R.S. 119" ("Act on the Forms of Draft and Hire, 1900"), *PKPS*, XVII, 528–531.

[51] "Prakat phoemdoem phrarachabanyat laksana ken čhang" ("Announcement of an Amendment to the Act on Forms of Draft and Hire"), *PKPS*, XVIII, 230–231.

[52] "Phrarachabanyat kep ngoen kharachakan, R.S. 120" ("Act on Collecting Money for Government Service, 1901"), *PKPS*, XVIII, 224–230.

[53] "Phrarachabanyat ken thahan, R.S. 124" ("Act on Drafting Soldiers, 1905"), *PKPS*, XX, 302–314.

When he succeeded to the throne, Thailand was ruled by the ancient system of government dating back for centuries. At the time of his death the kingdom had irrevocably turned its back on many of the traditional modes of society and government and had plunged into a vigorous and imaginative effort to bring itself to a state which was amenable to the standards of the contemporary world. No effort has been made here to trace in detail the many changes which took place.[54] Rather, an attempt has been made to emphasize the features which were particularly pertinent to later political developments. The power to establish policies and undertake activities throughout the entire kingdom had been brought together in a more centralized administration, and therefore the throne was more powerful at the end of the fifth reign than it had been at the beginning. In assuming this power, Rama V justified the many actions of his reign in terms of his determination to seek justice and also in terms of the vision and effectiveness of his administration. Moreover, from time to time he cast doubts on the king's place in the realm of magical supremacy by accepting the fact that the kingship, as well as all other offices, was bound by the imperatives of the principles of justice. In addition, through rationalization of the administration along functional lines, the principle that government officials were qualified by virtue of their skill as well as by virtue of their loyalty was introduced into the political system. This principle was to lead to profound modifications in the attitude of officials in later years. Finally, by the introduction of the principle of universal legal relationships in place of those of personal master and follower, the lines which tied the political and social order to the throne were weakened.

[54] For further consideration of the period of change see Walter F. Vella, *The Impact of the West on Government in Thailand* (Berkeley and Los Angeles: University of California Press, 1955).

Rama VI

Rama V was succeeded by his colorful heir, Prince Wachirawut (Rama VI). Although each of the two men left his mark on modern Thailand, there is considerable contrast between them. Whereas Rama V busied himself with administration and law, Rama VI was by nature a poet and a moralist. Rama VI was the first Thai king to receive extensive education in a foreign land: he spent nine years in England, at the military academy at Sandhurst and as a law student at Oxford. He was nevertheless very much a Thai and a king so that he combined in his own person the two great trends which have dominated modern Thailand, the European and the Southeast Asian traditions. He spoke and wrote fluently in English and at the same time is held by many to be one of the leading figures of modern Thai literature.

Rama VI's outstanding contribution to the political life of modern Thailand was the creation of a spirit of nationalism. The traditional mode of binding the political and social structure was through allegiance of the lesser to the greater—the loyalty of the people to the chiefs, the chiefs to the officials, and the officials to the king. The reforms of the fifth reign struck at these bonds but provided no new ideas to replace them. Rama V had faith in the traditional oaths and believed that the people would follow him because he was striving for their benefit. He called often for unity among the officials to face the task at hand.[55] It remained for Rama VI, however, to

[55] Cf. Čhulalongkǫn, *Phraboromarachathibai rüang samakhi* ("Royal Lecture on Unity"), first delivered about 1903 (Bangkok: Fine Arts Dept., 1946).

make the attempt at inculcating a spirit of national allegiance.

Among the more curious and yet characteristic devices used in the king's efforts to arouse a spirit of nationalism was the Wild Tiger Corps (*süa pa*). This was a paramilitary organization formed soon after the beginning of the reign. Bureaucrats and other leading citizens were encouraged to join, and membership became something of a social distinction. Its spirit was an amalgam of foreign ideas and slogans of Thai nationalism. In its organization the inspirational discipline of a British regiment was combined with the self-improvement attitudes of the Boy Scouts. The king, when he was a young prince in England, had observed these two institutions and conceived them to be suitable for his nationalistic purposes. Along with the adult Wild Tiger Corps, long since disappeared from the Thai scene, the king also founded the Tiger Cubs (*luk süa*), which continue today as the government-sponsored Boy Scouts.

The king, in his announcement of the establishment of the Wild Tiger Corps, gave three purposes to the organization. These were

in the first place to make the Thai people in general feel loyal to the leaders of the kingdom in accordance with the wise customs; secondly, to love the nation and respect the religion; and, finally, to feel unity with the group and not do harm to each other. These three ideas are the permanent principles which will make our nation continue free and prevent the sacrifice of any bit of ground where our ancestors have planted our nation within these Thai borders. . . . Our nation is not yet dead. It will grow and prosper.[56]

[56] "Phrarachadamrat" ("Proclamation"; 1911); quoted in S. Wathanaset, *Kiatthikhun phramongkut klao* ("The Virtue of Rama VI"; Bangkok: Watthana Phanit Press, 1957), pp. 36–37.

Troops of the Wild Tiger Corps were set up in Bangkok and various provincial towns. They were splendidly uniformed and met for regular weekly drill. The king took great personal interest in what should presumably be called the indoctrination of these corps. He drilled personally with the Bangkok troop and wrote much inspirational literature for the edification of the members. The themes of this literature were loyalty to religion, king, and nation (God, king, and country of the British army officer) and service to the community.

Clearly Rama VI revolted against the gradual diminishing of the Thai realm under pressure from colonial powers and was determined to arouse the nation to oppose the process. His early writings on the Wild Tiger Corps were sprinkled with refusals to sacrifice another inch of territory. In the course of events, he never had to face the issue.

Moreover, his writings also pressed the national question forward on two different lines. The first was that Thailand must hurry with its improvements and reforms so that full independence could be regained in treaty relations.[57] The general principle which he affirmed again and again was co-operation for progress. He was evidently deeply concerned about the individualistic character of his subjects and hoped through his energetic moralizing to weld them into a unified nation.

His second theme was the Chinese problem. He took a lively interest in the progress of the Chinese revolution and at the same time undertook to discourage nationalism among

[57] Asawaphahu (Rama VI), *Khlon titlo* ("Mud on the Wheels"), in *Pramuan bot phrarachaniphon nai phrabat somdet phramongkut klao čhaoyuhua* ("Collection of Royal Writings of Rama VI"; Bangkok: Fine Arts Dept., 1955), *passim*, particularly the last chapter.

the many Chinese in his kingdom. The object of his attack on the Chinese was the growing tendencies among them to perpetuate their national characteristics and look down on the Thai.[58]

Rama VI was one of the outstanding early Asian nationalists. His ideological contribution to his country has been neglected outside of the kingdom because of the undramatic quality of political events during the reign. Nevertheless, his legacy of ideas has been important to Thailand since his time. The slogans and symbols which he developed—religion, king, and nation; the attitude that the Thai should justify their nationhood by their progressiveness and adaptation of Western standards; and the fear of the Chinese role in the country— all remain today as potent instruments and ideas. This king was and is a figure of controversy. He played favorites at the expense of orderly administration; he was flamboyant and extravagant; he was cliquish, arrogant, literary, and a little odd. One has the feeling that at his death in 1925 the country sighed with relief. But his influence on modern Thailand is unmistakable.

For temperamental, political, and economic reasons, Rama VII was not able to maintain the dynamic qualities of the throne characteristic of his three predecessors. As a prince, Rama VII was not thought a likely successor to the throne. He was the youngest brother of Rama VI, and there were at least three other possible preceding heirs.[59] By a series of untimely deaths and unapproved marriages he became the heir of Rama VI. Probably the fact that he was not reared to be a

[58] Cf. Asawaphahu (Rama VI), *Mai chǫp thai* ("Don't Like Thai"), *Thukbangkhap hai pen čhin* ("Forced to Be Chinese"), and *Kan phai nai müang čhin* ("Affairs in China"), variously reprinted by the Fine Arts Dept.

[59] *Čhaofa prachathipok* ("Prince Prachathipok"; Bangkok: Surirat Press, 1949), p. 24.

king but in the shadow of kings made him a diffident young man.

At the very beginning of his reign, he came under the strong influence of older members of the royal family, some of whom had been aggrieved during Rama VI's reign. Their influence was not used to press forward with new reforms. Faced with financial difficulties, the government was, in fact, largely preoccupied with economy measures and of no mind to make changes. It is generally understood that although Rama VII himself was in favor of establishing a constitutional monarchy, he was dissuaded by his older counselors.[60] The trend of change was not to be resisted, however.

It was the destiny of Rama VII to lend dignity to the dissolution of royal power in Thailand and thereby to preserve the monarchy. His policy toward the group which established the consitiutional government by force was one of conciliation. The attempt of Phraya Mano, the first constitutional Prime Minister, to rule by decree and the Bǫwǫradet rebellion in 1933 embittered the relations between king and government, however, and the influence of the throne shriveled away. In early 1934 Rama VII left the kingdom for medical treatment and never returned. In a long correspondence between him and the government, he sought to reestablish his right to have a voice in government policy, but the Phahon government, which followed Phraya Mano, would not yield.[61] Finally, in March, 1935, Rama VII issued a bitter statement against the government and announced his intention to abdicate. The government accepted and selected as his suc-

[60] Baron de Lapomarède, "The Setting of the Siamese Revolution," *Pacific Affairs*, VII (Sept., 1934), 254.

[61] *Thalaengkan rüang phrabat somdet phraboromintramahaprachathipok phra pokklaočhaoyuhua song sala rachasombat* ("Announcement concerning the Abdication of King Phrapokklao"; Bangkok, 1935), *passim.*

cessor a young prince at that time in school in Switzerland.

The position of the throne and the circumstances that have surrounded it since the abdication of Rama VII have been somewhat unusual, and final judgment on the role of the throne as a permanent factor in the political system is not possible. Between 1935 and 1950, with brief exceptions, the reigning king was still not an adult and also was living out of the country. In such a situation the question of the ultimate relationship between the throne and the political leadership of the country could be avoided. Since the coronation of King Phumiphon in 1950, there have been indications of tensions between the king and the politicians. For example, when the constitution of 1932 was reinstated in 1951, the king's effort to influence the constitutional situation met with some slight success.[62] In 1955, the king made a ceremonial progress to the northeast region of the country and was enthusiastically received by the people. It is said that the government was dismayed by the potential popularity of the king and refused to finance any more such trips.[63] Again in 1957 at the time of the great public celebration of the twenty-five hundredth anniversary of Buddhism, the king declined to attend the elaborate government ceremonies in which he had been scheduled to take a major part. It was widely rumored, although officially denied on both sides, that the king's failure to attend was a result of his personal displeasure with the government. There is no question that by not attending this celebration the king contributed to the general decline of the prestige of the gov-

[62] *Bangkok Post*, Jan. 3, 17, 19, 21, 1952; Phairot Chaiyanam, *Khamathibai kotmai rathathammanun priap thiap* ("Lectures on Comparative Constitutional Law"; Bangkok: Thammasat University, 1952), II, 151–154.

[63] This was told to the author by a person close to the king and perhaps is somewhat exaggerated. The king, however, made no more public trips outside the capital until after the coup of 1957.

ernment and thereby to its ultimate overthrow. In September, 1957, when the government was overthrown, it was understood that the king was not displeased.

The fact that the throne is now occupied by an adult who can manipulate some of the great prestige of the institution would certainly indicate that the political problem of the position of the throne must be faced. Whether the political influence of the king will gradually increase or will suddenly be cut off as it was in 1935 depends largely upon the discretion of the monarch.

IV

NATIONAL LEADERSHIP

THE foundation of political life in Thailand is the clique, with a leader as the nucleus. A clique is fundamentally a face-to-face group because the characteristic ties binding it together are personal in nature—ties of personal love and loyalty based on the relationship between the leader and the follower. It would appear that there is a strong tendency for these ties to direct themselves up and down while lateral ties among the followers within the clique are not necessarily very strong. It is quite possible that different persons or elements tied to the same leader may be antagonistic to each other as rivals for the leader's favor and perhaps even for the succession.

Cliques may develop out of other kinds of groups. For example, family ties, which provide the pattern for the sort of attitudes of loyalty and obligation upon which cliques are constructed, are quite likely to carry over to some extent into political cliques. Centuries of bureaucratic social organizations have produced other structured patterns of loyalty. The relationships within units in the bureaucracy, between teacher and student, between schoolmates, also provide types of loyalty. The clique is not, however, the same as any of these other institutions. Rather it is an extension of the various patterns of relationship felt in other institutions of Thai society. Thus the clique, which is a personal relationship, may include persons whose ties to the leader began in another institution but have become strengthened because of continued contact.

It would seem reasonable to assume, although no study has been attempted on this question, that there is a limit to the kinds of personal tie characteristic of cliques. A certain amount of attention is required in the renewal of the less institutionally linked ties, and therefore at the outer limits they would become increasingly unstable and tenuous. For example, a clique might be temporarily enlarged by the distribution of rewards when they were available. But these obligations of a temporary and opportunistic kind might prove unreliable in the long run.

The clique has no formal organization. It is not likely to have meetings, it has no name, and it has no established list of members. It is a web of obligations which may spread out into a number of groups and organizations of other types. Probably no one knows all its ramifications, if it is a large clique, other than the leader himself. It may not even be considered by him as a coherent group. As a rule the clique is not suitable for taking a specific course of action in a specific circumstance. Rather the members will work generally to further the leader's causes and will do certain things for him as he suggests.

Six Leaders

Insofar as clique coherence is necessary for stable political careers, it is clear that the qualities of a leader, i.e., the capability to attract and hold followers, are crucial. Political leaders are not popularly chosen in Thailand. They thrust themselves on the country. If six men are selected as examples of top political leadership and their biographies combined with certain things known about Thai modes of thought and political attitudes, some tentative conclusions may be made about the very complex and difficult phenomenon of leadership. These six men are Phraya Phahon Phonphayuhasena, leader of the *coup d'état* of 1932 and Prime Minister from 1933 to 1938; Field Marshal Phibunsongkhram, second-echelon leader of the 1932 coup, former Minister of Defense and supreme commander of the armed forces, and Prime Minister from 1938 to 1944 and from 1948 to 1957; Dr. Pridi Phanomyong, intellectual leader of the 1932 coup, former Minister of the Interior, Foreign Affairs, and Finance, former regent, Prime Minister in 1946, and elder statesman; Khuang Aphaiwong, participant in the coup of 1932, former Minister of Communications and vice-president of the national assembly, Prime Minister in 1944–1945, 1946, and 1947–1948, and leader of the Democrat Party from 1946; Field Marshal Sarit Thanarat, former Minister of Defense, from 1957 supreme commander of the armed forces, and from 1959 Prime Minister; and General Phao Siyanon, former Minister of the Interior, director-general of the Police Department, and secretary-general of the Seri Manangkhasila Party.

Phraya Phahon was born in 1887 in Bangkok. He was the son of a military man who also held the title of Phraya and the rank of colonel. His education was begun early by his father, and he entered military academy at the age of 12. He graduated at the age of 16, first in his class. He was sent to Germany to continue his military training, apparently one of the earliest nonroyal students to go abroad. He had been in Europe, in both Germany and Denmark, as a military student for about nine years when he was recalled. It is reported that he was recalled after he, with other students, outraged the chief of staff, Prince Čhakraphong, by asking for a higher allowance.

From his return to Thailand shortly before World War I until 1932, he served in a variety of military posts and rose to the highest rank available to a nonroyal officer. In 1932 he was the leader of the *coup d'état* and served in the first governments of the constitutional period. In 1933 he sided with the anti-Mano faction and served as leader in seizing power from Phraya Mano. He was the natural candidate for the Prime Minister's office, which he held until he retired in 1938. From 1932 to 1938 he also held the position of commander in chief of the army.[1]

Field Marshal Phibunsongkhram was born in 1898 in a village not far from Bangkok. His father was a farmer. He is said to have been a quiet and thoughtful child as a result of poor health. He early entered the temple school near his birthplace and later went to another in Bangkok. He is reported to have been an industrious student throughout his educational career. He applied for admission to the royal military academy and graduated at the age of 20. After World War I he was selected to continue his military studies in France, where he met Pridi Phanomyong, Khuang Aphaiwong, and other Thai students, many of whom were participants in the coup of 1932. Returning to Thailand, he served in various posts in the army and rose to the rank of major by 1932.

He was an active promoter of the coup among young army officers and served in the first governments of the constitutional period. He is reported to have early entered into a rivalry in the army with Phraya Song Suradet, one of the four colonels

[1] Thai Noi, *Phraya phahon* (Bangkok: Phrae Phitaya and Odeon Store, 1954), pp. 32–59.

who were the top coup leaders, for control—a rivalry which ended with Song's fleeing the country under the charge of treason in 1939. Phibun joined with Phahon in overthrowing Mano's government in 1933. He was put in charge of the suppression of Prince Bǫwǫradet's rebellion in October, 1933, and won great renown by his success in that episode. In 1934 he became Minister of Defense in Phahon's government and immediately gained a reputation for building up the armed forces. He inaugurated the Youth Corps (*yawayon*), a kind of quasi-fascist youth group in 1935. He escaped three attempted assassinations between 1935 and 1938, and this gave him a reputation of having a charmed life.[2]

In 1938 he succeeded Phahon as Premier, and he also held the portfolios of Interior and Defense. Apparently he was designated for the Prime Minister's position by the retiring Phahon.[3] He led the government into an intensely nationalist policy against the Chinese minority. He challenged the French in Indochina in 1940 and regained title to former Thai territory in Cambodia and Laos. In this affair he had himself made a field marshal and appointed supreme commander of the armed forces. During the period of his prime ministership from 1938 to 1944, he made many pronouncements on the value of leadership. After the invasion of the country by Japan, he established a dictatorship under the slogan, "Have faith in the leader and the nation will be safe." His career in this

[2] Čharun Kuwanon, *Chiwit kan tǫsu khǫng bukkhon samkhan* ("Lives of Important People"; Bangkok: Aksǫn Čharoen That Press, 1953), pp. 252–257; W. Čh. Prasangsit, *Pathiwat rathaprahan lae kabot čhalačhon nai samai prachathipathai haeng prathet thai* ("Revolution, *Coup d'Etat*, and Rebellion in Thailand during the Democratic Period"; Bangkok, 1949), pp. 108–112.

[3] Khuang Aphaiwong, *Kan tǫsu khǫng khaphačhao* ("My Struggle"; Bangkok: Pramuansan, 1958), p. 59; Thai Noi, *Phraya phahon*, p. 418.

period is remembered for his arbitrary regulations on Thai "culture." These included the forbidding of the production or consumption of betel nut, the forced wearing of shoes, hats, ties, and coats, and the simplification of the Thai system of writing. His government was overthrown in the national assembly in 1944. At the same time he was stripped of his position as supreme commander.

In 1946 he was charged under a law on war crimes, but the law was thrown out as unconstitutional. He played the role of the man behind the scenes in the *coup d'état* of 1947, emerging only to take over the Prime Minister's office in April, 1948. He held the office until 1957, when he fled into exile after the coup in September. During that decade there were several attempts to overthrow his government by force, but at least once, in June, 1951, it was the declared intention of the rebels to ask him to continue in the Prime Minister's office. In the election of 1957 he was a candidate for a seat in Bangkok. He campaigned as the "Founder of the Thai Nation" and as the source of many improvements in the country. He ran ahead of all candidates, and there is no reason to think this did not reflect the mood of the public.[4]

Dr. Pridi Phanomyong was born in 1900 in Ayutthaya Province. His father was a farmer and merchant and apparently of good financial standing. Pridi was educated in local schools

[4] There is, of course, a vast literature on the career of Field Marshal Phibun, and no single source is particularly reliable since he has always been a man of controversy. Cf. Čharun Kuwanon, *Chiwit kan tosu khong čhomphon p. phibunsongkhram* ("The Life and Struggle of Field Marshal P. Phibunsongkhram"; Bangkok: Akson Čharoen That Press, 1953); M. R. Khükrit Pramoj *et al.*, *Čhomphon nai thatsana khong khaphačhao* ("My Opinion of the Field Marshal"; Bangkok: Wibunkit Press, 1949); Damri Pathamasiri, *Samkhan thi phu nam* ("Mark of the Leader"; Bangkok: Bangkok Municipality Press, 1939); and many others.

from the age of five to 11, when he was sent to school in Bangkok. He completed secondary school at the age of 15 and entered the Royal Law School at 16. He was apparently an unusual student, for he had earned the degree Bachelor of Law First Class by the time he was 19.

He is reported to have made a reputation very early by winning an extremely difficult case. But it was his first and last case because he then entered the civil service. In 1920 he won a government scholarship to study law in France. His young life has been described by a biographer as

the life of the sons of ordinary people, the sons of poor people like all Thai. In his youth he grew up in a rural environment and received his early education in temple schools and was a good temple boy. But he was industrious and ambitious for education and by means of good behavior advanced in life and in education.[5]

While a student at the University of Paris, Pridi had his first taste of political activity. Together with other students in France, including several subsequent leaders of the 1932 coup, he formed a club which took it upon itself to complain to the Thai minister that the Thai students in France were being discriminated against in their government allowances. This created a series of difficulties which very nearly resulted in the cancellation of his scholarship. He did finish his studies, however, and received a doctor's degree.[6]

Pridi returned from France in 1929 and entered government service as the secretary of the Department for Drafting Legislation and as a teacher in the Royal Law School. He was

[5] Sawai Sutthiphithak, *Dr. pridi phanomyong kap kan pathiwat* ("Dr. Pridi Phanomyong and the Revolution"; Bangkok: Sirithamnakhon, n.d.), p. 5.

[6] Düan Bunnak, *Than pridi rathaburut awuso* ("Mr. Pridi, Elder Statesman"; Bangkok: Soemwithaya Banakhan, 1957). pp. 8–13.

given the title of Luang Pradit Manutham. As a teacher he was in an excellent position to gather followers, and this was no doubt important in his later political career.[7]

Pridi along with other students from France had been considering, scheming, and planning the eventual replacement of the absolute monarchy with a constitutional regime. He was an early participant in the planning of the 1932 coup and took the role of intellectual leader. He has been credited with writing the provisional constitution of June, 1932. He also worked on the drafting of the permanent constitution of 1932.

His most dramatic contribution to the developments of the postcoup period was the Economic Plan, a radical scheme for the reorganization of the economic system. Pridi frightened a good many conservative politicians with his plan, and he became the center of the conflict between the government and the national assembly. He left the country under charges of being a Communist.

While he was abroad, the government of Phraya Mano was overthrown by the military, and Phraya Phahon asked him to return for an investigation of the Communist charges. A special commission investigated the case, and Pridi was cleared.

Pridi had an extraordinarily productive career after his return to the country. He served first as Minister of the Interior. While in that office he established the University of Moral and Political Science. Its purpose was to train lawyers and civil servants. He also developed the first serious attempt at local self-government in the Municipalities Act of 1933. After serving as Minister of the Interior he took the portfolio of Foreign Affairs and presided over the negotiation of new treaties with the world powers. This series of pacts finally returned Thailand to complete legal and fiscal autonomy after

[7] Sawai, p. 6.

80 years of restriction. In Phibun's first government Pridi held the Finance portfolio and worked on the revised revenue code promulgated in 1940.

In late 1941 he resigned from the government over the issue of collaboration with the Japanese and was appointed a regent. From that office he engineered the overthrow of Phibun in 1944 and also assumed leadership of the underground Free Thai organization. From 1944 until 1947 he was unquestionably the most powerful man in the kingdom. His prestige and position were undermined, however, by a number of developments, including inflation, corruption, and the death of the king. By the end of 1947 he had many more enemies than he had in 1944, and his power collapsed after the coup of 1947. Since the coup he has been living abroad.

Khuang Aphaiwong was born in 1902 in Phratabong (Battambang), a Cambodian province, at that time a part of the kingdom of Thailand. His father was governor of the eastern circle and a descendant of the family of hereditary rulers of Thailand's Cambodian realm whose line dated from the Thonburi kingdom. In the early years of Khuang's life his family had to move from their traditional home when Thailand yielded sovereignty to the French protectorate of Cambodia.[8]

At the age of five Khuang was sent by his father to start school in Bangkok. He studied first at the Royal Temple School of Thepsirin. At the age of nine he entered the French missionary school, Assumption College. His father accompanied Rama V on a trip to Europe, and the experience is said to have convinced him that he should have his children educated in Europe if possible.[9] At the end of World War I, Khuang at the age of 16 was sent to France to study engineering.

[8] Khuang, pp. 2–5.
[9] Bunchuai Sisawat, *Phantri khuang aphaiwong* ("Major Khuang Aphaiwong"; Bangkok: Rapphim Press, n.d.), p. 52.

While studying in France, Khuang became involved in the student group which was subsequently so important in the *coup d'état* of 1932. In 1929 Khuang returned to Thailand after completing his engineering course. He was employed in the Telegraph Department as an engineer.

Khuang's early friendships with the student group in France brought him into the civilian group promoting the *coup d'état* of 1932. As a result he was appointed a member of the first national assembly. He also remained in the Post and Telegraph Department as a civil servant and within a year had risen to be director-general. Khuang seems to have been an active and effective speaker in the assembly and rose to some prominence among the members. In 1937 he was appointed minister without portfolio in Phahon's cabinet. In the first Phibun government, he was Deputy Minister of Public Instruction. In the second Phibun government, he was Minister of Communications.[10] In 1943 and 1944 he was also vice-president of the national assembly.

At the time Phibunsongkhram's government was overthrown in 1944, Khuang was Pridi's candidate for the office of Prime Minister. His qualification for that office seems to have been, in large measure, his acceptability to a number of factions. He was neither pro- nor anti-Japanese. He was an old friend of both Pridi and Phibun. He was popular in the national assembly and also sympathetic to political figures of a royalist tendency who had been long excluded from politics. But it would not be fair to him to give the impression that his acceptability was a result of his being a nonentity. A more accurate explanation is probably that he is not an overly ambitious man. His social status and financial position were high.

Khuang served as Prime Minister until the surrender of Japan in 1945, when he resigned. In 1946 he ran for a parliamen-

[10] *Ibid.*, pp. 197–198.

tary seat in Bangkok, from which he has been returned in every subsequent election except 1952, when he did not run. Following the 1946 election he was again appointed Prime Minister with Pridi's support. During the first months of this government, there was evidently a falling out between Pridi and Khuang. When the government was reconstituted after the promulgation of the new constitution in 1946, he was opposed for the office by Pridi himself. In the meantime he had announced his separation from the Pridi group by assuming the leadership of the newly formed Democrat Party.[11] From that time he has been most prominent as an opponent of the government.

At the time of the *coup d'état* of 1947, however, he had another brief term as Prime Minister under the sponsorship of the Coup d'Etat Group. He was able to provide this group with respectability before the Allied powers, who were dubious of the return of Phibunsongkhram. He led an election campaign in which the majority of successful candidates were nominal members of the Democrat Party. Two months after the election, he was ousted from the office, virtually at gun point. He then returned to the position of leader of the parliamentary opposition. His following among members of the assembly dwindled, however, under the persuasive pressure of the Coup d'Etat Group.

After the "silent" coup of November, 1951, he, along with his closest associates, refused to stand for election under the constitution which provided that half the members of the assembly were to be appointed.[12] But he continued as an active commentator on politics.

In 1955, after the enactment of the law on political parties,

[11] "Kiat," pseud., *Phongsawadan kan müang* ("Political Chronicles"; Bangkok: Kiatthisak Press, 1950), pp. 1–45.
[12] Bunchuai Sisawat, p. 577.

the Democrat Party was revived under Khuang's leadership. He led a slate of candidates in Bangkok against a government group headed by Phibunsongkhram. Khuang ran second to Phibun. The Democrat Party was again a leading part of the parliamentary opposition to the Phibun government, although Khuang played no open role in the army coup of September, 1957. Khuang once more headed a slate of candidates in Bangkok in the December, 1957, election which won all the contested seats.

Field Marshal Sarit Thanarat was born in 1908 in Bangkok. His father was an army officer. He entered the military academy at the age of 11 and finished at the age of 20. There is no indication that his early military career was exceptional. His outstanding posts seem to have been deputy commander of the army infantry school, commander of an artillery regiment, and commandant of the military academy.[13] At the time of the *coup d'état* of 1947, he was commanding officer of an infantry battalion in Bangkok.[14] The fact that he was on active duty then indicates that he had had no previous political commitments.

In the 1947 coup he was an active participant, however, and thereafter his career was one of rapid rise. He was appointed commander of the first (Bangkok) military circle in 1948. In February, 1949, he was the officer in charge of the suppression of a naval and marine rebellion. Immediately thereafter he was raised to the post of Commander of the First Army. Within another two years he was deputy commander of the army, and within three more years commander in chief of the army.

After the "silent" coup of 1951, he became Deputy Minister of Defense in Phibun's cabinet. He remained in that post until March, 1957, when he was appointed Minister of Defense. In the period between 1952 and 1957 he became deeply involved

---

[13] W. Čh. Prasangsit, p. 339. [14] *Ibid.*, p. 179.

in a variety of nonmilitary enterprises. He was on the boards of directors of at least 20 corporations of various kinds. He was also chairman of the board of the National Lottery Organization.

By late 1954 it was evident that he was a rival of Police General Phao Siyanon for succession to Phibunsongkhram. In the campaign for the election in February, his role was particularly ambiguous. Although he was a deputy leader of the government political party of which General Phao was secretary-general, he conspicuously did no campaigning. At the same time people known to be his supporters campaigned against the party, and two newspapers owned by him vigorously opposed the government and especially the activities of the party.

It was in the period immediately after that election in March, 1957, that he emerged as something of a popular figure. He was appointed supreme commander of all the services in a declared emergency following the elections. He expressed his sympathy with the students who protested election practices and suddenly became popular with the antigovernment group. With his power as commander in chief of the army he became the great hope of the enemies of Phibunsongkhram and Phao Siyanon.

Finally, after several months of tension, the split between Field Marshal Sarit and the government was uncovered as an issue which could be resolved only by radical means. Sarit was the leader of the army group that overthrew the government in September, 1957. Because of extreme illness, however, he took no position other than supreme commander of the forces, from there playing the role of power behind the throne. During the first nine months of 1958, he was out of the country. In October, 1958, he suddenly returned to set up a military dictatorship, and he adopted a tough line against activities ranging from arson to communism which threatened stability. He became Prime Minister in February, 1959.

One of the most striking aspects of Sarit's career is the sudden transformation that took place. From an inconspicuous battalion commander before the 1947 *coup d'état*, he rose within a few years to be an extremely powerful political general. In 1957 he was transformed in the public eye from one, and by no means the least, of the rather corrupt government group into a man on a white horse who would set the nation right. There is so little evidence available about the man's personality that it is impossible to go beyond speculation to explain his rise. One is forced to recognize in him a keen sense of doing the right thing at the right time, a quality much admired among Thai people.

Police General Phao Siyanon was born in 1909 in Bangkok. His father was a civil servant under the monarchy. General Phao was educated in the royal military academy and graduated in 1930. At about the time of the suppression of the Bǫwǫradet rebellion in 1933, Phao became the aide of the then Colonel Phibunsongkhram. His close relationship with Phibun continued from that time on. After Phibun became Prime Minister, Phao served him in a number of important but not first-rank positions, such as administrator of the Crown Property Department. During this period he married a daughter of a close army associate of Phibun, General Phin Chunhawan, who was one of the leaders of the 1947 coup. When Phibun was retired from the office of Prime Minister and supreme commander of the forces in 1944, Phao was also put on inactive service. A peculiarity of Phao's career up to that point was the fact that although he was an army officer he had virtually no experience in the regular service but was occupied in his close association with political figures.

General Phao's rise toward great power began with the 1947 coup. In the planning stage he is reported to have acted as contact man with Phibun.[15] His previous close association with Phibun and his relationship with General Phin admirably qualified him for this task. After the success of the coup he was appointed deputy director-general of the Police Department, unofficially in charge of political police activity. The first event that brought him prominence was the arrest in October, 1948, of a number of army general staff officers on charges of plotting a rebellion. In that affair he demonstrated a talent as a strong man, which he exercised with vigor during the subsequent years.

In 1949 four very prominent supporters of Dr. Pridi were shot while in the custody of the police, a piece of brutality which was to plague Phibun and Phao until their overthrow in 1957.[16] In 1950 Phao was instrumental in the enforced exile of Lieutenant General Kat Katsongkhram, who had been the number two man in the coup group. He was also active in suppressing the June, 1951, revolt. Soon thereafter General Phao became director-general of the police.

After the "silent" coup of November, 1951, General Phao was appointed Deputy Minister of the Interior and also became the organizing genius behind the government's parliamentary group. Moreover, in 1953 he was appointed Deputy Minister of Finance, giving him an extraordinary set of powerful offices. Like Sarit he became very much interested in business enterprises after the November, 1951, coup and held positions on the boards of directors of at least 25 corporations.

[15] *Ibid.*, pp. 173–174.
[16] See "Khon Khaw Itsara," pseud., *Büang lang khadi lüat yuk asawin phayong* ("Behind the Bloody Affair of the Period of the Bullying Knights"; Bangkok: Sombun Woraphong at Aksoraborikan Press, 1957), for a sensational account of political murders by the police, first published in one of Field Marshal Sarit's weekly magazines.

In November, 1952, he organized the suppression of the so-called peace rebellion during which a number of leftist politicians, Chinese businessmen, and other dissident elements were arrested. He managed the passage of the Anti-Communist Act on the floor of the national assembly in late 1952.

By 1955 it was clear that he had enemies not only outside the government but within it as well. While traveling abroad, he was suddenly removed from his position as Deputy Finance Minister. Scandals began to be bruited regarding his connection with opium smugglers and with some of the brutalities of the police under his administration.

He had a central role in the election campaign of late 1956 and early 1957, both as a target for the opposition and as the organizer of the government's political party. Although he was not a candidate, he was an active campaigner and staked much on a triumph for the party. The party managed to win only a bare majority of the elected seats, and this relatively poor showing was accompanied by widespread belief that the election was badly corrupted—facts which went a long way toward undermining his personal authority. Field Marshal Sarit, in his role as keeper of the peace after the election, contributed to this process by subscribing to the idea that the election was corrupted. He also took the opportunity to make some public statements disdainful of General Phao.

The police general was clearly a major target in the attack on the government in the press and the national assembly before the coup of 1957. With all his supposed power he made no effort to resist the army in September, 1957, and he accepted their offer to let him go into exile. He left the country three days after the coup. He died abroad in 1961.

General Phao was rather different from what may be expected of prominent persons in Thailand. He was very imposing in appearance, tall and broad, and commanding in behavior. He smoked cigars. His reputation was as a fierce and ruthless man. He appears to have had unusual ability to organize, as he demonstrated in his administration of the police, in the construction of the government's parliamentary group and political party, and in some of his spectacular business enterprises.[17] It would appear that fear and favors were the foundation of his support, however, which seems to have dissolved after his exile.

As already mentioned, six examples are not sufficient to draw any general rules about leadership, but some significant elements may be extracted. First, four of the six come from official families, Phahon, Khuang, Phao, and Sarit, and two from rather low status backgrounds, Phibun and Pridi. Secondly, all six had careers in the bureaucracy before they entered politics. Phao may be excepted because he was a military aide to Phibun from the time he left the military academy. Thirdly, all six are well educated by Thai standards. The fact that the four older men had a substantial period of education in Europe and the two younger men did not is a current trend in leaders. Linked to this is the fact that of the four men of the older generation, two are civilians. The younger two men are both soldiers.

The one characteristic which all these men share most strikingly in their careers is prominent participation in *coups d'état*. All four of the older men were leaders of the coup of 1932, although Khuang was by no means as prominent as the other three. Both Sarit and Phao were leaders on the second level of the coup of 1947. Analogous similarities related to the rise of second-level leaders to the top is the role Phibun, Sarit, and Phao played on different occasions in the suppression of countercoups—Phibun against Bǫwǫradet, Phao against the October 1, 1948, army staff group, and Sarit and Phao together in 1949 and 1951. In this kind of experience those who rise to

[17] For example, the National Economic Development Company.

the top possess an ability to commit themselves to one group which as it presses forward cuts all lines of retreat—an ability that takes considerable daring when the stakes may be exile or execution. This trait is not widespread among Thai bureaucrats, who by and large find it the better part of valor to be discreet. The proper and routine attitude of the officeholder is one of respect and deference to his constituted superiors but without a deep commitment. In competing groups, the proper official will keep his lines open in all directions if possible. If one is to rise to the top, however, one must, at some stage in the conflict, make a complete commitment of loyalty to the individual or group. Since changes at the very top come suddenly by the replacement of one clique by another, one must be prepared to risk failure to gain success. And failure in this sort of enterprise is complete if not final in Thai politics.

If it takes daring to get on top, it takes other personal qualities to stay there. These are the qualities by which loyal followers are induced to support the leader's position in the face of competing alternatives. These personal qualities are the stuff of Thai social relations. Tolerance, generosity, articulate persuasiveness, even physical attractiveness are all important in the build-up of a network of followers. These qualities are not peculiar to Thailand and Thai leaders if they are considered as merely overt patterns of behavior. In order to understand this aspect of such qualities, as well as the relationship of leader and follower which they vitalize, it will be necessary to discuss some of the forms of thought that give them meaning.

The first of these is the complex of merit and fortune. The second is the complex of benevolence and obligation. Both of these are operative in the building up of cliques. According to Thai thought, moral goodness results in good fortune, and therefore good fortune is a sign and proof of moral goodness. The content or manifestation of good fortune includes profit or wealth, fame or high rank, praise or good reputation, and happiness. The moral goodness of a man is determined by his merit, which is considered as a cumulative result of his good deeds in many lives and thus a state at least in part beyond his control. The same idea may be associated with astrological ideas as well as with the accumulation of merit, but it still is beyond the control of this life. Within this framework of thought, good fortune, i.e., the rise to high rank, status, and power, is self-justifying. Moreover, it tends to be cumulative. The higher a man goes, the manifestly better he is and the more deserving of being obeyed and respected. Other elements come into this form of thought as well. For example, the three unsuccessful attempts to assassinate Field Marshal Phibun have been adduced to demonstrate his goodness. After relating his rapid rise and dwelling for some length upon the attempts to kill him, one of his biographers concludes: "On the basis of this brief biography of Field Marshal Phibunsongkhram it is very clear that he has built beautiful qualities and goodness which become manifest little by little so that even if his enemies would endanger him in anyway it would not succeed." [18]

Such a circle of reasoning from moral goodness to good fortune to social and political success and back to moral goodness is an effective stimulant to a band-wagon attitude toward leaders. A man on the way up will find his following increasing by geometric steps and the rate of his rise accelerating. It will be brought out below [19] that by getting into office a political leader has access to the traditional authority of the bureaucracy which he can use to reinforce his position. A similar accelerating effect is to be found in the informal lines of loyalty and obligation which run between a leader and his followers. From the point of view of the leader, it is unfortunate that the opposite is also true. The decline of his power and influence can

[18] W. Čh. Prasangsit, p. 112.   [19] See Chapter V.

be as precipitous as his rise. With a break in his fortune followers of this kind fall away at the same geometric rate.

The leader has some control over the process, however, in
terms of the benevolence and obligation complex. Part of the
system of thought which equates goodness with good fortune,
success, and power also associates these qualities with benevolence and generosity. A man in power must be gentle and
soft-spoken with his followers, undemanding, and ready to
give benefits to them. Such benefits should be tangible to be
most effective. They may range from free dinner parties to
good and rewarding opportunities. This kind of benevolence is
a demonstration of the quality of *bunkhun* [20] in the leader and
ought to be reciprocated with a sense of obligation and a willingness to serve him. Demands for generosity from the leader
explain a good deal about the rise of corruption and the difficulty of fighting it. A rising politician needs money as much as
anything else to cement to him followers who are not obligated
by more personal ties of loyalty. As the leader gains power, he
is then in a position to grant jobs and privileges to his followers
either in the government itself or by means of the power of
the government. These privileges are of the kind that will enhance the status of the follower so that he in turn may gather
followers. Since such a need for money and privilege is an outgrowth of the principles of organization of political power,
the very position of the leader forbids the dissolution of such
practices among his own group, although he may be able to
attack it in a rival group.

Just as those not entirely explicable personal qualities which
persuade others that he is a good person, a person of good fortune, and a person of great benevolence are essential to the po-

[20] *Bunkhun* is a quality which combines the goodness of meritful
life (*bun*) with a good (*khun*) which implies both virtue and benefit.
It suggests generosity and calls up obligation.

litical leader in Thailand, so is the opportunity to gain followers. Several of the six men cited as examples of top leadership have demonstrated the usefulness of a successful career in the bureaucracy for accumulating a following. Phibunsongkhram, in his years as Minister of Defense, devoted considerable attention to building up the army and at the same time attached to himself many officers who rose to positions of authority. Pridi, whose outstanding quality was his intelligence, won the loyalty of many of his students in the law school before the coup of 1932 and later in Thammasat University. Field Marshal Sarit in his career in the army, including a period as commandant of the military academy where he could win the loyalty of cadets, attracted many followers. His rapid rise, which was a result of his loyal and forceful support of the top leadership of the Coup Group of 1947, was no doubt helpful in drawing followers to him. General Phao, in the police force, had a network of followers he sought to distinguish by granting them special status as *asawin* (knights) which permitted them to wear an insignia ring.

In sum, a clique is a group of persons the organization of which takes its pattern from the fundamental social relationships recognized in Thai thought—family ties, bureaucratic ties, teacher-student ties. These ties ideally partake of love, loyalty, and respect. The pattern is hierarchical, and at its apex is the leader. The leader must exhibit the characteristics which pertain to a person of high status—rank, education, good looks, good manners, articulateness, and benevolence. Traditional modes of thought which link success and moral goodness reinforce and support the binding ties of the clique. The degrees of stability and strength of such ties vary a great deal with the nature of the case. A distinction between ties which are actually personal and those which are only quasi-personal may be useful. Where ties between the leader and his followers are really personal, they will be stronger and more stable. If the leader goes down, these followers—his children, his loyal students, and his friends—will go down too. But those followers whose ties to him are of an opportunistic kind—and the larger and more successful a clique the more of these there will be—will soon depart. This sort of distinction is clearly understood in the actual course of events so that many supposed followers of a fallen leader will remain in their positions by switching loyalty to the rising star.

The Prime Minister

The office of Prime Minister (*nayok rathamontri*) during most of the period since the establishment of the constitutional regime has been the point at which the formal power of authority has joined with the informal power of leadership. Together with the cabinet, which is discussed in the following chapter, the office of Prime Minister has provided an effective set of roles within the politics of changing Thailand. In its relationships to the apparatus of the cabinet and the administration, the Prime Minister's office is in terms of authority the successor to the throne. In this respect the notion of a powerful and responsible nonroyal official as the head of government is precisely comparable to the office of Prime Minister in parliamentary regimes of Europe after which it was modeled. In contrast to its model, however, the Prime Minister of Thailand draws power from bureaucratic constituencies by means of cliques rather than from popular constituencies by means of parties.

On the basis of historical evidence, the Prime Minister's office must be filled by the leader of the ruling clique in order to operate successfully. It was actually held by 10 men before Field Marshal Sarit Thanarat, who became Prime Minister in 1959. Of these only three have had tenure of much more than a year. The average of the other seven is somewhat less than seven months each. (See Table 1.) Khuang Aphaiwong held the office on three different occasions for a total of one year and nine months. Phraya Phahon held it consecutively for five and a half years. The most conspicuous length of tenure was that of Field Marshal Phibunsongkhram, who held the office for two different periods with a total of 15 years.

The institutional structure of the office of the Prime Minister gives further evidence of the power involved. It should be recalled that the Thai government is effectively institutionalized in that the ministries and agencies are well established in terms of their authority, and the service is inculcated with strong traditions of proper procedure and patterns of behavior. From the point of view of the ruling group, its major task, after it has arrived in a position of dominance, is to maintain a more or less effective control over the administration. The cabinet is the principal agency for such control, and the Prime Minister is the focal point of the cabinet.

In the model of cabinet government a Prime Minister is first among equals but by all rules of Thai social relations such a role is impossible. At least in the long tenure of Field Marshal Phibunsongkhram and, more especially, in the period of Field Marshal Sarit Thanarat thus far, the Prime Minister has been the leader of the ruling group and the government.

This fact was somewhat confused for many years by the legal arrangements based on the principle of cabinet supremacy and collective responsibility. The institutional capstone of the government was the Office of the Council of Ministers (*samnak-ngan khana rathamontri*). The name suggested that the office was responsible to the cabinet collectively, but in fact the Prime

Minister ran the affairs of the extremely powerful complex of functions.

Table 1. Prime Ministers in the constitutional period

Name	Period	Length of tenure
Phraya Manopakǫn	June, 1932, to June, 1933	1 year
Phraya Phahon Phon-phayuhasena	June, 1933, to Dec., 1938	5½ years
Luang Phibunsong-khram	Dec., 1938, to July, 1944	5½ years
Khuang Aphaiwong	Aug., 1944, to Aug., 1945	1 year
Tawi Bunyakhet	Aug., 1945, to Sept., 1945	3 weeks
M. R. Seni Pramoj	Sept., 1945, to Jan., 1946	4 months
Khuang Aphaiwong	Jan., 1946, to March, 1946	3 months
Dr. Pridi Phanomyong	March, 1946, to Aug., 1946	4 months
Admiral Thamrong Nawasawat	Aug., 1946, to Nov., 1947	14 months
Khuang Aphaiwong	Nov., 1947, to April, 1948	6 months
Field Marshal P. Phi-bunsongkhram	April, 1948, to Sept., 1957	9½ years
Phot Sarasin	Sept., 1957, to Jan., 1958	4 months
General Thanǫm Kit-tikhačhǫn	Jan., 1958, to Oct., 1958	9 months
Field Marshal Sarit Thanarat	From Feb., 1959	

The Office of the Council of Ministers, though including secretariats for the cabinet and the Prime Minister, developed duties more far-reaching than the secretarial. Within it there were three organizations of investigation and control of the bureaucracy, namely, the Civil Service Commission, the Administrative Inspection Department, and the Office of the

State Audit Council. It is problematical how thorough or systematic control of the bureaucracy has actually been, but there is little question that the negative limits of administrative autonomy have been maintained.

In addition to organizations for control, the Prime Minister had available to him in the Office of the Council of Ministers the facilities of the Public Relations Department, which operates the national radio and handles government press relations. Also under this office was the Department of Public Works, which supervised much government construction. Three organizations with the function of providing information and technical advice were under the Office of the Council of Ministers as well: the Central Information Department, an intelligence agency; the National Economic Council, a fact-finding and advisory body; and the Legislative Council, which provides expert legal advice. The Prime Minister's secretariat, which is part of this organizational structure, also had in more recent years the power to spend certain unbudgeted funds available from the National Lottery and special welfare revenues.[21]

The arrangements under the provisional constitution of 1959 have made explicit and, presumably, more convenient control by the Prime Minister. The Office of the Council of Ministers has been renamed the Office of the President of the Council of Ministers, and its functions have been reorganized in order to simplify lines of authority from the Prime Minister.[22] This administrative simplification is consonant with

[21] Manual of Organization of the Government of Thailand (Bangkok: Institute of Public Administration, in draft).

[22] Kiat Thanakhum, "Naew kan borikan rachakan phaendin nai yuk pathiwat" ("Methods of Administration in the Revolutionary Period"), *Rathasapha san* ("Journal of the National Assembly"), March, 1960, pp. 10–23; April, 1960, pp. 34–44; "Act on the Organization of the Office of the President of the Council of Ministers, B.E. 2502 (1959),"

the independent position of the Prime Minister as specified in the constitution.[23] The institutional position of the Prime Minister is obvious in the list of bureaus and agencies grouped under his explicit authority in the new office. They are:

(1) Office of the Undersecretary of the Office of the President of the Council of Ministers

(2) Office of Government House

(3) Executive Office of the President of the Council of Ministers

(4) Budget Office

(5) Office of the Secretary-General of the Council of Ministers

(6) Central Intelligence Department

(7) Public Relations Department

(8) Office of the State Audit Commission

(9) Office of the Juridical Council

(10) Office of the Civil Service

(11) Office of the National Security Council

(12) Office of the National Economic Development Council

(13) Office of the National Education Council

(14) National Power Authority

(15) Office of the National Research Council

(16) University of Agriculture

(17) Čhulalongkǫn University

(18) Thammasat University

(19) Medical University

(20) Fine Arts University

(21) Office of the Commission for the Investigation of Performance Relative to Taxes

---

Royal Thai Government Gazette (*from the Thai Version*), LXXVI, pts. 24–25 (Feb. 28, 1959), 123–128.
23 See Appendix B.

(22) Office of the Export Promotion Commission
(23) Atomic Energy for Peace Office [24]

With this structure of information, control, planning, and educational agencies reporting to him and under his direction, the Prime Minister's great personal authority as the leader of the powerful cliques is institutionalized in the form of legal access and control in the bureaucracy.

[24] "Act on the Organization of the Office of the President of the Council of Ministers (no. 7), B.E. 2503," *Royal Thai Government Gazette (from the Thai Version)*, LXXVII, pts. 30–31 (May 14, 1960), 226–232.

V

THE CABINET AND BUREAUCRATIC GOVERNMENT

THE institution of the cabinet is deeply rooted in Thai traditions of government. On the basis of its continuous development and vitality from the time of its modern creation in the fifth reign through its transformations down to the present, it must be judged a successful institution. Today it is the institutional focus of power in the Thai political system, both in law and in fact.

The powers and functions of the cabinet as set forth in the various constitutions were little changed from version to version until the provisional constitution of January, 1959. It is made up of a Prime Minister and a number of ministers. The cabinet is appointed by the king on recommendation of the Prime Minister. Excepting again the January, 1959, constitution, the cabinet has legally held power by virtue of the confidence of the assembly. Its primary function is to administer the affairs of state, and therefore it has control over the bureaucracy. Its members may come from the assembly or not. The cabinet has been an extremely strong branch of the government in the past quarter century. Those changes that have developed in the constitutional period have tended to strengthen it rather than otherwise.

Basis in Tradition

The ancient office of the king's minister (*senabodi*) and the royal audience held periodically for high officials form the traditional basis of the modern Council of Ministers. But there are some rather sharp differences to be noted between the traditional and modern systems, the dynamics of which contribute to the developmental forces behind the changes of government. Each of these ancient ministers was accountable for an administrative organization in which responsibilities were territorially localized. This kind of responsibility was especially associated with the Ministers of the North and of the South who were in effect viceroys for those areas of the kingdom. They held generalized powers to rule—to draft *corvée* labor and soldiers, to collect cash revenues, to keep the peace, to administer justice, and to defend the realm. The other four ministers (City, Palace, Fields, and Treasury) held responsibilities of a quasi-functional nature. In time, however, they also came to hold generalized power in specific localities.

Because of the minister's having such broad powers, it may be assumed that there was little need, except under unusual circumstances such as war, for them to coordinate their activities. Each could administer his bailiwick as he saw fit. The fact that they had different degrees of status would work against coordination.[1] Moreover, they were all completely subordinate to the king. Such coordination as there might have been was through the king rather than through any collectivity of senior administrative officials. It seems unlikely that the various ministers met often as a group to discuss affairs of state.[2] On the other hand, it is likely that in extraordinary circumstance the king consulted with them collectively as well as individually.[3]

A transformation of these ancient ministerial offices took place in the fifth reign.[4] In preparation for the reorganization of the government in the 1880's the ministers, senior departmental heads, and senior princes met together regularly as a "committee"[5] in planning the proposed changes. At the time of the announcement of the changes in 1892, it was intended that this committee should continue in the form of a cabinet of king's ministers. Thus, in the royal proclamation it said:

When the great ministries have been arranged, let there be meetings together to consult on government affairs in accordance with duties which are related to each other. This will be a meeting of the twelve ministers and will be called the Council of Ministers [*senabodi sapha*] which will have both combined responsibilities

[1] See above, Chapter III.

[2] Prince Damrong Rachanuphap, *Thesaphiban* ("Administration"; Bangkok: Klang Witthaya Press, 1952), pp. 6–7.

[3] Düan Bunnak and Phairot Chaiyanam, *Kham athibai kotmai ratthathammanun kap kotmai lüak tang* ("Lectures on the Constitution and the Election Law"; Bangkok: Thammasat University, 1935), pt. III, p. 9.

[4] "Prakat tang tamnaeng senabodi" ("Announcement of Appointment to Positions of *Senabodi*"), PKPS, XIII, pt. 2, 93–98.

[5] Damrong, *Thesaphiban*, pp. 8–9. The word *kommitthi* was used for this body.

and separate responsibilities as will be set forth in an act later. Moreover, it is ordered that each of the ministers will be of equal dignity in every way.[6]

The reorganization introduced the principle of functional ministry to replace the traditional territorial ones. Such a shift from functionally diffuse to functionally specific administrative organization raised the problem of coordination. As was stated in the proclamation, it was this question of "duties which are related to each other" that lay behind the establishment of the Council of Ministers. In the new council all members were of equal rank, and they met together regularly. It is not completely clear how often these meetings were held and whether or not the king regularly attended. Two British observers who were employed by the government during the fifth reign report that the council held regular meetings. Ernest Young says that the king might or might not attend, and Graham reports that the king served as his own Prime Minister.[7] Prince Damrong, the first Minister of the Interior in the new arrangement, in his account of the setting up of the new ministries is somewhat obscure on the point.[8] It is authoritatively said that the Council of Ministers was established with the European model in mind, and thus seems likely that the pattern of meetings was regular and that the king probably attended. As Phraya Maha-ammat has written:

As can be seen, the great change in the government of Thailand followed the model of Councils of Ministers in advanced countries, with modifications to make it suitable for Thailand and

[6] "Prakat tang tamnaeng senabodi," pp. 93–98.
[7] Ernest Young, *The Kingdom of the Yellow Robe* (Westminster, Eng.: Archibald Constable, 1898), pp. 219–220; W. A. Graham, *Siam* (London: Alexander Moring, Ltd., 1924), II, 237–238.
[8] Damrong, *Thesaphiban*, pp. 8–9.

genuinely useful for governing the country. By having the king as Prime Minister or leader of the Council of Ministers this organization was of use in ruling the country from the fifth reign in 1892 until 1932.[9]

It is quite clear that after the throne itself the Council of Ministers was the most powerful organ of the government at that time. Members of the council sat as one category of members in the Council of State,[10] and the ministers had direct and regular access to the king if they so desired.

The cabinet continued in an orderly development throughout the remainder of the fifth and sixth reigns. During the seventh reign there was a major modification which indicates the emergence of a fundamental fact about the hierarchy of political power in the kingdom. Almost immediately upon his accession to the throne in 1925, King Rama VII established the extraordinary office of Supreme State Councilor (*aphirathamontri*). The purpose of this office was, to quote the king's proclamation: "To provide the king with continuing counsel on all matters in order to strengthen his judgment on all affairs of state." The qualifications for the office of Supreme State Councilor were "long experience in affairs of state and a sufficient reputation in both *expertise* and ability to inspire the confidence of the king and all the people."[11]

Between 1925 and 1932 there were altogether five or six members of the Supreme State Council, all of whom were

[9] Phraya Maha-ammattayathibodi, "Rüang Mahatthai" ("On Interior"), in *Anusǫn nüang nai ngan chalong wan thi ralük sathappana krasuang mahatthai khroprop 60 pi bǫribun* ("Memorial Volume on the Occasion of the Sixtieth Anniversary of the Ministry of the Interior"; Bangkok: Ministry of the Interior, 1952), p. 72.

[10] "Phrarachabanyat rathamontri, R.S. 113" ("Act on the Council of State"), sec. 1, *PKPS*, XIV, 214.

[11] Prasoet Suphamatin, *Kotmai pokkhrǫng* ("Administrative Law"; Bangkok: Thammasat University, 1937), p. 189.

high princes, either uncles or brothers of the king. Some of them also held office concurrently as Ministers of State. The Supreme State Council, together with the king, represented the apex of political power in the kingdom at that time. By creating the Council an attempt was made to bolster the throne in relation to the increasingly authoritative and independent bureaucracy which was, at least in part or potentially, represented in the cabinet. The Supreme State Councilors met with the king to consider highly confidential and important affairs of state. They also had the right to attend meetings of the cabinet. The creation of the Supreme State Council was implicit recognition of the divergence of the interests of the royal family and the administration, as well as the relative diminution of the overwhelming authority of the throne. The institution of an inner, or counter, cabinet designed to dominate the cabinet and through it the administration may be interpreted as admission of weakened authority. This new institution was set against the trend of development of the government toward a more competent and expert administration eager to take on more responsibility for the management of the country. It was so obvious that it could become the institutional target for the *coup d'état* of 1932 in which bureaucrats moved to take over power from royalty. In that respect, its existence may have made possible the preservation of both the throne and the cabinet.[12]

The Supreme State Council was the first clear-cut appearance of what has become a common phenomenon in Thai politics—rule by a small clique. In the fifth and sixth reigns the throne was strong enough to maintain the appearance of

[12] W. Čh. Prasangsit, *Pathiwat rathaprahan lae kabot čhalačhon nai samai prachathipathai haeng prathet thai* ("Revolution, *Coup d'Etat*, and Rebellion in Thailand during the Democratic Period"; Bangkok, 1949), pp. 12–14.

absolute personal rule. Rama VII was not capable of doing so. It was necessary, therefore, that the ruling clique, in this case senior members of the royal family, be vested with extraordinary authority. Such authority was insufficient, however, to maintain their power after they had lost their roots in the bureaucracy.

In the preconstitutional period the cabinet was a link between the throne and the Supreme State Councilors on the one hand and the administration on the other. In this position it fulfilled the dual function of representing the administration at the seat of power and of representing royal authority in the ministries. Cabinet ministers were professional bureaucrats distinguished by their loyalty to the throne and their administrative competence. Some were princes and some were not. The ratio of royal to nonroyal ministers was about four to three over the 40-year period from 1892 to 1932. The average period in office was about six years. The range in tenure was from one year in the case of Phraya Maha-ammat as Minister of the Interior to 31 years in the case of Prince Thewawong in the Ministry of Foreign Affairs.

Constitutional Cabinet

In the constitutional period, the cabinet continued to be the most important center of government power. Its main modification under the constitution was the ending of royal participation in cabinet work. The transformation of the cabinet of the period of absolute monarchy (*senabodi sapha*) into a constitutional system (*khana rathamontri*) reveals certain characteristics and problems of the role of the Thai cabinet. The provisional constitution of June 27, 1932, established a council called the People's Committee (*khana kamakan ratsadǫn*) which was to assume responsibility for ruling the country. The People's Committee was formed in the following manner. The president of the committee was elected by the national assembly. He thereupon chose the members of the committee. The committee was then confirmed collectively by the assembly.[13] The committee was, in effect, a creature of the assembly. It was not appointed by the king, and it was charged with the duty of supervising actual administration of the country by the executive offices. It was not, therefore, intended to be a royal cabinet but rather a watchdog committee of the national assembly. This is made clear by the fact that during the period of the provisional constitution the office of *senabodi* continued separate from the People's Committee. The *senabodi*, who were administrative heads of the ministries as well as representatives of the throne in the administrative organization, became responsible to the People's Committee in all their activities. The situation has been described as follows:

Anything which was opposed to the orders or regulations of the People's Committee or was not permitted by the constitution was held to be void. Moreover, according to Section 35 the appointment and dismissal of *senabodi* was a royal prerogative, but it could be used only in accordance with the advice of the People's Committee. *Senabodi* was a permanent position, and some members of the People's Committee also held positions as *senabodi*. This was due to the fact that *senabodi* was a position continuing from the period of absolute monarchy and was not immediately abolished at the time of the change to constitutional rule.[14]

[13] Phairot Chaiyanam, *Khamathibai kotmai rathathammanun priap thiap* ("Lectures on Comparative Constitutional Law"; Bangkok: Thammasat University, 1952), II, 41.

[14] *Ibid.*, p. 42.

Under the permanent constitution of December 10, 1932, the situation in regard to the cabinet was changed. Following the model of European constitutional monarchies, the cabinet was appointed by the throne but could rule only with the confidence of the national assembly. The name of the cabinet was changed from People's Committee to Council of Ministers (*khana rathamontri*). The constitution also provided that all members of the cabinet need not be members of the national assembly. It should be noted, however, that according to law the Council of Ministers did not rule at the king's pleasure but, once appointed, stayed in office (1) throughout the life of the assembly which gave it a vote of confidence, (2) until the assembly passed a vote of no confidence, or (3) until the Prime Minister resigned. Otherwise membership in the cabinet came to an end individually by death, resignation, loss of certain qualifications, or vote of no confidence. This provision, of course, limited to some extent the power of the Prime Minister over his individual cabinet colleagues. Under the permanent constitution the position of *senabodi* was assimilated to that of cabinet minister, and the functions of administrative and political control of ministries were combined.

This withdrawal from the radical concept of the executive as a committee of the representative assembly to the more conventional form of cabinet was completely consistent with the generally conciliatory atmosphere which prevailed in the latter part of 1932 on the part of both the promoters of the *coup d'état* and the throne. The outstanding public demonstration of the mood of conciliation was the elaborate ceremony of asking the king's forgiveness by the Coup Group just before the promulgation of the December constitution.[15]

Although the minutes of the commission which drafted the

[15] *Bangkok Times Weekly Mail*, Dec. 12, 1932, p. 24.

permanent constitution have not been published, one of the two matters of contention brought into the house in connection with the draft was the name to be given to the cabinet. A certain group was holding out for the term People's Committee, but the throne and more conservative politicians wanted the term Minister of State (*rathamontri*) adopted.[16] This public conflict over terminology suggests that the throne and conservative elements were concerned that the cabinet should remain essentially executive and administrative. There was presumably hope that the throne could have some influence in both the make-up and deliberations of the cabinet. The subsequent course of events went in another direction, however, and royal influence was finally destroyed. But the novel position of the People's Committee as a purely political and representative council was diluted by the resurgence of the traditional role of king's minister. The cabinet continued to be the "summit" of the administration as it had been in the preconstitutional period.[17] As such it absorbed much of the prestige of the *senabodi* in the eyes of the bureaucracy and much of the attitude of the *senabodi* toward popular representatives.

But the *coup d'état* broke the chain of authority from the throne through the cabinet to the administration. The political power of the king was preempted by the promoters of the *coup d'état* who assumed the ruling clique role of the throne and Supreme State Council. The promoters' group, the precise composition of which is still rather obscure,[18] had access to both the cabinet and the House of People's Representatives. The promoters' group was able to dominate because of its prestige, powers of appointment, and ultimate control of sub-

[16] The other matter of contention was sec. 11, which barred members of the royal family from politics.

[17] Prasoet Suphamatin, p. 326.   [18] See below, Chapter IX.

stantial military power. Through the cabinet the ruling clique controlled the administrative machinery of the government.

The modern cabinet is made up of the Prime Minister (*nayok rathamontri*), or President of the Council of Ministers, and a varying number of members. Members may hold different ranks, including Deputy Prime Minister, minister with portfolio, deputy minister with portfolio, minister acting for a portfolio, and minister without portfolio. The constitutions have put limits on the size of the cabinet. The constitution of December, 1932, specified that there should be at least 14 ministers from among members of the national assembly, but no upper limit was set. The constitution of 1946 specified that the cabinet should be made up of from 10 to 18 members. The constitutions of 1947 and 1948 set the figure at from 15 to 25 members. The 1952 amended version of the 1932 constitution specified that the cabinet should consist of from 14 to 28 members. In the postwar years the membership of the cabinet has tended to reach the upper limits set by the constitution. The Thai system does not have the distinction of ministers in and ministers not in the cabinet. The ruling clique, although usually in the cabinet, has no special legal status there. All ministers of whatever rank or power are members of the cabinet.

There are at least six categories into which virtually all members of the cabinet since 1932 may be divided. The first category is the coup leader. Such a man, because he is a leader of the organization which carried out a major shift of political power, is a natural candidate for membership in the cabinet and control of an important administrative agency. The second category is the loyal and competent follower. Such a person may or may not have been a participant in a *coup d'état*, but he has, over a period of time, demonstrated his ability and willingness to control an administrative organization in the interest of the Prime Minister or the group dominating the cabinet. The third category includes leaders of important organized forces. Commanders of military units in Bangkok, the man who controls the military airport, the chief of police—such men are likely candidates for ministerial posts. Their command over these forces may well be a result of their previous participation in a *coup d'état* and their proved loyalty. Their importance and power, however, are enhanced by their control over these organizations, and this will lead to their inclusion in the cabinet. The fourth category is the rewarded client. A man who has performed service in the national assembly by mustering support for the ruling group, who has performed services in elections, or who has served the same interest in some other manner may be rewarded with a post in the cabinet, albeit probably a minor one. The fifth category is the expert. Judges appointed to the Ministry of Justice, diplomats appointed to the Ministry of Foreign Affairs, and financiers appointed to the Ministry of Finance fall into this category. The final category is the front man who through his popularity or reputation is able to screen and implicitly justify shifts of power and policy going on behind the scenes.

The major qualifications for membership in the cabinet are the same as in the preconstitutional period, loyalty and competence. A minister's loyalty may be a personal attachment or long-standing association with the Prime Minister. On the other hand, it may be loyalty to that ruling clique which a cabinet purports to represent, such as the Promoters of the Coup d'Etat or People's Party, the Coup d'Etat Group, or the Military Group. There is, of course, nothing unusual about loyalty as a touchstone of cabinet qualification. It might well be equated with the qualification of party regularity in a cabinet system associated with well-developed political parties.

The question of competence as a qualification in the cabinet is a difficult one to analyze. Ministers throughout the history of the cabinet have come mainly from administrative backgrounds. Of 211 men who have held seats in the cabinet between 1932 and 1958, 84 had had previous careers in the civil service, 68 had previous careers in the military service, and only 13 could be clearly identified as nonbureaucratic. The previous careers of the remaining 46 are unknown, but it may be taken as assured that a high proportion of these also had bureaucratic backgrounds. To what extent this can be interpreted as a desire for administrative competence in the cabinet is not at all clear. Since the groups that seized power in the *coup d'état* have had their origins in the civil or military service, it is not surprising that bureaucrats should predominate in seats of power. The argument of competence as part of the general argument for the tutelage principle has been a recurring element in the justification of the various devices for limiting the participation of nonbureaucratic politicians in the actual manipulation of power. The justification for the use of appointed members of the assembly and for the establishment of upper houses has generally been that in a transitional period there is a need for training as well as restraining the representatives of the people. The fact that at least from time to time men have been appointed to cabinet posts for no other apparent reason than their competence does, however, lend an element of credibility to this argument.

A man may be appointed to a cabinet post for his competence if there is no evidence that he is committed to a counter or competing group. This sort of appointment is most likely to occur at times of crisis. For example, in the Phot Sarasin cabinet, after the *coup d'état* of September, 1957, the portfolios of Agriculture, Cooperatives, Culture, Education, and Justice, as well as the prime ministership itself, were held by men whose main qualification was a special competence. Phot Sarasin, the Prime Minister, was persuaded to accept the office not because he was known to be fiercely loyal to the Military Group but because of his competence in foreign affairs.

It was feared by the Military Group that the events leading up to the coup of 1957 had shaken the confidence of the United States in the firmness of Thailand's commitment to an anti-Communist foreign policy. Phot, because he had been ambassador to the United States for a number of years and had very recently been appointed Secretary-General of the Southeast Asia Treaty Organization, was no doubt the man best qualified to persuade the United States that no change in foreign policy was contemplated. In the case of Agriculture, Cooperatives, Culture, and Education, men were promoted from high civil service positions to the post of minister. As for Justice, an elderly lawyer of unimpeachable integrity was asked to take over the portfolio. It should be noted, however, that even in this caretaker cabinet the Ministries of Defense and Interior were held by senior leaders of the Military Group, and most other appointments were given to loyal followers of one faction or another, sympathetic to the group.

Popularity or reputation, under certain circumstances, may also be an important qualification. For example, Khuang Aphaiwong has no important base of power which he can call his own. He controls no military units. He has no influence in the police. He has no network of loyal followers in the civil service. He was not a front-rank leader of any *coup d'état*. But because he is a good speaker and has a reputation for independence, he is extremely popular with the political public of Bangkok. Largely for this reason he has held the office of Prime Minister at three separate times—twice under the aegis of Pridi Phanomyong and once under that of the Coup Group of 1947. On two of these three occasions he served as a mask for behind the scenes political maneuvering designed to make secure the position of others. On both occasions, when his usefulness was past he lost his job. Popularity would seem to be no substitute for powerful organized backing. Unpopularity, at least with special groups, has also been known to drive men out of the cabinet. In forming his cabinet after the election of February, 1957, Phibunsongkhram was forced to drop two loyal followers of long standing mainly because they were unpopular and unsupported by any group.

Authority

The relationship of the cabinet to other institutions of government has been for the most part a dominant one since 1932. The authority which inheres in the position of cabinet minister is supported by both tradition and law. That is to say, the unquestionably high degree of authority of cabinet ministers derives from the fact that the king's ministers have ruled the country for centuries, as well as from the legal sanctions embodied in the constitutions and statutes. The position of cabinet minister fits without difficulty into the hierarchy of status traditional in Thai society, and the authority vested in the office by law does not conflict with any Thai conception of what constitutes proper authority.

The attainment of the position of cabinet minister is desirable not only because of the authority in government which it confers upon the incumbent but also because of the public affirmation of his status. The prestige associated with this publicly affirmed high status extends far beyond the more restricted legal authority of a cabinet minister and brings to him those psychological and material perquisities so dear to

the hearts of politicians. This authority-status-prestige complex is a vital element in Thai social organization with roots
deep in tradition. Because office gives rise to authority,
prestige, and status, the cabinet is the objective of aspiring
power groups. By getting into office they have won more than
half the battle—they have won the weapons and resources
which will affect the likelihood of their remaining in office.
Appointments to the cabinet itself offer an example of this
process. When a small ruling clique succeeds in seizing power,
it can proceed to bolster its power by rewarding sympathizers
and followers with the extremely attractive offices in the
cabinet. In that way many cabinet positions are a form of
political patronage as rewards for services rendered or as
inducements to future loyalty.

The critical and interacting relationship between the institution of the cabinet and the ruling clique is pivotal in the structure of informal power and formal authority. In most of the
twenty-odd cabinets of the constitutional period, the leaders
of the ruling clique have held the most important portfolios
in the cabinet. These posts are the Ministry of Defense, the
Ministry of the Interior, and the Prime Ministry. As has been
suggested, there have been times when the ruling clique was
not in the cabinet, but such cabinets have been brief and for
the most part unsuccessful.

During the year in which Phraya Mano was Prime Minister
(1932–1933), the ruling clique, at the time the Promoters of
the Coup d'Etat of 1932, left the major cabinet positions in
the hands of older civil servants still deeply imbued with the
traditions of the absolute monarchy. The difficulties in han-
dling Pridi's Economic Plan, the resulting closing of the
national assembly along with the period of decree rule, and
evidently some suspicion of a countercoup led the Promoters

of the Coup d'Etat to seize power a second time and take over the cabinet.

During the brief period from November, 1947, to April, 1948, when Khuang was Prime Minister, the cabinet was drawn from his party and the Coup d'Etat Group remained in the background. This situation continued only until the necessary election was held and the government recognized by the still-suspicious Allied powers. Then the ruling group stepped in rather unceremoniously.

Royal power is circumscribed legally by all constitutions. Although the lack of effect of many important constitutional provisions is a notorious element in Thailand's contemporary political system, this limitation on the power of the throne has in the constitutional period been made good. The inter-position of the ruling clique between the throne and the cabinet and the assumption by the clique of the role and function of the royal will provide the solid reality behind the legal phrases. As has been suggested above, however, the influence of the throne in the reign of King Phumiphon has apparently increased.[19] This trend leads in the direction of a possible renewal of tension between the throne and the ruling clique which was removed in 1935 by the abdication of Rama VII. As part of any final constitutional settlement, the politicians of Thailand will be required to resolve the problem of the throne's political position.

In contrast with the simplicity of the position of the throne, that of members of the national assembly has been very complex. Even if one disregards the organizational difficulties of a large body of men attempting to dominate a smaller body and also the matter of cabinet power to appoint members of the assembly, the fact that the position of members of the

[19] See above, pp. 114–115.

assembly is anomalous according to Thai traditions might well make it impossible for the assembly to sway the cabinet. The egalitarian rather than hierarchical relationship which the member has both as regards other members and as regards his constituents makes his status dubious. At the same time the authority of the assembly, while indisputable in terms of constitutional law, knows no traditional equivalent. As has been pointed out in the discussion of the national assembly,[20] this institution has not succeeded in countervailing the extensive power located in the cabinet. The assembly's supposed control over the purse and legislation has yet to be realized.

Moreover, control of the cabinet is control of the administration which puts under its domination thousands of officials. In its day-to-day operations the cabinet is essentially an administrative committee to which many decisions must legally be submitted. In this regard the cabinet serves as arbiter among various demands on the resources of the country from segments of the government. While the process of policy formulation and implementation is only tangential to the question of gaining and holding power, there is considerable evidence that in the final analysis the cabinet and, in this context, the power clique are sharply restricted in use of the power they possess.

A clear-cut example of what is involved here is revealed in the following comment which appeared in a report of a Thai government committee concerned with economic development:

[The economic adviser] noted the absence of organized political strength behind alternative schemes for economic development—that is to say, the absence of articulate democratic opinion in support of one line of development rather than another. This, he

[20] See Chapter VII.

said, led to a state of affairs in which competing claims of alternative development schemes became competing claims of different segments of the governmental bureaucracy. There is no inherent machinery for resolving conflicts between ministries for funds; there tended therefore to be a process of settlement of the conflicts by compromise; with the result that no ministry got enough money to carry out the projects most urgently needed in the sector of the economy for which it was responsible.[21]

This situation in regard to economic development is generally characteristic of the role the cabinet plays in policy formulation and implementation. It arises from the relationship of the cabinet and the bureaucracy which in turn is determined by the character of the power complex in Thai society. The ruling clique seizes the seats of power by a sudden coup, and then uses these positions to establish and maintain its authority. But the constituencies of the members of the clique are of the bureaucracy itself. These are primarily the military, as will be discussed below, but also, to a greater or lesser extent, all agencies. A minister, when he steps into his ministry, possesses the traditional authority of the office, and he can expect to get the deference, respect, and obedience from his subordinates which tradition demands. He is obligated by tradition to look out for these subordinates, however. In order not to disturb his authority and perhaps that of the whole clique, he must look to this obligation. His ministry then becomes his constituency, and he represents it in the cabinet. He fights for its budget, and he protects its employees. The success with which he does this depends upon his relative position within the ruling clique, although the best he can expect is a compromise with his fellow ministers.

[21] Thailand, Ministry of Finance, Economic Survey Group, *Report on Economic Development Plans* (mimeographed; Bangkok, 1957), p. 1.

Such a tendency is not unusual in any governmental organization. The distinctiveness in the relationships of the Thai organization is the small number of articulated claims and pressures that come into the bureaucratic structure from outside. Such a deficiency makes extremely difficult the establishment of a hierarchy of values useful in judging and resolving the competing bureaucratic claims. The lack of a structure of multiple constituencies for the men who decide which agencies are to get what makes for conservation of existing patterns of allocations in which rich agencies get richer and poor ones stay poor. In order to bring about any substantial redirection of government resources, an extensive and sustained series of acts of will would be required. A structure more conducive to such an effort may be emerging under the Sarit regime (post-1959), in which the Prime Minister's choice of cabinet is simplified and he is insulated from a part of the complexities of the problem of maintaining loyalties.

There are 12 ministries and the Office of the President of the Council of Ministers in the government. In addition, there are a number of quasi-autonomous organizations, such as the Railroad Organization and the Port of Bangkok Authority, which come under the supervision of the cabinet or a particular minister. The ministries are Defense, Interior, Finance, Foreign Affairs, Justice, Agriculture, Cooperatives, Education, Economic Affairs, Communications, Public Health, and Industry. Each of these is organized in a similar manner. The minister's office has authority for policy supervision. The undersecretary's office has authority for administrative supervision. Each ministry has a number of departments with specialized functions.

As a general rule, the department and its chief, titled director-general, make up the unit of most cohesion. There are about 60 in the whole government. The director-general receives a royal appointment so that he is in a direct relationship to the Prime Minister who must approve it. At the same time, the department is usually the level of organization with the greatest coherence of activity and program, and it is the fundamental unit in budgeting. Because the departments have a simple internal structure, which is subdivided into only two further levels—the division and the section—the director-general is in a position to know his subordinates well. In keeping with Thai traditions of hierarchy and subordination, he can expect to call upon their personal loyalty, deference, and respect. The director-generals and the undersecretaries are a kind of elite group in the bureaucracy. But because their lines of loyalty run up to the minister and down to their subordinates, there is no more than a minimum of cooperation among them as a group. In fact, because the major aim of a director-general is to expand the activities of his department, he is often in competition with his counterparts for the resources of the government.

The tendency of the bureaucracy to break up into competing groups because it is under no pressure from articulate expressions of interest from constituencies outside the government results in a dispersal of power to make policy. From the point of view of the ruling clique, the limits of the dispersal of power and the criterion of judgment on policy are negative ones. Let there be no programs—this would be the dictum if the criterion were to be expressed—let there be no programs which threaten our position.

VI

MILITARY BUREAUCRACY

MILITARY leaders have played a dominant role in the politics of Thailand for a long time. This role has not gone unchallenged, and it has experienced its ups and its downs. But for the better part of the period of constitutional regime the military, particularly the army, has been nominated to rule. Army officers have led the ruling group and dominated the institutions of government. There are both historical and organizational reasons for this dominance.

An appreciation of the position of permanent government organizations is fundamental to the understanding of Thai politics. Government goes on regardless of which leader or group of leaders is in power, and moreover it goes on much the same course. The fact that the ruling class is small and largely overlaps the bureaucracy is basic in this situation. The ruling class is responsive to a political public which to a large extent reflects its own outlook on life. Other insitutions which might reflect divergent forces of public opinion, e.g., the national assembly and the private press, are deficient in organization. Political parties and interest groups are feeble because of the nature of the national social structure. Commercial interests are often considered alien and are politically intimidated. They seek their ends by means of influence. The great and fundamental class of cultivators is absorbed in an isolated peasant's world of work and religion, remaining largely free from socially revolutionary pressures. They are politically inarticulate. The issues upon which political fortunes turn are narrow, if not actually personal. The fundamental questions of politics have revolved around political status—how shall the rewards of goods, prestige, and power be distributed within the ruling class?

The group of military officers in modern Thailand has its roots in the traditional bureaucracy, where a formal distinction was maintained between civil and military officials, but this distinction seems scarcely to have extended to function, training, or general outlook. It seems to have corresponded approximately to such other distinctions as left and right, north and south, and inner and outer which were elements of the magico-cosmological organization of the state. The fact that these distinctions appear to the modern student as functionless should not be understood to mean that they were empty or meaningless. In a system wherein symbols, signs, paraphernalia, and regalia were seen to have a vitality and power of their own, the forms of organization cannot be thought of as "mere formalties." The forms were real and essential while the content was accidental. This understanding suggests that the distinction "to be a soldier" (*pen thahan*) is an old one. This in turn suggests the existence of a persistent set of group loyalties.

Although there was a formal distinction between military and civil officials, a distinction which could serve as the foundation for persisting group loyalties along these lines, there was little distinction between the roles assigned to civil and military officials in the system of government. Both groups served the king's business as their primary duty, and both groups did it in approximately the same fashion. As has been pointed out above, the two senior ministers of the king were equal in title, rank, and authority, and each administered about half the kingdom. One of the distinctions between these two positions, which went along with the designations of left and right and north and south, was that between soldier and civilian.

The actual function of fighting in time of war was widely dispersed throughout the traditional bureaucracy. Each minister and governor was expected to defend his own bailiwick when necessary, and he had the power to draft soldiers for the purpose. Whatever standing military organizations there were appear to have been more or less independent and attached directly to the throne.

It seems unlikely that any group existed in traditional Thailand which would correspond to the modern professional military services and officer corps. Fighting was not an esoteric art to be maintained by a cult or school. As has been suggested and as might be expected in a quasi-feudal system of government, all political leaders were soldiers in some sense of the word, and all were necessarily prepared and able to organize and lead armies. But the Thai system was feudal only in that rule was divided territorially. There was no feudal warrior class. In fact, the ruling group was bureaucratic. All officials, both military and civil, were equally subordinate to the throne.

Thus it can be seen that in the traditional system of organization there is a basis for a distinction of loyalty in terms of military and civil. At the same time there is a basis for both military and civil officials to take equivalent roles in politics.

The present military officer group is the heir to these traditions and the attitudes which derive from them.

Professional Military

During the period of transformation of institutions corresponding approximately with the fifth, sixth, and seventh reigns of the Čhakkri dynasty, the relationship between civil and military officials and organizations had been substantially modified. By the end of the fifth reign, the armed services had been reestablished on an entirely new basis. Professional training had been introduced, control had been brought into a single ministry, and universal conscription provided a regular and sufficient source of manpower. By the 1920's the distinction between military and civilian had become fully functional. The military was a separate institution and as such epitomized the new conditions of the Thai bureaucracy. Outstanding characteristics of this new condition were centralization, professionalization, infusion of a spirit of nationalism and also of institutional pride, and, finally, a high degree of organization. The army is the main concern in this discussion because it has been army officers, for the most part and most successfully, who have used their organization as a political base. The first step in the process of professionalization of the army was the establishment in the fourth reign of a military pages' corps trained by English officers on loan from the government of India. This special troop was uniformed and drilled in contemporary European style, and thus the basis was laid for a professional attitude toward military affairs. In the words of an official history of the army, "If we speak historically, this troop was the origin of the army of the present." [1] It and others like it were evidently of great interest to the king.[2] In 1870, King Rama V organized a European-style military troop among his pages and recruited princes and sons of high officials to serve in it. This troop was called the King's Guard Regiment, and the king was commander.[3] With this auspicious beginning there was throughout the fifth reign a gradual development of a variety of specialized military corps trained in the Western manner.[4]

Until 1886 each of these various organizations operated autonomously under direct authority from the king. In that year all land and naval forces were brought together in the Military Affairs Department with a single commander. This step marked the beginning of the organization of centralized armed forces. In the same year, a military cadet school was organized for the training of professional officers. Regulations were also issued to standardize ranks, positions, training methods, and pay.[5]

In 1892, when the cabinet was established, the chief of the Military Affairs Department was made a member, and the department temporarily became a ministry. Two years later the Military Affairs Ministry was again reduced to department status, with responsibility for the land forces, although its chief retained his cabinet position. The navy and certain other units were transferred to the Defense (*kalahom*) Ministry. Over the next decade all military matters were gradually consolidated in this ministry.[6] In 1905 the position of commander

---

[1] Thailand, Ministry of Defense, *Thi ralük wan sathapana krasuang kalahom 8 mesayon 2430—8 mesayon 2495* ("In Commemoration of the Anniversary of the Ministry of Defense, April 8, 1887—April 8, 1952"; Bangkok: Ministry of Defense, 1952), p. 167.

[2] *Ibid.*   [3] *Ibid.*, p. 173.   [4] *Ibid.*, pp. 174–178.   [5] *Ibid.*, p. 180.

[6] *Ibid.*, pp. 184–192. During the same period *kalahom* lost its function of local civil administration to *mahatthai* (Interior).

in chief of the armed forces was created and assigned to the crown prince.[7]

In addition to the reorganization of the armed forces along Western lines and continuous effort to bring the command of all forces under central control, the recruitment of soldiers was put on a new footing. In place of the traditional system of impressment which was a part of the general obligations of all freemen to the government, a system of universal conscription of youths was instituted. This system was modeled after European methods. At the age of 20 every youth became liable for two years' service in the military. He would then have certain obligations as a reserve for another 14 years. Set up by stages in different parts of the country, with both the Ministry of Defense and the Ministry of the Interior cooperating, the system seems to have succeeded in providing the army with a stable source of manpower.[8]

While the military was being professionalized, it should be noted that it was not unpolitical. In 1905 an act was promulgated which established the position of commander in chief of all the forces. This position was to be held by the crown prince, much as the heir apparent (*uparat*) in the traditional system of government had been a senior general.[9] Since the crown prince at that time was still a youth, the act provided for an acting commander in chief to be appointed on a year to year basis.[10] Moreover, most of the highest officers of the military were princes who had been sent to study in the military academies of Great Britain, Germany, and Russia.[11] The king, in the process of reorganizing and strengthening, was careful to keep control of this powerful instrument in the hands of loyal princes.

[7] *Ibid.*, p. 214.   [8] *Ibid.*, pp. 194–198.   [9] *Ibid.*, p. 214.   [10] *Ibid.*
[11] The crown prince (later Rama VI) graduated from Sandhurst, and upon his return to the kingdom served as chief of staff.

Rama VI considered himself a soldier. When he came to the throne, he took considerable personal interest in military affairs. Perhaps his most important act in these affairs was the creation of the Council of National Defense. This body, a sort of military cabinet, put military affairs on a governmental footing approximately equal to all civil affairs combined.

The king acted as president of this council himself. Membership included the Minister of Defense, the Minister of the Navy (which had been again separated from the Defense Ministry), the commander of the army, and the commander of the navy. Other ministers could attend meetings of the council if their advice was required.[12] This special position for the military was continued in the seventh reign by the reorganization of the Council of National Defense, which now included the king as president, the Supreme Councilors of State, and the Ministers of Defense, Navy, Foreign Affairs, Interior, Finance, and Commerce and Communications.[13] The council had the function of deciding national defense policy and coordinating the activities of the military ministries with related activities on the civil side.[14]

The military was a source of considerable pride to the government in the 1920's. The fact that there was a modern military force had made possible Thailand's joining with the Allied powers in World War I. This effort, which included sending a small expeditionary force to France, was one of the primary talking points in the negotiations that led to a complete revision of treaties by 1925. Moreover, national pride was not obscured by any question of credit to be accorded to foreign advisers in the building up of the modern army. The army was reorganized and rebuilt by Thai officials alone. This process could not but have had its influence on the *esprit* of the national elite. As one careful observer of the Bangkok scene of the 1920's said:

[12] *Ibid.*, p. 220.   [13] *Ibid.*, p. 223.   [14] *Ibid.*

As a school of training and as a safeguard of internal peace and order, the maintenance of armed forces sufficient adequately to reinforce the gendarmerie and police is not only desirable but absolutely necessary whatever may be the nature and extent of their foreign political value. Moreover, the working of the military law as exemplified by the smart appearance and orderly behavior of the men concentrated in Bangkok for the periodical reviews held there, is calculated to astonish the sceptics and upset all their theories, and encourages the belief that under good organization, the Siamese peasant may be turned into a good soldier. . . .

Self-defense, the preservation of internal order, discipline (more especially amongst the officer class), and the dignity of the crown, are all arguments strongly urging the maintenance of serviceable warlike forces.[15]

Military dominance in politics during the constitutional period is in part an outgrowth of the relationship among the parts of the government before 1932. In a system in which the sovereign power is an absolute monarch, the relationship of a ministry or agency to the throne is of such importance that it will overshadow certain other potential difficulties. The ministries draw their authority and budgets from the throne, and whatever conflict or competition there is among units of government takes the form of seeking greater influence with the throne. Such conflict was no doubt present in Bangkok before 1932. Graham makes the following remarks in regard to allocation of funds which indicate that there was debate about the configurations of the budget:

The question of funds is, however, a difficulty. There are many demands upon [Siam's] purse, and irrigation, improvements of communications and other works tending to the development of her natural resources, are of the utmost immediate importance if

15 W. A. Graham, *Siam* (London: Alexander Moring, Ltd., 1924), I, 317-318.

her future welfare is to be assured. At present she is trying to finance her economic reform and to build up a strong war machine at one and the same time, and there are signs of an inclination to starve the former for the latter.[16]

Moreover, for much of the period from the late nineteenth century until the *coup d'état* in 1932, the distinction between political and administrative functions of the government was obscured by a broad common interest in modernization, maintenance of independence, revision of treaties, and expansion of government activities. With the declining urgency of the struggle for independence and legal autonomy, especially after the renegotiation of treaties in the early 1920's, the impact of world economic decline on the national budget, and the divisive effect of Western antimonarchist thought, the question of political power became more distinct. It developed into an issue which was esentially the same for both military and civil officials. They were opposed to either military or civil princes. Any potential conflict between soldiers and civilians was submerged in the actual conflict between royalty and nonroyalty.

The Military in Politics in the Constitutional Period

The military was subject to the various influences which contributed to the *coup d'état* of 1932. Military officers had been regularly sent abroad for study in Europe from the late nineteenth century and were infused there with a taste for progress and modernity if not for democracy. But any sense

[16] *Ibid.*, pp. 318–319. *Plus ça change, plus c'est la même chose.*

of self-importance and *expertise* acquired abroad by officers was frustrated in the monopoly of top posts and decisions by high princes and their intimates. Phraya Phahon Phonphayu-hasena, leader of the 1932 coup, once said:

At the very base [of my reasons for joining in the coup] was the birth of the feeling that in the government at that time high officials and princes acted according to their whim and were not willing to pay heed to smaller people even though there were reasons for believing them. The big boys mostly felt that the quality of the opinion of lesser people was not important. What was important was whether or not it pleased them.[17]

In addition to this general frustration of the aspirations of lower officers, the Ministry of Defense was disturbed in the early 1930's by substantial budget cuts. The extent of this disturbance was indicated by the fact that Prince Bǫwǫradet, Minister of Defense from 1928 to 1931, resigned over the cut-back in the military budget. Such a political resignation was in itself an important event. It could not fail to contribute to the dissatisfaction among the military. The impact of the resignation among those officers who participated in the coup was sufficient to persuade them to support the noble prince for the position of Prime Minister after the coup in June, 1932.[18]

The nature of the successful *coup d'état* within the kind of narrow political system which Thailand had at that time lends a certain inevitability to the eventual dominance of the military. The literature on preparations for the coup which appear to

[17] Kulab Saipradit, *Büanglang kan pathiwat, 2475* ("Behind the Revolution of 1932"; Bangkok: Chamlǫngsan Press, 1947), p. 110.

[18] W. Čh. Prasangsit, *Pathiwat rathaprahan lae kabot čhalačhon nai samai prachathipathai haeng prathet thai* ("Revolution, *Coup d'Etat*, and Rebellion in Thailand during the Democratic Period"; Bangkok, 1949), p. 30.

have begun many years before in Paris gives no indication that any other method of political action was contemplated.[19] It is difficult to imagine any action which would have been successful without military participation. But evidently the military aspect caused no concern to the civil participants in the coup since the most important problem was to isolate and intimidate members of the royal ruling clique.

As a result the military had an important role in the events of June, 1932, and their political power has been, with the exception of the four years from 1944 to 1947, on the increase. A résumé of the important steps in the process will be useful in providing an explanation of why and how the military has been able to reach and stay on the top.

The first 16 months of the constitutional regime were crucial. In that period the pattern of military action was established and reinforced. First of all, the decision to carry out a *coup d'état* determined the need to include, even to depend upon, the military. The fact that the four senior leaders of the coup were colonels is sufficient evidence of the dependence upon military forces for success. Initially the military was not overwhelmingly dominant, however. In the list of persons appointed to the House of Representatives, only 16 out of 70 were military officers. The first Prime Minister was a civilian chosen, it has been reported, in preference to the candidate of the military.[20] The first constitution was written by a civilian, and the committee for drafting the permanent constitution was mainly civilian. Civilians might have continued to rule if they had stuck together. But they did not. There was an important division among the civilians in the first constitu-

[19] Khükrit Pramoj *et al., Čhomphon nai thatsana khọng khaphačhao* ("My Opinion of the Field Marshal"; Bangkok: Wibunkit Press, 1949), pp. 137 ff.
[20] W. Čh. Prasangsit, p. 30.

tional government. On the one hand, younger men who had promoted the coup were fired with the idea of revolution. On the other hand, older and more conservative bureaucrats had been brought in after the coup to lend solidity and respectability to the government.

Actually in the first part of 1933, i.e., in the second half year of the constitutional regime, there were a number of fractures in the government. But the foremost issue was between Dr. Pridi Phanomyong, the youthful intellectual leader of the coup, and Phraya Mano, the older more conservative bureaucrat who was serving as Prime Minister. Their dispute, which initially revolved around an economic plan, developed into a virtual countercoup, in which Phraya Mano closed the national assembly. This was a blow at the Coup Group as a whole. The reaction was military. A group of military leaders of the Coup Group seized power and reopened the assembly. Thus for the second time in a year the proponents of constitutional government revealed their dependence upon military support.

The indispensability of the army having been demonstrated, the important question for the future concerned who would turn the army into his own constituency. The period of Phraya Phahon's governments between 1933 and 1938 was a time of inner conflict in the military. Within the ruling group as a whole the military and civilian elements were in a sort of uneasy balance. Luang Phibunsongkhram,[21] because of his role in the seizure of power from Phraya Mano and in the suppression of a rebellion in October, 1933, became the most prominent of the young army officers. In 1934 he became Phraya Phahon's Minister of Defense. Apparently the dynamic manner in which he built up the military, as well as his ruthless suppression of opposition to himself and the

[21] Later Field Marshal P. Phibunsongkhram.

regime, increased his control over the army organization. During his tenure as minister the budget of the defense establishment doubled. He also undertook a campaign of public relations which emphasized the indispensability of the military for the nation. He made speeches comparing his administration favorably with the royal administration and saying that a strong military was necessary to prevent other countries from bullying and oppressing the kingdom.[22] In this way he constructed a solid constituency in the army. Thus based he surpassed the influence of his main rival, Dr. Pridi, and was Phraya Phahon's successor as Prime Minister in 1938.

Between 1938 and 1944, Phibunsongkhram and the army were firmly in control of the country. Phibun pressed forward a nationalist policy initially against the Chinese minority in the country and then against France on the borders of Indochina. The latter conflict brought Thailand into the scope of Japan's developing strength in Southeast Asia. In December, 1941, Phibun took Thailand into Japan's camp along with his own future and the army's political position.

Phibun's coming to power and the increasingly warlike situation in which the country found itself meant greater influence for army officers in the government. Civilians continued to cooperate although with less and less enthusiasm. One by one the more important civilians withdrew or were ousted from the government. Thus the military established their political role.

The declining fortunes of Japan and increasing hardship in Bangkok provided the opportunity for the civilians to engineer a parliamentary defeat of Phibun in 1944. By means of a certain amount of political legerdemain, he was eased out of

[22] Kenneth P. Landon, *Siam in Transition* (Chicago: University of Chicago Press, 1939), pp. 54–55.

office. The presence of Japanese troops in the country seems to have persuaded him not to force his way back.

The Postwar Period

The overthrow of the Phibun cabinet in 1944 was a challenge to the role of the army in politics. It was the first open split between civilians and military politicians. From that time until the *coup d'état* of November, 1947, there was a total of only five army officers who held posts in the eight cabinets.

In a revision of the constitution of 1946, supported by Pridi and his followers, who were now heavily relying on parliamentary strength, the civilians attempted to draw on the rationale of a professional government service to throw up a barrier to military politicians. Section 66 of that constitution prohibited permanent officials from holding political posts. This provision stood through the three constitutions used between 1946 and 1951, but the military officers found no problem in rising above it.

The *coup d'état* of 1947 was fundamentally an action by the army against the major parliamentary civilian group led by Pridi. Initially it had the cooperation of the Democrat Party, but this cooperation dissolved before many months. A list of the 36 leading figures of the Coup d'Etat Group shows 33 army officers, two air force officers, and one police officer.

One of the stated purposes of the coup was to "exonerate the honor of the army which had been trampled underfoot." [23] In addition, the military leadership assumed the authoritarian role of saving the nation from "the dishonesty and evil of

[23] W. Čh. Prasangsit, p. 170.

various kinds in the government circle." [24] By this coup the military took on as its trust the guarantee of orderly and good government. Such an idea served admirably to rationalize the authority of military leaders in politics.

But the leaders of the 1947 coup were only one group in the struggle for power. Their constituency was the army while competing groups were based in the navy and marines and in the national assembly. The coup leadership beat back two serious attempts to overthrow it by other military groups— one in 1949 and one in June, 1951. In 1948 an attempt to undermine their control of the army itself was scotched. The growing encroachment of parliamentary politicians was tolerated while these other military groups were a potential threat, but in late 1951, after the defeat of the naval attempt to seize power, the national assembly was dissolved. It was replaced by a revival of the system of tutelage used from 1932 to 1946, with half of the assembly appointed by the government. By means of this coup against the assembly, the leadership of the Coup d'Etat Group assumed overwhelming political power.

The army has been able to maintain its control and authority over the bulk of the government organization since that time by putting loyal army officers or other followers into the controlling offices.

The question of how one leader or clique within the army can be displaced by another is a subtle problem. It is difficult to distinguish by observation between an army leader with a political role and a politician whose constituency is in the army. But analytically there is such a distinction. It is clear that only an army officer can call upon the loyalty of the army to support him. But it is not clear at what point in his political-military advancement he is cut off from personal contact with

[24] *Ibid.*

the fundamental units of action (say the regiments) in such a way that his support by the army depends upon his political manipulation or placation of other officers who have open to them several alternatives.

The events of 1952 to 1957 are instructive in this regard. After the coup of November, 1951, the Coup d'Etat Group was firmly in control of all the military services, the police, the administration in general, and the national assembly. Within the Coup Group there were three cliques or potential cliques. The first was the Phibunsongkhram clique. The second was the Phin Chunhawan–Phao Siyanon clique. The third was the Sarit Thanarat clique. In retrospect it appears that in 1952 the leaders of these three cliques were each in a different stage of army control. Field Marshal Phibunsongkhram lost his direct contact with the army commanders of regimental level probably no later than 1944, when he was retired from the supreme commander's post by Pridi. When the Coup d'Etat Group came to power in 1947, Phibunsongkhram was important because of his great fame and because he symbolized the honor of the army. But it was General Phin Chunhawan who was active in recruiting army commanders to the coup.

In 1952 Phin was in his last stand as army commander. His political activities already had extended far beyond the army into business and a variety of other areas. His clique was being transformed by his son-in-law, Police General Phao Siyanon, into a broad, complex organization which included control of the police and the government parliamentary group as well as other activities.

In 1952 General Sarit, who had joined the 1947 coup as a regimental commander, was in command of the army in Bangkok and thereby probably in effective control of the army's political activities. In 1954 he replaced Phin as commander in chief of the army and was promoted to field marshal. By this time the Coup Group was in a process of dissolution. What evidently happened was that as General Phin became more involved in political activities outside the army he lost control of the army. His position came to depend on the power of General Phao, who was not influential in the army at all. At the same time Field Marshal Phibun's position was dependent upon the support of Field Marshal Sarit, controlling the army, and of General Phao.

These two men, Field Marshal Sarit and General Phao, both about the same age, were inevitably in competition for the succession to Phibun as leader. The rise to the top of either would be incompatible with the expectations of the other. Their two cliques were mutually exclusive.

The events of 1955 to 1957 culminating in the coup in which Sarit ousted both the Phibun and Phao-Phin cliques can be interpreted as mainly a succession conflict. In the struggle both sides sought allies against the other, and both sides encouraged discussion of issues which undermined the authority of the other. When a situation of considerable tension had developed in the Bangkok political scene, the Sarit clique moved with the army to take over the government and "clean up the mess."

The Army as a Political Organization

What are the reasons behind the historical fact that the relative power of the army among the various bureaucratic agencies has proved overwhelming? Is it not because an army is a bureaucratic agency par excellence? There are certain characteristics implicit in an army which provide it with advantages over other organizations. Not the least of these characteristics is control over arms. But this is not a sufficient although certainly a necessary part of the explanation.

It is the nature of the army's organization that is outstanding. This organizing principle of a modern army is unequivocal hierarchy. The principle has created some difficulty in the armies of modern Western democracies, but in Thailand it is admirably fitted to the traditional modes of social organization. Even though the Thai army is historically a modern innovation, this hierarchical principle was completely harmonious with Thai attitudes.

Research in connection with the psychological content of social organization carried out in the village of Bang Chan in central Thailand by associates of Cornell University is very suggestive in this context. Due respect must be paid to scholarly caution. The research is based on limited sources, namely, a few villagers, and extrapolation involves the usual risks. The homogeneity of Thai society, however, has encouraged the extension of some of the conclusions beyond their immediate point of origin. These conclusions make good sense in Thai social organization, urban as well as rural, political as well as domestic, military as well as civilian.

The essential of the analysis is that the Thai understand social organization only when patterned in subordinate-superordinate terms. In the words of L. M. Hanks, Jr., and Herbert P. Phillips: "Group coherence depends on status inequality. It is difficult for an equal to give anything of value to an equal or to command his 'respect.' Indeed he stands as a potential competitor for favors. Group solidarity requires . . . framing unambiguously the relative rank of each." [25]

[25] Lucien M. Hanks, Jr., and Herbert P. Phillips, "A Young Thai from the Countryside," in B. Kaplan, ed., *Studying Personality Cross-culturally* (Evanston, Ill.: Row, Peterson and Co., 1961), p. 642.

The military is, of course, very successful at "framing un-ambiguously the relative rank of each." It is contended here that in a society which has such a sociopsychological taste for hierarchy a military organization will very likely be a strong one, particularly in comparison to groups which seek to follow more egalitarian principles.

To reinforce the strength of such hierarchical organization the army can call upon the disciplines of loyalty and swift punishment. Respect, deference, and loyalty to one's superiors is also a large element of traditional Thai social thought, and the modern army is able to tap these feelings without being embarrassed by more novel ideas of equality and freedom. Ideas which lead naturally toward good discipline can also be reinforced by a system of courts-martial.

The army has additional means of developing solidarity and *esprit de corps*. With distinctive uniforms and insignia, ranks, titles, and other symbolic apparatus of the organization as a whole or of particular units, members of the army can be expected to have an allegiance to the organization as well as to individuals in it. Members of the army, particularly the officers, become concerned about the place and role of the organization on the national scene. The army's honor becomes an issue of personal honor. The fate of the army is the fate of each officer. This *esprit* built upon an in-group psychology can be reinforced by a general attitude of patriotism. The army's role as the defender of the nation makes it appear uniquely important that its dignity and honor be upheld.

Moreover, soldiering is now a profession. The esoteric arts of government are combined in the army with the esoteric arts of warfare. The management of large units of men is matched by the management and operation of large machines and weapons. The sciences of tactics and strategy are in the possession of the army. The fate of the nation depends upon the degree to which army officers are permitted to practice these arts and sciences unencumbered by petty and niggling demands.

Such an *esprit de corps* and in-group attitude are not unique to the army in Thailand. While practically nonexistent outside of the bureaucratic organizations, they are to some extent characteristic of all governmental units.

A deficiency of solidaristic corporate organization is typical of Thai society. Therefore while the society is faced with the tensions and strain of social change, there is premium value on any organization which may be available. The military, particularly the army, is one of the few such organizations which can mobilize large numbers of men for coordinated activities. The sum effect of these organizational characteristics is the ability to act with decision at the proper moment.

Good communications are an important element of the modern army's ability to coordinate action. The army units based in Bangkok are the most important insofar as the army's role in politics is concerned. They are under the single command of the First Army. Precisely how many troops there may be in the Bangkok area is a fact not available to the public —the number is certainly much higher than any other group could muster. The men are all compactly located to the north and east of the city, and units can be rapidly activated by telephone. Included among the troops stationed in Bangkok is at least one battalion of tanks which inevitably appears at each periodic declaration of emergency. Since the declaration of an emergency, which will bring out troops, is not an unusual occurrence, one may assume that the army has a standing plan for such occasions. This orderly establishment of patrol by army units at key locations in the city is one of the more impressive displays of organized activity likely to be observed in Bangkok. The significance of this impression is surely not lost on politicians.

Within the Ministry of Defense, the army is the dominant service. Since the beginning of the constitutional regime, the Minister of Defense has always been an army officer. The same is true of the permanent undersecretary. The army's share of the defense budget is always greater than that of the other services. At the same time the Ministry of Defense has a high degree of autonomy. Its budget is succinctly stated in a few lines in the annual budget act, and there is no indication of any inquiry into the expenditure of hundreds of millions of baht. The Ministry of Defense has its own section in the National Audit Council. Moreover, most officials in the ministry are officers under discipline.

The ministry also operates a number of industrial enterprises, including a fuel distribution organization and factories which are producing batteries, leather goods, glass, woven cloth, and canned food. Various military units operate the majority of commercial radiobroadcasting stations in the country. The ministry is a major shareholder in the Military Bank (*thanakan thahan*), a private commercial bank. This type of administrative autonomy is not exclusively characteristic of the military. To some extent it prevails throughout the bureaucracy.[26] In the military organization, however, it is

---

[26] The type of administrative autonomy under discussion here is a peculiar aspect of the Thai government which requires substantially more investigation. For example, every ministry and every department of the government has the status of a legal person. As such, these organizations are empowered to enter into a variety of relationships with other persons, legal or natural. The extraordinary organization of radiobroadcasting is perhaps an illustrative case. The kingdom has one national radio system, which operates a noncommercial domestic

somewhat more extreme for two reasons. One is simply that the army wants it that way and can insist on its being that way. The second reason is that the military gets a larger share of the national budget and thus controls far greater resources than other ministries. Such administrative freewheeling is quite likely to become increasingly difficult to bring under the control of outside influence.

In addition to this administrative autonomy, the military is, of course, juridically independent. Soldiers live under strict military law and are tried in military courts. The sway of military law has at times been extraordinarily broad. For example, in 1939 when a group of conspirators was tried for revolt, it was decided by the government, then under Phibunsongkhram's firm control, that all of them would be tried

---

and foreign service and is under the control of the Public Relations Department in the Office of the President of the Council of Ministers. There is also one quasi-private broadcasting company, Thai TV, which operates a commercial radio and television service. These are the only services which have a regular legal status. In addition, however, there are as many as 20 other broadcasting services. Most of them are operated on a commercial basis by a number of government departments, including the Public Relations Department, the Post and Telegraph Department, the army signal corps (which also operates a television station), the regional army radio service, the armored division, the air forces, the navy, the police, the Ministry of Education, and the royal palace. Moreover, the Ministry of Defense is not the only government organization which owns shares in a supposedly private corporation. The key institution in this sort of commercial activity appears to be the so-called revolving fund which each department is authorized to maintain for the purpose of covering petty expenses. It appears that, at least in some cases, these revolving funds become the core of elaborate departmental commercial complexes. Another aspect of this kind of autonomy is duplication of activities resulting from a reluctance to cooperate interdepartmentally. The duplication of control of government industries in the Ministries of Defense and Industries is an example.

in a special court under military law because some of the accused were army officers.[27] This practice created an extraordinary amount of resentment outside the military.

Finally, the most important aspect of the autonomy of the army and the military is perhaps the recruitment and training of its own personnel. These activities are particularly important in regard to the officer corps. The army, as well as the other services, maintain cadet academies which because of the prestige of the military officer's role receive large numbers of applicants. Therefore they are able to select candidates whom they want. This selection process in itself contributes to the tradition of the military as an elite group, and the graduates of the military academies are the elite of the military services. The more routine administrators are graduates of universities who are obliged to spend a period of time in the service.

Control over the education of its elite permits the army to mold the candidate officer's mind. A uniformity of attitude toward politics is almost certain to result from this uniform education, especially since the life of a cadet is entirely given over to education and academy life.

The extent to which there is such a thing as a military mind and the extent to which the Thai military mind is different from military mind as a universal phenomenon will here be bypassed. Military officers in Thailand do share certain common attitudes and ideas, however, which distinguish them from civilians.

A few elements of this Thai military mind may be isolated and will help to explain the role of the soldiers in politics. The first is the attitude of nationalism. One of the most important justifications for the maintenance of the military is as a symbol of national status in the world, bearer of the national honor, the defender of national independence. In a

27 *Bangkok Times Weekly Mail,* Feb. 6, 1939, p. 23.

selection of messages to the army on Army Day, 1955, are found the following:

It is a matter of certainty that the Thai army is an up-to-date army equal to the army of other countries. . . . It is a certainty that the army is capable of maintaining the independence of the Thai nation very firmly and as is fitting to the honor of the Thai nation as well.[28]

Thailand is a country which is independent and fully sovereign, and it must have an army to shield, defend, and maintain its independence and sovereignty undivided. . . . During the time when I was commander in chief of the army, I tried to the best of my ability to bring about rapid progress in the army so that it would be the equal of the armies of independent nations of the same rank, and I tried fully to have our army go ahead speedily into a state of development greater than that of our neighbors which have just recently joined the ranks of independent nations.[29]

The highest duty of a soldier is to shield and defend the nation from the threats of its enemies so that the people can live happily and at peace. Soldiers receive the highest honor and trust from the nation.[30]

A second aspect of the military mind of the Thai soldier is brought out in the uncomplex virtues which are inculcated into his character in the academy. The highest of these are love of duty, love of honor, and love of nation. Chart 1, reproduced from the Army Day Book, provides an example. It is introduced with this statement:

The present cadets department has heavy activities in conducting affairs for the cadets. It is necessary to work 24 hours together

[28] Field Marshal Phibunsongkhram in Thailand, Ministry of Defense, *Wan kong thap bok, 2498* ("Army Day, 1955"; Bangkok: Ministry of Defense, 1955), unpaged.
[29] Field Marshal Phin Chunhawan in *ibid*.
[30] King Phumiphon in *ibid*.

without finishing. But pride may be surely taken in the elements combined in the plan for the inculcation of character in the academy.

Finally, the soldier is oriented for action and for leadership. The military academy puts a great deal of emphasis upon qualities of leadership in the training program. One may assume that within the army itself qualities of decisiveness and even aggressiveness are rewarded to a greater extent than elsewhere in the Thai bureaucracy.

Aspects of the Thai military mind which influence the soldier's attitude toward politics may be summed up as follows. He believes himself to be a part of the organization upon which the fate and honor of the nation depend. This tends toward the belief that what is good for the army is good for the country. Coupled with this sense of the vital importance of the army itself is a very limited view of politics and government. The highest virtues of duty, honor, and nationalism do not lend themselves to a subtle sense of restraint and patience. These simple virtues encourage moral self-confidence. In the experience of the army officer, for example, this is reenforced by the fact that he is not questioned by those who are his subordinates. The soldier, with such moral self-confidence, is less likely to be troubled when making decisions necessary to press forward his case and that of the army itself. In addition to the quality of decisiveness, his training supports a tendency of character which demands action.

The Thai army is unusual in the non-Western world because it has a ready supply of fresh recruits. Universal conscription has been in effect since 1905. It produces more than adequate numbers of young men who serve for two-year terms on active service. The effect of conscription is to keep

Chart 1. The inculcation of character in the army academy

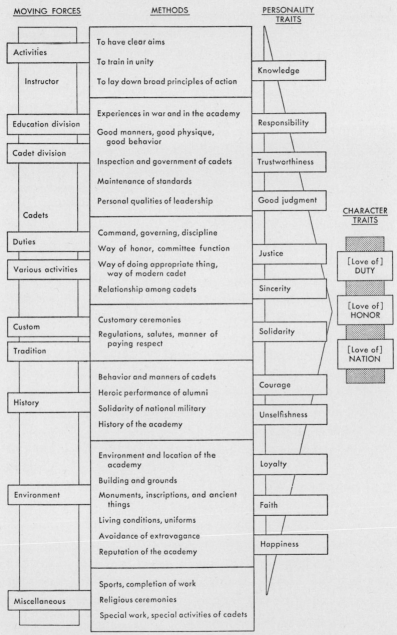

Source: Thailand, Ministry of Defense, *Wan kong thap bok 2498* ("Army Day, 1955"; Bangkok: Ministry of Defense, 1955).

the main, subordinate body of troops politically indifferent and docile.

Recruits are by and large from the villages. They have at best only four years of elementary education. Their social horizon is not likely to extend far beyond the village environment, and national politics is of little concern to them. They are unlikely to have any attitude at all toward such sophisticated questions as that of the military's role in politics. In the army they receive no political education beyond loyalty and obedience to their superiors, to the army, and to the nation.

The strength of organization and certain tendencies of character—which serve the army leaders well in the game of bureaucratic politics—are not exclusively associated with the army, but related advantages give the army an edge over other agencies. These advantages fall under three heads: force or strength, leisure time, and effective rationale for political action.

In the long list of coups and revolts which have occurred since the first in June, 1932, the army has never had a failure. Each of these episodes has involved a show of force by the army, and several have involved sustained fighting. On the six occasions when the army has taken the offensive to change the political situation—June, 1932; June, 1933; November, 1947; November, 1951; September, 1957; and October, 1958 —the seizure of key points in the city and the arrest of certain leaders have proved sufficient for success. On the three occasions when fighting has taken place—October, 1933; February, 1949; and June, 1951—the army has successfully beaten back moves to oust it from power. In the Bǫwǫradet rebellion in 1933 the fighting was in fact between certain upcountry garrisons and the combined force of the Bangkok army garrisons and the navy ground forces. In both 1949 and 1951 the army fought with the cooperation of the air force and the police against naval and marine troops. The history of the use of force in politics clearly indicates that in the event of a clash of arms the army is sufficiently determined and strong to impose its will on its opponents.

Yet the army, large and well organized, with its leadership trained in an attitude that is vital to the life of the nation, is idle for much of the time.

The function of an army in a small state such as Thailand is peculiarly ambiguous. There are, in fact, at least three different functions which it may undertake. First of all, there is its symbolic function as part of the apparatus of an independent state. No self-respecting nation can be without a military force. In this role the Thai army has on several occasions been the instrument of national diplomacy. For example, essentially symbolic forces were dispatched during World War I to France and during the Korean war to Korea. Neither of these episodes involved the defense of the country. Rather they were expressions of Thailand's diplomatic commitment.

The second function of the army is national defense. On the only occasion since the founding of the modern Thai army when the actual defense of the kingdom was at issue, namely, at the time of the Japanese invasion in December, 1941, the army surrendered. This surrender was, of course, not an unreasonable course of action. There was little chance that the Thai army could do more than momentarily delay the passage of Japanese troops through Thailand. There must be serious doubts about the Thai army's function as an instrument of national defense, however.

Such doubts arise not from any views on the capability or willingness of the army to fight. It is rather a question of whether the defense of Thailand has ever been or will ever be a matter of its own independent military action. In the early twentieth century, Thailand was squeezed by France and Britain; and its only defenses were diplomatic. From 1909 to 1941 Thailand lived at peace under the protective influence of European imperialism. Japan replaced France and Britain in 1941 with little resistance from Thailand, and it was changed back again in 1945 without fighting. At present Thailand is on the marches of the free world, and its fate is largely in the hands of the United States and China. Regardless of its capabilities, the Thai army's function as defender of the nation from external attack has been largely unexercised.

The army leadership has therefore had a great deal of leisure time in which to consider its proper place in the nation, to contemplate its honor, and to plan its actions. In this the military has an advantage over all government organizations. While it has a substantial and effective organization which is for the most part idle, other organizations have continuing administrative obligations to keep them occupied. For example, the police, which shares the use of force with the military, is charged with such a variety of duties that there is no time or excess of manpower to undertake strong political action against the military.

The third function of the army is to maintain internal security. A conception of duty along this line is either implicit or explicit in the army's political activites. A question of what actually constitutes a threat to internal security is a subtle one, as any student of the history of civil liberties knows. In the recent history of Thailand, the military has on various occasions taken it upon itself to judge this question and has in the name of civil order overthrown governments, suppressed dissident elements, and beaten back countercoups.

The pattern which guides the army in its relationship with other groups and institutions is subordination rather than destruction. There is no indication that the army's leadership has any desire to revolutionize the nation's social or economic system. In general, the army's rule has been conservative and in some respects reactionary. This is true in spite of the fact that dominance by the army is an outgrowth of the reduction of royal power.

The events of 1932 resulted in a realignment of the relationships among the institutions of the government and the locations of political power. As a result the system made up of these elements became somewhat more complex.

In the seventh reign before the coup the government consisted of two major organizations of approximately parallel powers and structure. These were the military establishment and the civil administration. Each of these two had a council at its apex which served as the over-all administrative control. These councils linked the ruling group with the administration of the two organizations. At that time the ruling group consisted of the king and the Supreme State Council.

Following the *coup d'état* and establishment of the constitutional regime, the basic structure of the government organization was retained, but the ruling group was no longer royal. In fact, it was quite explicity nonroyal. At the same time the novel insititution of the national assembly was introduced, in part to lend legitimacy to the authority of the new ruling group and in part to have it function as an institution representing parts of the society presumed to have previously been ignored.

The three fundamental institutional structures—the military, the civil administration, and the national assembly—have been potential competitors for domination. As noted, throughout most of the quarter century since the establishment of the constitutional regime the military, in particular the army within it, has been the institution which has been the base and origin of the dominating group. This has not, except for relatively brief periods, resulted in a military dictatorship, however. Rather, the result has been the overlapping and interlocking of the three institutions much in the style of the monarchy with a clique of army leaders playing the role of the ruling group.

VII

THE DIFFICULTIES
OF THE NATIONAL
ASSEMBLY

THE history of Thailand's efforts to establish and maintain some sort of representative assembly is the story of many of the difficulties that the country has faced in organizing a constitutional government by transforming its institutions. The various forms of national assembly specified in the procession of constitutions from 1932 to the present give some evidence of this story. But clearly the success or failure of a national assembly to exert its will and to be an effective political institution is more than a matter of law. It is also a matter of the interrelation and the action and reaction of the various organized power structures, both those which are institutionalized and those which are not.

Thailand is not entirely lacking in precedents for legislative councils. As long ago as 1874, Rama V attempted to establish

some sort of corporate responsibility in the drafting of legislation and to bring together a number of persons for the
purpose of discussing and debating the law. His Council of
State set up in that year was in fact a kind of parliament of
officials whose collective knowledge and wisdom were sought
in formulating state policy. It is not unreasonable to imagine
that the king intended to involve the interests of a number
of high and powerful officials in his efforts to modify some
of the state's institutions as well as to gain their wisdom.
Nevertheless, the Council of State was a quasi-legislative
assembly.[1]

The Council of State was made up of members chosen by
the king from among his officials. It met regularly to discuss
matters put before it by the king. Members also had limited
powers of initiative. One peculiar regulation of the council,
which indicates that membership was probably not altogether
a sought-after honor, was the provision that members who
wanted to resign from the council had to resign from all their
official positions.[2] Both the king and his ministers had a veto
over the decisions of this council.

The Council of State was changed into the Assembly of
State Councilors in 1894. The act establishing the new council
prescribed that the Ministers of State or their representatives
were to be ex officio members. In addition, there were to be
at least 12 members appointed by the king. There were in
fact three officers—chairman, vice-chairman, and secretary
—and 39 members.[3] The king also charged this council with
the function of advising on legislation. It is said to have been

[1] "Prakat wa duay tang khaosin lae phrarachabanyat" ("Announcement about Establishing a Council and an Act"), *PKPS*, VIII, 115.

[2] Nathawut Suthisongkhram, "Sapha kanphaendin nai müang thai"
("Government Councils in Thailand"), *Rathasapha san* ("Journal of
the National Assembly"), VI, no. 27 (June, 1958), 20–21.

[3] *Ibid.*, VI, no. 29 (June, 1958), 10–12.

extremely active in its first four years and then to have gradually fallen into disuse. No meetings are recorded after 1907.[4]

Sufficient evidence is not available to judge the actual workings of these councils, but in view of the vast amount of legislation which was enacted during their existence—much of this is known to have been considered by them—it is likely that they labored in an earnest and thoughtful manner. The effort was not altogether successful, however. The tremendous amount of work required by the administrative reorganizations of that period may have contributed as much as anything to the demise of the councils. Amendments to the regulations of the Assembly of State Councilors in 1895, which excluded from the quorum count members away on business, indicate that demands of administrative duties on the member's time were slowing up the meetings. It is quite possible that when the great press of new legislation was over in 1907, the king allowed the council to wither rather than risk the development of a permanent institution to challenge the royal will.

Rama V was rather doubtful about the idea of a parliament in Thailand in his time. The councils were advisory only, and he clearly and unequivocally retained the final authority and sovereign power for himself. His councils were designed to bring him closer to the administration, to inform him of what was going on, and presumably to seek for prior agreement among the powerful officials on his proposed policies. In his correspondence it is clear that he foresaw the eventuality of a constitutional regime, but it is also clear that he did not expect to see it in his lifetime.[5]

The quasi-legislative councils in the reign of Rama V were the nearest approach to a kind of parliament in the history of Thailand up to 1932. During the reign of Rama VI there

[4] *Ibid.,* VI, no. 30 (July, 1958), 9–14.   [5] *Ibid.,* p. 15

was no attempt to revive the use of such a council. Rama VI evidently was not a systematic administrator but was a man of strong opinions. It may be assumed that deliberate discussion and slow decisions had no appeal for him. Rama VI continued the Privy Council which his father had set up as a personal advisory body. He appointed many of his friends and cronies to it as an honor, but he seldom consulted it.

When Rama VII succeeded, he revived the idea of an advisory council. One such institution of this reign was called the Supreme State Council (*aphirathamontri sapha*) and was constituted of high princes who were half brothers or uncles of the king. It bore little resemblance to a representative assembly. Actually it served as a kind of super or inner cabinet rather than a legislative council. Its members attended cabinet meetings and also had direct access to the king. In fact, the Supreme State Council was a kind of antiparliament which ensured that the final control of state policy would be in the hands of the royal family. This council is said to have discouraged Rama VII's intention to grant a constitution to the country on his own initiative.[6] If this is really the case, the council contributed by this act to the course of events that culminated in the revolution of 1932 and ended royal control over the government.

In 1928, Rama VII also reorganized the Privy Council in such a way as to make it useful as a quasi-legislative assembly. The entire Privy Council, as it had been inherited from the previous reign, was too large and apparently not altogether qualified to accomplish much. Under the new plan, however, a committee of the Privy Council consisting of 40 councilors selected by the king had special status. This committee was to be organized according to parliamentary principles in order

[6] Baron de Lapomarède, "The Setting of the Siamese Revolution," *Pacific Affairs*, VII (Sept, 1934), 253.

to consider such matters as the king might submit to it. Moreover, five members could petition for discussion of an issue which they felt to be important to the well-being of the country. The opinions of the committee were merely advisory, however.[7] It is reported that the king intended this council to serve as a training ground for a future parliament.[8]

Constitutional Period

When, with the constitutional regime, an ostensibly genuine parliament was established which was based on the principle of popular representation and given legal authority to control legislation and administration, its condition and behavior served as a symptom of the regime's difficulties. In view of the traditions and precedents of government the difficulties of the national assembly are small cause for wonder. In the situation of the time a representative assembly of great power was logically, but not practically, necessary.

Consider that the revolutionary group was made up of officials of the government trained in the atmosphere and manner of bureaucracy. The task of the revolution in 1932 Thailand was not to release and articulate into the political system the interests of a previously excluded social group. In that sense it was not democratic. Rather its task was to shift control from one faction to another within the ruling class as it was then constituted.[9] This shift of control was not

[7] Nathawut, VI, no. 42 (Oct., 1958), 9–14; no. 43 (Oct., 1958), 9–14.

[8] Lapomarède, p. 253.

[9] Sawai Sutthiphithak, *Dr. pridi phanomyong kap kan pathiwat* ("Dr. Pridi Phanomyong and the Revolution,"; Bangkok: Sirithamnakhǫn, n.d.), p. 96.

without some social significance since the new men represented the trained expert rather than the amateur. But the
vocabulary of the revolution was that of constitutionalism
and democracy. No duplicity is suggested here but merely
the fact that the revolutionaries in seeking ideological and
legal justification for their actions looked to their previous
experience for models. Many of them (perhaps most) had
studied in Europe after World War I, a setting of intellectual
and social strife, and thus many had had contact with European ideas of democracy, constitutionalism, and revolution.
They found in the current notion of constitution a device
which in part served them admirably. A constitution limits a
king. But a constitution also has a representative assembly
whether representation is in demand or not. Thus they had an
assembly.

Approaches to such a national assembly from such a group
as the leaders of Thailand's 1932 coup were rather ambivalent
in concept. The bureaucratic background of the leaders gave
them an inclination toward strong executive government and
suspicion of the unprecedented and unpredictable nature of
a body of undisciplined men each of whom had his own personal sources of power. Therefore, a more or less traditional
conception of an assembly as a group of wise but gentle
counselors which would express the consensus of the nation
for the guidance and information of the government was a
natural and acceptable one. But there was another view current as well. This was the doctrinaire conception of an assembly as a watchdog of the public interest or even as the
embodiment of a general will which commands government.
The more radical idea, which came home in the luggage of
returning students and had little in tradition to support it,
was the origin of unforeseen consequences. It came to be held
by the men who were elected to the national assembly. The

tensions implicit in this confrontation of ideas contribute to the basic problem of the national assembly.

Although its constitutional position has been powerful, the national assembly, struggling against this ambivalent role, has never succeeded in developing its potential authority. It remains a novel institution, and during its short life since 1932 it has suffered various indignities, such as being summarily closed, being dissolved, and, worst of all, being periodically reorganized. At the same time a distrust of its general representative nature and of its competence has been demonstrated in various constitutionally provided safeguards against the independence of elected representatives. In all, the national assembly has been unable to construct a tradition of power.

Another cause of weakness is that parliamentary groups have little strength outside of the assembly. As will be shown in the next chapter, party organization is feeble and lacks any substantial popular base. Individual members may be strong within their constituencies, but there are no national organizations to impose discipline within the assembly. These factors contribute to the overwhelming dominance of the government over that body. Bearing the immense prestige of his majesty's government and of the bureaucracy in general and having military backing in particular, the cabinet as a rule is able to rule the assembly firmly. Using fear, persuasion, corruption, and patronage, in addition to the power to appoint members itself, the government has, with rare exceptions, imposed an iron discipline on its majority and ignored what opposition there might be.

Tension, arising from the different conceptions of the assembly's role and from its failure to realize its power, is evident in the erratic history of the assembly in its various forms. The first assembly met on June 28, 1932, and was constituted of persons selected by the promoters of the *coup d'état* from

among their supporters. This group went little beyond the
concept of the advisory council of Rama V, although it also
was the first stage in the proposed House of People's Representatives. The second stage involved the election of an equal
number of representatives by a rather complicated two-stage
indirect election.[10] This procedure apparently assured firm
control by the leadership of the Coup Group over the election.
The assembly was then constituted, in accordance with transitional provisions of the constitution, of two categories of
members equal in number—one elected and the other appointed. The reasoning behind the provision to divide the
assembly into two categories was that "we have only just
introduced a constitution and familiarity with its workings
is not fully developed; therefore, there will be a category of
members which is thought to have experience so that they
may cooperate in the work of the assembly with the members
of the first category elected by the people." [11]

Doubts about the adequacy of the process of election in
producing an assembly with the desirable qualities are very
clear in this arrangement. In the words of a leading commentator upon Thai politics at that time:

The matter of having two categories of members is temporary.
It is needed because it is feared that first category [elected] members will not yet be proficient enough in the working of the
house. It is believed that there ought to be a second category of
members consisting of persons expert in government work to
cooperate in the beginning. When the first category members
have acquired proficiency in the workings of the assembly, within

[10] Prince Wan Waithayakon, "Pathokatha rüang kan lüaktang"
("Lecture on Elections"), in *Khumü rabop mai* ("Handbook on the
New Regime"; Bangkok: Bunthong Lekhakhun, 1934), pp. 97–111.
[11] *Raingan kan prachum sapha phuthaen ratsadon* ("Reports of the
Meetings of the House of People's Representatives"), sitting no.
34/2475 (special), p. 366.

ten years at the longest, then the second category will be abolished.[12]

There is no reason to think that the promoters of the coup were not acting in good faith in setting up this tutelage procedure, but from the point of view of the prestige of the assembly an unfortunate precedent had been established.

In less than a year from the first meeting, the assembly was faced with its first direct assault. The event turned around two issues—an order by the government that permanent officials could not belong to the People's Association (the People's Party club) and a radical economic plan submitted by a leader of the coup. Both these issues created sharp differences of opinion within the Coup Group and among members of the government. The Prime Minister, Phraya Mano, who had been chosen for the office because of his conservative outlook and connections, took the ensuing tension within the government and the assembly as an opportunity to prorogue the House on the grounds that the government could not get on with its business. Moreover, a new government was constituted which assumed the right to legislate by decree.[13] This event amounted to a coup against the assembly, which had to wait upon the military to put it back in session again three months later.

For the remainder of the first session, the assembly seems to have functioned quite smoothly although attempts to get greater powers away from the executive were rather quickly suppressed. For example, in 1934 certain members of the assembly submitted a bill to have the Office of National Audit moved out of the Office of the Council of Ministers and put under the direct control of the assembly. The government

[12] Prince Wan, p. 89.
[13] Kenneth P. Landon, *Siam in Transition* (Chicago: University of Chicago, 1939), pp. 250–251.

refused, however, and the bill was defeated.[14] Nevertheless, during the first session, the government was actually forced to resign twice. On the first occasion in 1934, the government found itself under considerable pressure over the issue of an international agreement to limit the export of rubber. The government's policy was ambivalent on the matter of the size of quota to be accepted by Thailand. A motion to decrease the size of the quota was defeated in the House, and the government resigned.[15] The cabinet was reshuffled and returned to office shortly thereafter. In 1937, the government resigned in the face of a potential scandal about the sale of crown property to cabinet ministers at bargain prices. Again the cabinet was reshuffled with certain members dropped.[16]

In 1938 in its second term, the role of the assembly, such as it was, began to decline. The first category of members in the second term had been elected by a direct election on November 7, 1937. The following year in the debate on the budget the assembly demanded further details on the bill. It got short shrift, however, and the government dissolved it forthwith. New elections were called. When the assembly met again, Phibunsongkhram, the acknowledged leader of the military segment of the People's Party, took the office of Prime Minister. Phibun lacked the conciliatory temperament of his predecessor, Phraya Phahon. From that time until the collapse of his pro-Japan policy in 1944, Phibun seems to have had little difficulty with the assembly. It does not appear that this development should be entirely ascribed to a love or respect of Phibun, nor should it be laid entirely to fear. It was in part a result of the fact that Phibun had the

---

14 *Raingan kan prachum*, 2d sess., 1934, pp. 179–199.
15 *Ibid.*, 2d special sess., 1934, pp. 1701–1722.
16 *Bangkok Times Weekly Mail*, Aug. 2, 1937, and following issues.

opportunity to appoint a number of second category members and in part a matter of a general feeling of crisis and unwillingness to rock the boat. But under Phibun's strong hand, the status of the assembly suffered decline. During the Indochina incident in 1940 and even more after the invasion by Japan in 1941, Phibun's personal power was vastly increased as a result of his tight control over the entire military establishment. Although the assembly was not the only institution to lose power in the course of this development, it was clearly in ebb from 1939 to 1944.

In 1944 Phibun's personal prestige and power began to decrease rapidly. Because the war was going badly for the Japanese and had created considerable hardship and discontent in Thailand, Pridi Phanomyong, Phibun's chief rival, was able to persuade a sufficient number of members of the assembly to join in an effort to overthrow the government. Two important government measures were defeated in parliamentary votes, and after some hesitation Phibun was finally induced to resign.[17] Phibun is reported to have been assured that the resignation would be a formality and that he would immediately be reappointed Prime Minister. This turned out not to be the case, and Pridi, after energetic political maneuvering, was able to sidetrack Phibun and have Khuang Aphaiwong appointed Prime Minister. This was the first occasion in which a major change of government was brought about through parliamentary action.

The successful completion of this maneuver must be credited largely to the fact that at the time Thailand was under great strain because of international events. The Japanese army was present in the country in substantial force,

[17] Čharun Kuwanon, *Chiwit kan tǫsu khǫng čhomphon p. phibunsongkhram* ("The Life and Struggle of Field Marshal P. Phibunsongkhram"; Bangkok: Aksǫn Čharoen That Press, 1953), pp. 248–256.

and any overt clash of political factions or dramatic evidence
of political instability might well have provided an excuse
for the Japanese to take over the administration of the kingdom directly. So it was thought at the time, at least.[18]

The overthrow of Phibun's government marked the beginning of a period during which the national assembly was
again to play a more important role in the political process.
This period lasted as long as Pridi remained the dominant
figure in Thai politics, i.e., until the end of 1947. The revived role of the national assembly as the political market
place can be explained by three interlocking elements of the
situation.

First was the fact that the army was in a state of confusion
as a result of the failure of the pro-Japan policy and was
also restrained from taking direct action to recapture the pre-
eminent position it held from 1938 to 1944 by the delicacy
of the international situation. Thailand was seeking in 1944
and 1945 to avoid any provocation of its Japanese guests and
thereafter to rehabilitate itself in the eyes of the victorious
Allies.

In addition to the disorganized and debilitated state of the
army there was the fact that Pridi found one of his main
sources of support among elected members of the assembly.
Pridi also leaned heavily upon his former students and followers who were numerous on the rolls of the civil service,
particularly the Interior administration.

Finally, as this period progressed, the developing opposition party of conservative "royalist" politicians that rallied
around Khuang Aphaiwong came exclusively from the assembly. Its members made up a sizable and vocal group, and
they had great public prestige. The struggle between the
Khuang and Pridi groups thus took place in the national as-

[18] *Ibid.*, p. 262.

sembly, but the continuance of the assembly's role as a focus for political activity was contingent on the continued inaction of the armed forces. As soon as the forces, particularly the army, made the decision to return to an active role in politics and to throw their weight on one side of the struggle between the two parliamentary groups, the focus of politics shifted, and the national assembly was again relegated to a secondary position.

During the period between early 1944 and late 1947 when the national assembly was playing an important role in the political life of the kingdom, it underwent its first major reorganization. The constitution of 1946 provided for a national assembly made up of two houses. The lower house was called the House of People's Representatives and was fully elected. The upper house was to be elected indirectly by an electoral college chosen especially for the purpose. In the first instance after adoption of the constitution, however, the House cf People's Representatives of that time elected the upper house. Membership in the upper house was restricted by special qualifications of age and education. Its ostensible purpose was to provide wise and deliberate consideration on legislation and advice upon the conduct of the government.

An immediate motive for the creation of the upper house is reported to have been a demand by appointed members of the previous national assembly that positions of dignity be prepared for them before they gave approval to the revised constitution. At the first election of the upper house, most of the candidates were in fact second-category members of the national assembly, and virtually all of these who agreed to support Pridi were elected to sit in the upper house.[19] Another motive in creation of the upper house lay in the de-

---

[19] "Kiat," *Phongsawadan kan müang* ("Political Chronicles"); Bangkok: Kiatthisak Press, 1950), pp. 97–101.

sire to extend the influence of Pridi's supporters for longer than the life of the elected lower house.[20]

The appearance of political parties on the parliamentary scene was a second novel element during this period. There were a number of such parties which were in fact only parliamentary groups, including the Progressive Party led by M. R. Khükrit Pramoj; the Constitution Front and the Cooperation Party, both of which supported the leadership of Pridi; and the Democrat Party under the leadership of Khuang Aphaiwong. These parties amounted to a recognition of the fact that the assembly had divided into a number of groups. Their creation was an attempt to stabilize the situation as far as possible. They also represented the first institutionalization of parliamentary opposition to the government. Their appearance may be taken as evidence of the important role that parliamentary activity was playing during that period.[21]

The *coup d'état* of November, 1947, put an end to the postwar period in which the national assembly played such a prominent part in national politics, and succeeding years have been witness to its decline. During that time it has been transformed in many respects into a kind of club for those members of the ruling class whose source of power lies mainly in their ability to win elections. At the same time there has been a related increase in the ability of the military, particularly the army, to act politically with little consideration for the expression of parliamentary will.

The *coup d'état* in 1947 also abruptly ended the life of a properly constituted national assembly which, although plagued by sharp divisions, was acting effectively. Again in April, 1948, the army cavalierly ignored the will and intention of a duly elected assembly by forcing the resignation

20 The term of office of members of the upper house was six years.
21 See Chapter VIII for a discussion of parties.

of Khuang's government, which had the confidence of a substantial majority. It is revealing that during this incident Khuang never appealed to the assembly. In the face of a demand from the leaders of the Coup Group that he resign immediately, he turned to his friends in the military. Apparently he never seriously considered asking the assembly to back him in his desire not to quit.[22]

Between April, 1948, and the end of 1951, the governments of Phibunsongkhram were not in a position to ignore the national assembly completely. During that period the assembly was constituted of two houses, a fully elected lower house and a royally appointed upper house. The Phibun governments were faced in those years with a variety of threats. Younger, disaffected military officers were unreliable; followers of Pridi staged a revolt at least once; and the Democrat Party under the leadership of Khuang maintained a vocal opposition in the national assembly. It was therefore necessary for the Phibunsongkhram governments to maintain a majority group in the assembly by a variety of means.

By 1951, however, after the suppression of the so-called Manhattan revolt (called thus because the opening events occurred on a dredge named "Manhattan") in June, the army group which was the core of the Phibun governments appears to have consolidated its position fully. In November, 1951, it was evidently felt by important figures in the government that the time was opportune for the reduction of their dependence on the unreliable good will or insatiable cupidity of elected members of parliament.[23]

[22] John Coast, *Some Aspects of Siamese Politics* (New York: Institute of Pacific Relations, 1953), pp. 46–47.

[23] Bunchuai Sisawat, *Phantri khuang aphaiwong* ("Major Khuang Aphaiwong"; Bangkok: Rapphim Press, n.d.), pp. 568–569; Prachuap Thongurai, *Sin yuk müt* ("End of Darkness"; Bangkok: Phrayun Phitsanakha, 1957), pp. 34–36.

The "silent" coup of November, 1951, may well be the low point in the dignity of the national assembly. By reestablishment of the constitution of 1932 the principle of tutelage was again imposed on an assembly which had been free of it for six years. The government was then able to appoint half the members of the single house and no longer faced serious difficulty in organizing a majority group to support it. Khuang and his close associates expressed the extreme outrage with which parliamentary politicians viewed this development by refusing to participate in the election of February, 1952.[24]

Between 1955 and 1958, as the split between the police and army factions in the ruling Coup d'État Group developed, the center of political acitivity shifted back toward the national assembly. The general election of February, 1957, became the focus of an effort to discredit Phibunsongkhram, the government political party, and General Phao Siyanon who, in addition to being director-general of the Police Department, was secretary-general of the Seri Manangkhasila Party. During the campaign a loose coalition came together in an informal way and was centered on the determination to carry through this effort against Phibun. Khuang and the Democrat Party returned to active politics in an enthusiastic attempt to regain a substantial parliamentary representation. The army supported the campaign against Phibun by indirection. At the same time a parliamentary left wing emerged to join in the effort although at least in part the motive of this group was to modify the government's foreign policy. Phibunsongkhram and General Phao were not passive. They were determined to broaden their respective bases of power by means of an election as an endorsement of their leadership.

Following the election, which was in fact a moral defeat for

Phibun, Phao, and the Seri Manangkhasila Party, the scene of the effort to discredit them shifted from the hustings to the national assembly. There were bitter discussion and debate in the House until the coup of 1957. The climax of this two-year campaign to undermine Phibun and his immediate associates was a so-called general debate staged just prior to the coup. The general debate was itself inconclusive, but it contributed to the tense atmosphere which provided the backdrop for the action of the military.

After the coup the army appears to have been reluctant or unable to muffle parliamentary activity even though the assembly had been dissolved during the coup. A new election was organized for December, 1957, which in effect was a ratification of the coup. The army group seems to have been too confident of their ability to control an elected parliament, however, and the government of Thanọm Kittikhačhọn set up in January, 1958, was harassed in the house and in its own party. Finally, in October, 1958, the life of the national assembly was ended and the constitution completely suspended in the second stage of the military's taking over power. The interim constitution of January, 1959, provided for an assembly appointed by the throne to act concurrently as a legislative assembly and a drafting commission for a new constitution.[25] The concept of the assembly had come full circle again to that of a body of wise and trusty counselors to the government.[26]

---

[25] *Bangkok World*, Jan. 30, 1959.

[26] An interesting comment on the military attitude toward the assembly was revealed in an editorial in one of Field Marshal Sarit's newspapers on the occasion of the first meeting of the new assembly in Feb., 1959. Expressing the hope that the new assembly would do better than the old one, it said: "At this time there are not a few people who are interested in the attitude of the new assembly and who intend that the new assembly should be different from the old, espe-

Legislation

In order to throw further light upon the position of parliament, some explanation of the legal system and the legislative process is in order. According to the constitution, sovereignty is exercised by the king. As long as the constitution is in force, the legislative power is exercised "by and with the advice and consent of" the national assembly. In concept this role is presumably similar to that of the United States Senate in treaty making. The general body of the law is included in the codes—penal, civil, commercial, and procedural—which for the most part historically predate the constitution. These rest upon the sovereignty of the throne. At the same time the sovereign has a variety of legislative and quasi-legislative acts available to it. Among these the most important are the royal act (*phrarachabanyat*), the royal ordinance (*phrarachakamnot*), the royal decree (*phrararchakrisadika*), and the royal command or rescript (*phrarachaongkan*). Lesser orders of quasi-legislation in the form of ministerial regulations, notifications, military commands, orders, announcements, and the like are widely utilized. The precise use of each of these actions is somewhat confused at the present time although the procedures for the enactment of each are clear.

Both the royal act and the royal ordinance (sometimes called the royal decree-law) must receive the consent of the assembly. An act is presented to the assembly in the form of a

---

cially in the use of harsh, cruel, and insulting language which was the habit of some members of the former assembly and in disrespect to the hallowed place [in which meetings are held] by inciting disturbances" (*Thai raiwan*, Feb. 7, 1959).

bill and after debate is passed or defeated by majority vote. The ordinance is available to the government for emergency action. An ordinance may be issued "when there is an urgent necessity to maintain public safety or to avert public calamity" at such time as the assembly is not in session.[27] It may also be used to enact such programs as taxes and currency regulations which would be damaged by prior publicity.[28] In any case the ordinance must be submitted to the parliament as soon as possible for its approval. If approval is withheld, the power of the ordinance is void. The ordinance is rarely used in normal times (there have been six issued since 1946) but was heavily relied upon during wartime. It is unpopular with the assembly since it presents them with an accomplished fact, often difficult to undo.

The most difficult legislative action to define is the royal decree. The constitution grants a broad mandate by declaring: "It is the prerogative of the King to issue Royal Decrees which are not in conflict with law." [29] This power has been much used by the government and serves as a demonstration of the dominance of the executive over the legislative branch of the state. In the period from 1946 to the middle of 1957, the government issued 782 royal decrees as compared with 468 royal acts. Many of the decrees derive authority not only from the constitution but also from grants of power to the government in royal acts. For example, the Act for the Establishment of Government Organizations of 1952 grants to the government the power to establish by decree, subject to certain limitations of form, any number of autonomous government corporations to engage in specific enterprises. In the intervening period, the government has set up a number of

[27] Constitution of the Kingdom of Thailand, 1932 as amended 1952, sec. 88.

[28] *Ibid.*, sec. 89. [29] *Ibid.*, sec. 95.

such organizations with activities ranging from the operation of the railways to the building of warehouses.

Legislation in general takes the form of the delegation of
certain authority to officials in terms of the most general
objectives. To a great extent the development and implementation of policy are left to the bureaucrat. A good many
departments of the government have no specification of their
powers and functions other than the act which creates them
and the granting of their annual budget. Beyond that the
specific role of the department is defined by the ministerial
regulations, orders, notifications, and so forth that are developed under the broad authority by which they were
created.

The budget is potentially a most vital and effective form
of control of the government and the bureaucracy. Under
the constitution (Section 68) the budget must be enacted as
a royal act with the approval of the assembly. Parliamentary
control is hedged, however, by the government's power to
make emergency expenditures in advance of parliamentary
approval (Section 69) and by the provision to extend the
previous year's budget if the new act is not passed (Section
68). Money bills may be introduced in the House only by
the government or with the approval of the Prime Minister.

Although the constitution declares that no state monies may
be spent unless sanctioned by the law governing the budget,
there are in fact substantial funds available to government
departments which are not accounted for in the budget. This
situation arises from the fact that each department has the
status of a juristic person and as such can own property and
enter into business. The profits of such activities are then
available to the departments for their own uses.

The Role of the National Assembly

Even though in fact the national assembly has never been able to exercise its specified constitutional powers, it has nevertheless become an important element of the political system. In the three decades since its establishment, its existence has been so fully institutionalized that it is difficult to see how it could be abolished. If it is true that constitutional government legitimates the present system, then the assembly in some form is indispensable. Moreover, it serves certain functions beyond the mere symbolic in the working of the system. Although it has often been buffeted about in a most undignified fashion by irritable ruling groups, the assembly's place has always been reaffirmed and its ultimate legitimacy has not been questioned.

Aside from its formal legislative powers, there are at least two political functions which the assembly performs. The first of these is related to regionalism, the most serious divisive force in the society of the kingdom. Regional feeling is strong outside the central area of the country, particularly in the northeast and northern provinces. In not too distant history, these areas have been outside the direct administration of the Bangkok monarchy, living under the rule of hereditary princes or governors. There is in these areas a pattern of opposition to the center on ethnic, economic, linguistic, and cultural, as well as historical, grounds. The national assembly provides a possible pathway for provincial notables to attain positions of prestige in the capital and to give vent to their regional grievances. To the extent that the assembly performs this function, it is an apparatus which links the parts of the country to the center and in large measure siphons off pressures which might lead to the development of more irascible proponents of localism. It would appear that most of the outspoken critics of the central government from the regions are in the assembly, or have hopes of being. There they have a platform from which to gain public notice for their purposes.

Related to this kind of expression is a broader, though still limited representation of a range of political attitudes. The changing and mobile nature of Thai society results in the circulation of a variety of ideas and attitudes from traditional and novel sources. A good many of these receive a hearing on the assembly floor. Thailand is almost completely deficient in organizations which might expertly present proposals in the interest of particular groups. Therefore the differing attitudes which are from time to time manifested in the assembly are not to be understood as evidence of pressure or interest groups seeking to modify legislation in a purposefully interested manner. Such expressed attitudes provide something more in the nature of a running commentary or editorial on the government and its affairs than a systematic presentation of special interests or group aspirations. It is revealing in this context that during 1956 and 1957 the national assembly was often linked with the press and Hyde Park speakers as the spokesmen of public opinion. The limits of the public opinion voiced by the national assembly are dependent upon the extent to which the members represent in themselves a social cross section.

In the following studies of five elected members of the assembly, it can be seen, however, that there is considerable divergence among members of the assembly. They do represent currents of opinion running in the interested political public. But at the same time a great part of the country's population goes wholly unrepresented by this system because assembly members are not part of the majority of people who elect them and these interests and aspirations, whatever they may be, are unexpressed. The bulk of the farm population is not represented by individual members, nor is it any more organized than any other Thai social interest group. It is therefore left without articulate spokesmen.

Members of the Assembly

Biographical sketches of five characteristic members of the assembly will give some idea of the sort of man the Thai parliamentary politician is. Whereas each of these men is an individual, they may be taken as representing characteristic types of personalities and attitudes on the middle level of Thai political life. Because this is so, they reveal together something of the role of the national assembly in the Thai political system.

Nom Upramai was born in 1911 in the town of Nakhọn Sithammarat on the southern isthmus. His father, also born in Nakhọn Sithammarat, was a well-to-do farmer who had only the traditional education of the local monastery. Nom married the daughter of a local doctor, and they have seven children, the oldest in his early twenties. Nom received his education in Nakhọn Sithammarat in government schools and also studied for a period in Penang. He has a law degree from Thammasat University in Bangkok and also holds a diploma from the Ministry of the Interior school for administrators and a certificate from a government teacher training school. Although Nom considers himself to be primarily a lawyer, he is best known in his province as Teacher Nom, the headmaster of a well-known private school. He says that he has not practiced law since he entered the national assembly.

After teaching school in Nakhǫn Sithammarat for 10 years, Nom entered government service as a district officer during World War II. Because of his ability to speak English, he served as liaison officer between the Thai administration and the Japanese and later between the administration and the Allies.

After World War II, Nom returned to Nakhǫn Sithammarat to practice law and operate his school. In 1948 he was elected mayor of the Municipality of Nakhǫn Sithammarat, a position which he held for two years. Nom says that he entered politics because it gave him an opportunity to use his mind and his ideas for Thailand. "I can't live more than 100 years," he comments, "and I want to serve humanity and the nation. I don't want property because I can't take it with me." As for his political interests Nom says, "I am interested in foreign affairs more than anything else. I am educated so I prefer to learn more and more." And he continues: "By nature I prefer to read history, politics, and international relations. Reading history lets me know different events and the activities of important men. I want to be an important man of the nation and of the world."

Nom is quite cosmopolitan. He studied in the Western-style city of Penang, and since he has been in the assembly, he made an extended junket to the United States and Europe in 1955 and was a Thai delegate to the conference of the Interparliamentary Union in Great Britain in 1957. In his home town he maintains a reading room of United Nations materials, and his house in the capital is decorated with UN posters. He knows a number of languages.

First elected to the national assembly in 1952, Nom, during

his period in office, has been a supporter of the government. In February, 1957, he was a successful candidate for reelection on the government Seri Manangkhasila Party ticket. In the next session of the assembly, Nom was rewarded with the office of vice-president of the House. At the same time he was holding a seat as a member of the municipal council of Nakhǫn Sithammarat and as a member of the provincial council of Nakhǫn Sithammarat. After the coup of 1957 he switched to Field Marshal Sarit's Unionist Party. Many thought his political career was finished because of this turnabout, but he won a hard-fought campaign for reelection in December, 1957.

Nom is an admirer of power—of power for service. He has no sympathy for the "captious" opposition of certain politicians. He believes that the purpose of government is to provide for the "safety and sovereignty of the nation and the peace and tranquillity of the people." The main quality he professes to admire in leadership is "sacrifice." His life gives no outward sign of personal enrichment, and it may be concluded that Nom has sought public office for more abstract motives than money.

Noi Thinnarat was born in 1924 in Mahasarakham Province in northeast Thailand. His father, who had a primary school education, is a farmer and had previously also been a schoolteacher; Noi describes him as poor. Noi is married to the daughter of a farmer, and they have five children. He holds a diploma of law from Thammasat University which he received in 1944, and he is still a part-time student for a Bachelor of Law degree. He makes his living as a lawyer and also by raising animals for sale.

Noi began working in 1938 as a schoolteacher and in 1939 came to Bangkok to study law. He supported himself in the university by riding a pedicab and engaging in petty commerce. He has never been a civil servant except in the tenuous position of a schoolteacher.

Noi's political career began in 1954 when he was elected to the provincial council, and he evidently gained some reputation as a stout opponent of the government. He describes this stage of his career as follows:

The people saw my character, my friendliness, and my struggle, and they elected me to be a member of the provincial council. At that time I became associated with some Bangkok politicians. In the provincial council I opposed the executive and won in some cases. And so I enjoyed being a politician. The *kamnan* [commune headmen], the headmen, and the teachers liked the results of my work.

When asked why he opposes the government, Noi said:

The government rules the people without sympathy, and they don't understand the people well. I think that the method of politics at this time is like France in the time of Louis XVI and Marie Antoinette, because the government believes in representatives who flatter them. They give privileges to politicians, and they pass extravagant laws. Even if the people object, the government does not pay any heed.

Noi is a simple man. He admires the life of Abraham Lincoln because, as he says, "It is like my life—coming from poverty too." The late Ramon Magsaysay, another man of the people, is a model for Noi. It would appear, however, that he has had little experience of the world outside Thailand. His only travel abroad has been a trip to Laos, and his knowledge of foreign languages is somewhat rudimentary.

Because of his success as a provincial politician, Noi decided to run for the assembly in 1956. He ran as a candidate of the Democrat Party. When asked why he joined the Democrat Party, he said: "I saw that the people wanted the Democrat Party, and I like the policy and the leader of this party. I liked the leader because he is a pure man, and he does not like cheating." Noi joined the party on his own application. During the process of campaigning, however, for some unexplained reason he got into trouble with the party leadership. He relates the affair in this way:

After I became a party member, I asked Khuang Aphaiwong to come and speak in seven places in Nakhǫn Račhasima. People liked him very much. Afterward there was the election campaign, and Mr. Khuang did not help me. For some reasons within the party he sent another person to be the candidate. The Democrat candidate damned me in the campaign, but because of the goodness which the people had seen and the fact that I campaigned without any transportation and walked from place to place, they took pity on me. They gave me money for my candidacy.

Noi ran third of six elected in Nakhǫn Račhasima Province.

After the election Noi was somewhat confused about his group allegiance. During the first session of the assembly, he said: "Now that I am an MP I am still of the Democrat Party, but they don't like me because I am not the man they sent to be a candidate. I intend to resign and be independent. I won't join the progovernment party. I am not sure whom I shall join." Noi's career in the assembly was prematurely cut short. Although he was a candidate for reelection in December, 1957, he was not successful.

Noi is something of a rustic and deficient in the suave and blasé ways of the Bangkok elite. He is, like Nom, a respecter of power and authority. But he demands that it be honest and "pure." He says, "People who would be the government should be honest," and continues:

When ministers are selected, their careers should be studied to see
if they have a bad history, if they are educated, if they are honest.
If after he becomes a minister he brings in bad men, then he is no
good. Phraya Phahon was the best Prime Minister because he was
honest with the country. The people love and worship the king,
because he is pure.

The upcountry lawyer, schoolteacher, or journalist, like
Noi, is not an unusual figure on the fringes of Thai political
life. He is a product of the extended educational system and
the broadening of political life. He may tend either toward the
conservative, as in Noi's case, or to the left. But like Noi his
career possibilities are limited for the present although he is
a symptom of the increasing complexity of political life which
is straining the traditional attitudes.

Yuang Iamsila was born in 1912 in Udǫn Province in northeast Thailand. His father was an army officer assigned to the
police and civil administration and rose to the position of
district officer. Yuang is a bachelor. He has a secondary education and also holds a teacher's certificate. During his early
years he was a government schoolteacher.

The most important experience of Yuang's life appears to
have been when there occurred what he says was an unjust
arrest and conviction as a rebel in 1935. He describes the
experience as follows:

I was outspoken in my views of the seizure of power from
Phraya Mano.[30] I helped to suppress the Bǫwǫradet rebellion. I
was an official and led Boy Scouts into the fight to help the military because I didn't want things to go back to the old way.

---

[30] The reference is to the seizure of the government by the leaders
of the 1932 *coup d'état* after the first postcoup Prime Minister, Phraya
Mano, had dissolved parliament and was ruling by decree in 1933.
(See above, p. 17.) Yuang was in favor of this action by the leaders
of the coup.

I was arrested in 1935. At that time I was still young and was of the anti-Bǫwǫradet group. In Monthon Udǫn there was a group which supported Bǫwǫradet and another which supported the People's Party. Later things were confused and some groups were falsely accused. I was arrested as a rebel and a Communist even though I didn't know what a Communist was.

Yuang maintains that his experience in jail aroused his interest in politics. He says:

I entered political life because of being in jail. I was sorry that I had been arrested because of other people's spite when I was only 24 years old. I studied politics in prison. There were 366 persons together in prison from the time of the Bǫwǫradet rebellion. I saw that those who were politicians were not playing politics in the right way. The state of the people was not improving. After studying politics I observed those people playing politics. When I had seen enough, then I wanted to play a little politics myself. I wanted to demonstrate my views.

After his release from prison in the general amnesty of political prisoners in 1945, Yuang became an active journalist in Bangkok. He says that he has been a columnist in almost every newspaper and has from time to time been a newspaper editor and owner. He is also the author of several books.

Yuang is a long-time follower of Pridi Phanomyong. In 1957 he was an official of the Free Democrat (Seri Prachathipatai) Party. Some of his attitude toward politics may be revealed by his opinions of political leaders:

I first met Pridi in 1945. He was a person who could think well. For anything he wanted to do he had a plan. He was firm in his effort to complete things. He was the most intelligent man in the People's Party, but he was hot-tempered. It was characteristic of him to use power. This was a characteristic of all the Promoters of the Coup d'Etat. They were rather inclined to dictatorship.

I first met Phibunsongkhram in 1948 when I was a newspaper man. He is a man who is firm in his intention to do things. He has some progressive thoughts. But he only does things which give quick and visible results. He is hot-headed like Pridi and nobody can oppose him. He is intelligent in taking care of his own place. I have known Khuang Aphaiwong since 1942. He is humorous. He works without a plan.

Democracy is defined by Yuang as "the ability to know how to respect the rights and freedoms of others and not to limit the rights of others and not to hoodwink others. The purpose of government," he goes on, "is to give most of the people happiness and bring about understanding among mankind throughout the world. . . . The happiness of the people is satisfaction and not feeling upset."

Yuang has been active in political life for many years, but until 1957 he was barred from running for office by his record as a rebel. In February, 1957, he was a candidate in Udǫn Province and was elected. He was a successful candidate for reelection in December, 1957.

Yuang has vigorous ideas on the role of parties and groups in Thai politics, and he comments:

The Political Parties Act should be changed because it is too broad. For example, a party can be established in only one province. There are many parties, and the people are confused about policy. Thailand should have three parties, one right, one center, one left, and then the people would not be confused. At this time the people do not understand parties, and at elections they vote individual by individual.

As for his own party experience he says: "At first I didn't feel that I should join a party, but later my friends, who had been ministers, were killed, and then I decided to be a candidate in order to fight. I joined the Free Democrat Party because its policy is that of the Constitution Front and the Cooperation Party." [31] But regarding the reliability of party leadership he has this to say:

Pridi's views were not constant. Politics in Thailand does not follow principle. Everyone seeks power. For example, near the end of the war Pridi joined the royalists. My group did not like that because Pridi was a left-winger. Why should he join with the royalists? Later Pridi was beaten by the royalists in the king's death case. Then Pridi came into the left wing.

In contrast to Nom and Noi, Yuang is a political sophisticate. In talking to him one has the impression of a man with reservations of principle about the system of Thai politics. In Nom and Noi one receives a hint of personal and private embarrassment or frustration but a general acceptance of politics as they are. But in Yuang there is the suggestion of a conception of politics as something completely different. For example, he says: "I respect nobody in particular because each person has his own virtues. No one is complete. For example, Mr. Pridi is good at economic problems, Phibun gets things done, Phao is intelligent, Sarit is other things. . . . I am a disciple of no one. I am a disciple of books, not of persons."

The combination in Yuang of the Thai quest for personal autonomy and something like the European liberal virtues is not unusual among Thai politicians although such persons are uneasy in the society of Thailand. There is a similarity between Yuang and Noi in this respect, but while Noi is persuaded thereby to a conservative opposition, Yuang inclines toward the radical and shows something of the revolutionary's taste for machination. In leadership, he admires in-

[31] Parties supporting the Pridi and Thamrong governments in 1946 and 1947.

telligence and ability to plan and get things done. Yuang and those like him are a radical threat to the old system.

Khlai La-ongmani was born in 1909 in Songkhla Province in southern Thailand. His father, also born in Songkhla, was a successful farmer with only the rudiments of formal education. Khlai's wife is the daughter of a merchant in Surat Province, and they have four children. Khlai received most of his secondary education in Songkhla but also studied for a period in Singapore, where he passed the senior matriculation for Cambridge. He also holds a law degree from Thammasat University in Bangkok. His income derives from the practice of law and from rubber holdings in the south.

Khlai worked a number of years for the East Asiatic Company, a large European trading and shipping firm in Thailand. He was a clerk and translator for them. It was after his experience with the East Asiatic Company that he returned to school to study for his law degree. While studying, he was headmaster of a Chinese school in Surat. After receiving his degree he practiced law in Songkhla. Khlai is probably a third-generation offspring of a Chinese immigrant.

His experience with the East Asiatic Company, Khlai says, was very influential in his life and in his attitudes. This fact is confirmed in his personal behavior which to some extent reflects the model of a European gentleman. But he meant something else. He said:

I was very young. The method of a company which wants to get people to work for them is to give a high salary to start. Take, for example, two people who finish school together. Mr. A. becomes an official [of the government] at a low salary. I went to work at a foreign firm because I saw that the salary was better and [thought] that there would be a better future. But in the long run, Mr. A. progressed better. In a Western firm an Asian never gets a salary equal to Westerners even if he has greater ability. When I came to think like this, I changed my career even though I had worked for six years. Some people who work for ten or twenty years have no hope of being boss. When I came to this conclusion, I entered law studies.

It was in 1946 that Khlai was first elected to the assembly from Songkhla. He had this to say about it:

I entered politics because I like politics. I like it because it is a way that we ourselves can work for the country independently. Some jobs are not independent. If one is a politician, whatever one does, one does independently. I felt that I had the knowledge and ability to do anything in the way of politics. So I wanted to be a politician.

Khlai has been a member of the Democrat Party since he first entered the asembly. He has also been an active committeeman of the party. He explains his reasons for joining as follows: "At first I considered the individuals in the party. Some parties wrote good policies but acted badly. I saw that the persons in the party [Democrat] were good so I joined."

Khlai's political career has been remarkable only for its steadiness. He was first elected in 1946 and then was reelected in 1948, 1952, February, 1957, and December, 1957. During this entire period he has stayed with the Democrats. He has held no cabinet positions and seems not to be troubled by uncontrollable ambition. His attitude appears to be that which one would expect from a moderately well-to-do professional man—calm, conservative, and patiently hopeful. The purpose of government, he says, "is to cause the nation to progress and the people to be happy, i.e., to have a good living and live in peace."

Khlai seems to be satisfied with the political system except insofar as it is infected with "selfish" men. "Parliament has been changed because of events of the country which were not good," he commented. "This comes from the moods of selfish politicians. For example, the 'silent' *coup d'état* [in November, 1951] was an action for selfish reasons. They say they did it for Thailand. But from the results we can see that it was for themselves." Of Khuang Aphaiwong, the leader of his party, he says:

He is frank and straightforward. In government he doesn't think the country is his own property. If his ideas are not in agreement with others, he is willing to change. If he is thrown out, he goes. He does everything democratically. When it is time to resign, he resigns. He is not stuck to the chair. Resigning easily is a good thing. A sensitive person is a good thing. When the people think he is good, they will choose him again. To yield easily is better than to yield after difficulties. To be defeated and not to yield is not good.

Coupled with calm steadiness is a kind of lack of urgency often associated with conservative outlook. When asked what Thailand's fundamental problem is, he answered:

The economics and agriculture of the country. Thailand doesn't want to do much—only to have its economy, communications, and public welfare in good shape. The solution of these problems will help the country progress. The basic problem is a matter of people. This can be solved with the cooperation of many, many people, but it will only be solved gradually. It may take 40 to 50 years, or perhaps 100 years. It is like a school with disorderly and bad children or with bad teachers. If a good teacher comes to improve it, it will take a long time to make it orderly.

Wing Commander Thinnakǫn Bhandhugravi was born in 1919 in Nakhǫn Pathom Province in central Thailand. His father was a civil official who held the rank of deputy district officer in Phitsanulok Province, which Commander Thinnakǫn considers his home. His elder sister is Madame La-iad Phibunsongkhram, wife of Field Marshal Phibunsongkhram. Commander Thinnakǫn is an example of a young man with connections. He is married to the daughter of a civil official in the Ministry of Finance, and they have four children.

Commander Thinnakǫn received his secondary education at Assumption College, a well-known missionary secondary school in Bangkok. He received the B.Sc. in mechanical engineering in 1945 from Čhulalongkǫn University. He also studied for a year (1940) in the Philippines. In 1945 Commander Thinnakǫn joined the Thai air force. In 1949 he was assigned as liaison officer to the United States Air Transport Command and was sent to the United States. One year later he was transferred to be assistant air attaché in London, where he stayed from 1950 to 1953. Following that he was appointed assistant secretary to the Minister of the Interior; later, when the minister was transferred to the Ministry of Communications, Commander Thinnakǫn went with him. He has also been attached to the general staff of the air force, and he held the position of deputy manager of the Thai Sugar Organization.

In 1956 he decided to run for the parliamentary seat of Phitsanulok Province. "I entered politics," he said, "because I was working with politicians, and I decided to run for MP. I also wanted to serve my home town. After my decision to run for MP, I asked my sister [Madame La-iad] for advice. She did not want me to get into politics because she has had much experience in that field."

Commander Thinnakǫn retains his air force rank although he is on inactive duty. He ran in February, 1957, as a candidate of the Seri Manangkhasila Party and was elected. He received the post of parliamentary secretary to the Minister of Industry in the Phibunsongkhram government of March, 1957. After the *coup d'état* of September, 1957, during which his brother-in-law was ousted from the Prime Minister's office, Commander Thinnakǫn ran for reelection in December, this time as an independent. He was reelected.

His association with the Seri Manangkhasila Party is not surprising, but he has this to say about it: "I joined because I believed this party could bring progress to the country—there were individuals in it in whom I could believe." Commander Thinnakǫn, although a member of the air force, did not participate in the *coup d'état* of 1947 and has never joined the Coup d'Etat Group. When asked about the Coup d'Etat Group, he said: "I don't know much about that, but I know that the group are mostly military officers." He explained that new members are recruited to the group and then added: "I did not join because I took no part in the coup and I didn't want to take any advantage." When asked to explain what sort of advantage he meant, he replied: "The group has meetings and members give assistance to each other."

Commander Thinnakǫn's views on the national leadership are, for the most part, favorable without qualification. Of Phibunsongkhram, he said:

I feel that in work he has the intention of bringing progress to the people and not of thinking of his private advantage. He has won the hearts of the armed forces and also the people. I am a disciple of the Field Marshal because I have lived near him and know that he has worked well and for the advantage of the people. It is not because he is my brother-in-law. I respect all my seniors.

Commander Thinnakǫn's connection with Field Marshal Phibunsongkhram was, of course, an unusual advantage for him. There is no reason to think, however, that the rate of his advancement is uncommensurate with his ability. In talking to Commander Thinnakọn, one senses a well-educated, hard-working, and earnest young man. His attitudes are characteristic of the numerous young, technically educated members of the Thai ruling class. His running for the assembly, while unquestionably aided by the support of Field Marshal Phibunsongkhram, was in no way necessary for the furtherance of his career and seems evidence of the seriousness of his purpose. He may be taken as typical of such well-educated and modern young people who work in the traditional system but hope, perhaps, for some change.

VIII

POLITICAL
ORGANIZATIONS

THE clique, a quasi-kin group, is the received tradition of
social and political organization in Thailand. It has already
been mentioned above that the clique focuses on the person of
a leader and is bound together by lines of loyalty more or less
deeply felt. As the political institutions and the numbers of
people involved in politics have expanded with the establishment of parliamentary institutions on the one hand and the
development of a more elaborate bureaucracy on the other,
the cohesion of a clique has been severely strained. A tendency
for cliques to be transformed into more formal and impersonal
organizations is related to such strains. During the period of
the constitutional regime such a transformation tendency has
been evident in the appearance of political parties and a certain kind of bureaucratic faction which have assumed a special
political role for themselves.

Parliamentary Groups and Parties

As in so much of Thai social organization, personal relations and personality are fundamental in social relations, and the personal clique has been fundamental in parliamentary and election activity as well. Political parties remain, on the whole, personal parliamentary groups with more or less elaborate *ad hoc* electoral machinery. Leadership is the binding element of a political party or parliamentary group. Its representative function at its broadest does not extend beyond a clique or group of cliques. Thus the posture of the party or group depends largely on the temperament of its leader, and its continuity and vitality rest upon his political fortune.

From 1932 through World War II, there were no political parties in Thai politics. The People's Party or People's Association which emerged as the public organization of the Promoters of the Coup d'Etat of 1932 cannot properly be so described. The initial intention of the Promoters apparently was to form a large but exclusive party organization to support their position,[1] but they soon abandoned the idea. Shortly after the establishment of the constitutional government, it became public policy not to permit the organization of parties and the People's Party became the People's Association, which appears to have combined social activities with some genteel political education. The usage is somewhat confused, however, since the ruling group continued to refer to themselves as the People's Party. In this sense the term refers to the ruling group associated with the 1932 coup.

[1] Cf. speech by Sanguan Tularak in *Bangkok Times Weekly Mail,* June 28, 1932.

Several times during the 1930's the question of political parties was raised in the national assembly. The fundamental position of the government was that parties could be permitted to come into being only after the enactment of permissive legislation. Such legislation would have to wait, said the government, until the appropriate time.[2] In 1939 a private member's bill was introduced to authorize political parties. It was opposed by the government, again on the grounds that the time was not appropriate. It was defeated.[3]

It was not until after World War II that groups began to take on the name and form of political parties as they have emerged in recent Thai politics. These parties have played a relatively minor role in politics because of the instability and weakness of the national assembly. Their function has been primarily as parliamentary groups. They have also served as campaign labels in certain elections and occasionally as public relations devices.

Because they draw their vitality from maneuver in the national assembly, the degree to which parties play a part in politics depends upon the place of the assembly in the political situation of the moment. Thus during 1946 and 1947, when the Pridi group was based to a large extent on its parliamentary position, the attack by opposition parties contributed substantially to the weakening of the government's authority. Between 1948 and 1955, when the military-based Coup d'Etat Group was in power, the sounds of party debate in the house were drowned in the clash of arms or buried under the weight of appointed members. From the middle of 1955 to September, 1957, when the split appeared between the army on the

[2] Reply of the Minister of the Interior to a parliamentary question, Feb. 1, 1938, in *Raingan kan prachum sapha phuthaen ratsadǫn* ("Reports of the Meetings of the House of People's Representatives"), 2d sess., 2d set (ordinary; 1937–1938), II, 809–811.

[3] *Ibid.*, 2d sess., 3d set (ordinary; 1939), I, 119–147.

one hand and Field Marshal Phibun and General Phao on the other, the struggle was carried into the assembly again. Phibun and Phao sought to gain enough support in the assembly to resist the army, and they turned to the device of political parties for help. General Phao organized the great government Seri Manangkhasila Party for this purpose. After the coup of 1957, Field Marshal Sarit also tried to rule with the help of a political party but found that parliamentary debate was troublesome and unnecessary. In October, 1958, he closed the assembly and outlawed political parties.

During the brief history of the national assembly, there have been two basic forms of parliamentary groups. The first of these is the government group. In Thailand the rules of parliamentary government have not had a great deal of influence on the political system, however, and the fact that the government's parliamentary group is the larger is not a precondition but rather a result of the power of the ruling group. In a system of factional constitutionalism,[4] the ruling group starts out with some sort of advantage in the assembly. It may have the power to appoint members, or at least it has the powers of the bureaucracy and the treasury to help trusted friends get seats. To this core of supporters, a number of other members will gravitate naturally. Because the members of this group join for a variety of reasons, it is inevitably heterogeneous in terms of the position, status, and background of its members.

The second form of parliamentary group is the opposition clique which, because the government has the facilities to create opportunities for the opportunists, tends to be more homogeneous. The overriding quality of party activity is instability, however. Parties and groups are regularly reorganized in conformity with the shifts of the political wind.

[4] See below, Chapter IX.

The first of the big government groups was brought together in 1946 to support the governments which were headed
by or supported by Pridi. It was called the Constitution Front
and was modeled vaguely on the idea of a popular front. Following the election of 1946, the Constitution Front included
four groups, namely, the Promoters of the Coup d'Etat
(1932), the Cooperation Party, the Independents Party, and
the Communist Party (one member).

The first of these parties to appear was the Cooperation
Party (Sahachip). It was formed by supporters of Pridi who
were associated in the "Free Thai" movement of which Pridi
was acknowledged head. The party pronounced itself to be of
a leftist nature and in favor of a socialist policy.[5] A good many
of Pridi's supporters in the assembly were unwilling to join
the Cooperation Party for one reason or another.[6] These members, under the leadership of Luang Thamrong Nawasawat,
who later became Prime Minister, formed the Constitution
Front.[7] The Independents Party was a small residual group
of men who refused or were not qualified (either as Promoters
or Free Thai) to join either of the other two groups.

The Constitution Front collapsed when the Pridi group was
overthrown by the coup of 1947, and its role as the government party was assumed by a succession of groups supporting

[5] "Kiat," pseud., *Phongsawadan kan müang* ("Political Chronicles";
Bangkok: Kiatthisak Press, 1950), p. 89.

[6] *Ibid.* "Kiat" attributes their reluctance to the socialist policy of
the Cooperation Party. It is also indicated, however, that an important
consideration may have been the fact that the Cooperation Party
was associated with the Free Thai. The group which was reluctant
to join included Promoters of the Coup d'Etat (1932) who had not
been in the Free Thai. Since the function of both groups was the
same, i.e., to back Pridi, one may suspect that the distinction between
the two groups was related to their place in the groups and their respective conceptions of relative status.

[7] "Kiat," pp. 94–95.

the governments of Field Marshal Phibun from April, 1948, to September, 1957. The first of these was an organization not unlike the Constitution Front which took the name United Parties (Sahaphak). This organization was an agglomeration of small groups supporting the government in the assembly. The United Parties began the practice of having regular meetings of the government group before meetings of the assembly.[8] As has been suggested above, the period in which the constitutions of 1947 and 1948 were in force, which lasted until November, 1951, was a time when the government found itself with its hands full trying to control the assembly. Not the least of its troubles was the United Parties. In it there were a number of tiny groups whose *raison d'être* appears to have been expressed in the words of a perceptive but not altogether sympathetic commentator: "Each different party had several members—some more, some less—and all were combined in mind and body to support Field Marshal P. Phibunsongkhram, the Prime Minister, and to become ministers, one after another. This was a way of building up one's reputation or that of one's family." [9]

Such jostling for position was brought to an end when the assembly was reestablished with half its members appointed. As part of the new dispensation, parties were again forbidden. This situation led to the formation of a crypto-group called the Legislative Study Committee. It appears to have had some sort of official status as a committee of the cabinet.[10] This group was made up of the appointed half of the assembly plus those members willing to support the government. The man who created this group was General Phao Siyanon, who became its secretary-general. The Legislative Study Committee

[8] Pračhuap Thongurai, *Sin yuk müt* ("End of Darkness"; Bangkok: Phrayun Phitsanakha, 1957), pp. 33–34.
[9] *Ibid.*, p. 33.　　　　　　　　　　[10] *Ibid.*, pp. 40–41.

also held regular meetings to lay strategy for meetings of the assembly. With the advent of legal political parties in 1955, the Legislative Study Committee was transformed into the Seri Manangkhasila Party. It took its name from the mansion in which its meetings were held. Seri Manangkhasila collapsed after the coup of September, 1957, when Field Marshal Phibun and General Phao left the country.

After the election of December, 1957, which confirmed the rule of the military group led by Field Marshal Sarit, a new party called the National Socialist Party (Chat Sangkhom) was organized, and it followed the pattern of Seri Manangkhasila. Its core was the appointed category of members to which were added the Unionist Party (Sahaphum) [11] and other members willing to support the government. The National Socialist Party, which was never successfully brought into a state of discipline, was suppressed by the coup of 1958. The present dispensation in regard to the assembly provides for the appointment of all the members so that the matter of parties is irrelevant.

The motives for joining one of these heterogeneous government parties range from love to greed. One category of members includes those who have long been followers of the leadership of the ruling group and members of the inner clique. A second category includes those who respect and believe in the real or supposed principles and policies of the ruling group. A third would be those members who look to the ruling group for the resources to build up their political position in their constituencies. A fourth category includes those members who seek private profit. In satisfying these motives the

[11] The Unionist Party appeared in the months between the general election of February, 1957, and the coup of September. It was a parliamentary group opposing the Phibun government and backed quietly by Field Marshal Sarit.

state machinery is helpful to the ruling group. They have control of patronage, for example. For members themselves there are cabinet and parliamentary secretary posts. Friends and supporters of a member can also be given official positions or jobs in the various enterprises with which top-level politicians find themselves associated. The government has control of the pork barrel, too, so that in some cases money for the promotion of local improvements is given to a loyal member to be spent in his province as he sees fit. The government also has several kinds of privileges at its disposal to be granted to members, such as government contracts, permits to import or export scarce or controlled commodities, or access to scarce railroad cars. Finally, the government, having the use of considerable funds, is able to pay substantial stipends to supporters over and above the normal salary. All of these methods have been used from time to time.[12]

Because of the various devices at hand for disciplining this kind of government group and because of the variety of motives for adherence, the history of such groups has been a stormy one. The heterogeneity of motives for adherence to these large government organizations precludes the possibility of much uniformity throughout the membership. The ideas which the party professes to hold in common are those of a weak and vague nationalism and social justice. On the other hand, the opposition parties, having little to offer their membership, are small and always in danger of getting smaller. Those members who remain have some sort of commitment of social origin or ideals. The oldest of the opposition parties is the Democrat Party. In its original form it was actually the first party to proclaim its existence after World War II. In 1945, M. R. Khükrit Pramoj, a prominent intellectual, announced that he was forming the Progressive Party, made up of former

[12] Pračhuap, pp. 95–96.

political prisoners who had been amnestied after the overthrow of Phibunsongkhram's government in 1944. The stated purpose of the Progressive Party was to break off the monopolistic hold of the Promoters of the Coup d'Etat of 1932 on Thai politics. It aimed to open the way for the entry of "good men" previously barred from the political arena.[13]

The principal target of this challenge was Pridi, who was the acknowledged leader of the governing group at that time and, of course, a Promoter of the Coup. Following the election of early 1946, Khuang Aphaiwong, who had served as Prime Minister under the aegis of Pridi on two occasions, split away from him. He announced that he would establish a party of his followers in the assembly. Into this party, which was called the Democrat Party (Phak Prachathipat), was merged the Progressive Party, along with a number of other members.[14]

Since Khuang had been a Promoter of the Coup and was proud of it, the Democrat Party did not assume the policy of opposing the Promoters as such. The bulk of its members was made up of the kind of conservative, formerly monarchist persons who had been the basis of the Progressive Party, however. The Democrat Party has since that time represented this group.[15] Khuang was able to hold the core of the party together through all the exigencies of politics from 1946 to 1958. It was the leading opposition to the Constitution Front up until the coup of 1947, to the United Parties until 1951, and to Seri Manangkhasila until September, 1957. The Democrat Party had a brief moment of glory between November, 1947, and April, 1948, when Khuang was Prime Minister under the aegis of the Coup d'Etat Group. It took on some of the qualities of a government party in the election of early 1948, which

---

[13] John Coast, *Some Aspects of Siamese Politics* (New York: Institute of Pacific Relations, 1953), p. 31; "Kiat," p. 88.

[14] "Kiat," pp. 91–93.   [15] Coast, pp. 33–34.

it won.[16] But the formation of the United Parties group was already in progress, and when Khuang was forced by the Coup Group to resign in April, the Democrats reverted to their role of hard-core opposition.[17]

After the reestablishment of a national assembly with half the members appointed, the Democrats decided to boycott politics, and in that assembly the role of opposition fell to an unorganized group of members mainly from the northeastern region of the country. Many of them were former supporters of Pridi. From this group a number of small parties gradually emerged in 1955. All these parties professed a leftist ideology and were ultimately brought together in a Socialist Front in 1957.[18]

The Democrat Party and the Socialist Front differ widely in the groups they represent and the ideals they profess. The Democrat Party, as has been suggested, is mainly the home of that segment of Thai elite society which aligns itself with the throne and against the personnel, but not the general purposes, of the 1932 coup. That is to say, they hold to principles of liberal constitutionalism. In contrast, the Socialist Front upholds the suppression of royal power and to a large extent the antiliberal tendencies of the coup of 1932. On the basis of its representation of the depressed northeast, it would press forward with economic development. At the same time, it opposes the foreign policy which all governments since 1947 have followed and would align the country with the Asian neutralists.

Membership in a party is extremely unstable, and parties and groups are regularly reorganized. Individual members readily move from one group to another depending upon their calculation of the situation. The domination of the assembly by

16 *Ibid.*, p. 44.   17 *Ibid.*
18 *Bangkok Post*, Jan. 16, 1957.

the executive and the weakness of political organizations have
encouraged continuing instability. Under normal conditions
the executive is insensitive and largely invulnerable to the
influence of parliamentary opposition. From the point of view
of a member there is little hope that he will be heeded, not to
mention given preferment, so long as he persists as a member
of the opposition. He must ultimately cooperate with the government if he wants to be effective, either personally or publicly. It may be to his advantage to create a public image of
himself as a clear-eyed and courageous critic of the government so that when his time comes to cooperate his bargaining
position is that much stronger and his price that much higher.
This procedure is a risky one, however, and if the opportune
moment is missed, the member may be out in the cold.

A classic example of this kind of parliamentary behavior is
to be found in the career of Liang Chaiyakan, member from
Ubon, who held his seat from 1933. Liang was one of the organizing members of the Democrat Party in 1946 and a leader
of the opposition to the governments of Pridi and Luang
Thamrong. In 1947, Liang bolted the Democrats and organized his own People's Party. After the coup of 1947 he co-
operated with the Khuang government until it was overthrown in 1948, and then he carried his People's Party into the
so-called United Parties which supported the governments of
Phibunsongkhram. After the "silent" coup of 1951 he again
returned to opposition as an adamant opponent of the Coup
d'Etat Group governments from 1952 until the election campaign of 1956–1957. After announcing his intention to campaign on the ticket of his own party he suddenly went over to
the Seri Manangkhasila Party and became one of its leading
political advisers. His reward was a ministerial portfolio in
the Phibunsongkhram government of March, 1957.

The fate of the Democrat Party between early 1948 and

1951 is an example of the weakness of party organization. In the election of the House of People's Representatives in 1948, conducted under the auspices of the Khuang government, a majority of the members returned were nominal Democrats.[19] By 1951, a reporter of the situation said that "the number of members of the Democrat Party began to diminish, although by means of what trickery it is not clear." [20] The indication is that even though, or perhaps because, an election was near, members who had been elected on the Democrat ticket seemed to have little hesitation about shifting their allegiance. At the same time the party had no resources to prevent such attrition. No party is sufficiently strong or well organized to either guarantee or deny election to any candidate.

Election Organization

The basic electoral unit is the province. Because Thailand's provinces are historically determined areas, there is considerable variation in size and population. They range from about 180 to 7,200 square miles in area and from about 20,000 to 500,000 in population. From these figures it is clear that the electoral situation is by no means uniform.

From another point of view the basic electoral unit is the candidate. No party has had anything like a national organization, and there are only a very few provincial party clubs. Candidacy has been generally open to any qualified voter although substantial deposits have been required. Although this deposit is certainly restrictive, the country has never lacked

[19] Bunchuai Sisawat, *Phantri khuang aphaiwong* ("Major Khuang Aphaiwong"; Bangkok: Rapphim Press, n.d.), p. 503.

[20] *Ibid.*, p. 566.

for candidate material. In 1957, the nationwide average was between eight and nine candidates per seat. The candidate's party affiliation, if he has one, is a matter of accommodation between him and the central committee of the party. This accommodation, of course, varies in each case and is dependent upon the candidate's strength in his province; his compatibility with party leadership in terms of personal relationships, loyalty, and general ideological tone; and various monetary considerations. In any individual case the candidate may be wooed by one or several parties, or he may have to petition party leadership to give their endorsement. There are always many nonparty candidates, and ballots have no reference to party.

Local campaign machinery is generally the problem of the candidate. In provinces where there is more than one seat, the slate of a party generally but not always works as a team. The candidate looks to his clique, made up of family and friends, as a campaigning organization. He is often, therefore, independently based and free of obligation to the central party leadership.

The difficulty of putting together a stable and permanent national party organization for election purposes may be explained by various factors. First is money. It is generally agreed by party leaders that it is almost impossible to raise an adequate supply of money in any manner which will leave the party free of crippling obligations. Money has, in fact, been raised by contributions from local businessmen on a presumably *quid pro quo* basis, by tapping the government revenues in possibly illegal ways (obviously open only to the party in power), and probably by contributions from abroad, particularly from Chinese sources, both red and white. The second factor which inhibits organizational development is the very slow growth of local elected bodies which might provide opportunities for more or less continuous exercise. This situation may be modified if provincial, municipal, and commune councils continue to develop. The final factor of importance is the weakness of the party groups in the assembly itself. With the complete dominance of the executive over the assembly, there is a premium on a member's independence and availability to make a deal. He gets his results through his influence in the government, and his major source of influence (charm excluded) is his vote. It is easier to sell one's private vote than to bolt one's party.

In any election, the temptation of the government party with no better organization than any other is to utilize the existing governmental machinery. It is quite likely that the extreme example of this technique was in the Seri Manangkhasila Party's activities in February, 1957. Since General Phao Siyanon was at the same time chief of the national police, Deputy Minister of the Interior, and secretary-general of the party, the temptation to utilize the police and Interior service organizations for campaigning was no doubt beyond the limit of human resistance. Civil servants were dragooned into party membership, and their prestige and organization were utilized throughout the country. A district officer in the south was asked if there was a close relationship between the civil service and the Seri Manangkhasila organization. Frankly, but without pride, he said, "We were the Seri Manangkhasila organization." [21]

Any future development of political parties is linked with future forms of representation in the institutions of government. Since representative institutions have been the most troublesome during the constitutional regime, it is difficult to foresee what form may be adopted in any future constitu-

[21] See Bunchuai, pp. 361–362, for a report of similar practices in 1946.

tion. It is possible that some radically new device may emerge from the Sarit interregnum, but even this cannot be assured.

Khana

Larger political organizations are pyramided from cliques. The organizers and leaders of the three great coups of 1932, 1947, and 1957, as well as those who helped in the overthrow of Phibun in 1944, have served as the nation's leaders. These events produced corresponding organizations which here will be termed *khana*, the Thai term for a semiformal group. The *khana* have assumed the role of trustee for the attainment of the purposes of the coup. Their assumption of this role applies both to the overt protection of overt purposes and to the covert protection of covert purposes. The *khana* have names and established membership and hold meetings with fixed procedures. These groups are the Promoters of the Revolution (Phu Kǫ Kan Pathiwat), the Coup d'Etat Group (Khana Rathaprahan), the Military Group (later the Revolutionary Group; Khana Thahan or Khana Pathiwat), and the Free Thai (Seri Thai). A peculiar characteristic of these groups is that although they play a public role, they are exclusive as to membership and private in their conduct. Little is directly known, except by members, of what goes on within them.

Membership in these groups is determined initially and in principle by prior participation in the *coup d'état* or comparable event. For this reason the kind of commitment mentioned above as a requirement for top leadership is necessary also for inclusion in the ruling group. The fact that all have participated in the coup at the much-proclaimed risk of life and limb creates some sort of fellowship of "friends unto death" (*phüan ruam tai*). In spite of the exclusivity of joint risk, there is some indication that as time passes other persons have been invited to join these groups. It is likely that there is an attempt to co-opt rising young men, who if not included in the group might become a threat to it.

The fellowship of these groups has at least in the case of the Coup d'Etat Group been affirmed by a solemn oath:

Under the power of the Triple Gems and before all the divine beings who have supreme might, i.e., Phra Süa Müang, Phra Song Müang, Phra Lak Müang, and also all the divine beings who reside in all places including the king of the divine beings who protects the nine-tiered white umbrella, I want to swear that in this *coup d'état* I acted with the firm intention to serve the nation, religion, and king. I acted in order to end a time of trouble and bring coolness to the nation and carry it forward toward progress. I was without personal ambition in any way at all. I intend to hold firmly in my heart the decision to maintain good honor and discipline with all my courage. I shall not do that which I should not do and I shall do that which I should do. I shall protect and maintain the unity of the group. I shall not betray or envy persons who are endowed with *khunngamkhwamdi*.[22] I shall hold firmly to this oath with a stout heart and at each breath until I die.[23]

The distinction between these *khana* and the cliques from which they are formed, the open groups such as political parties to which they are in some ways similar, and the in-

[22] This term, which might be roughly translated as virtue, beauty, and goodness, implies the characteristics of moral goodness and high status which result from high merit. It may be interpreted to mean persons of high status, i.e., the leaders.

[23] W. Čh. Prasangsit, *Pathiwat rathaprahan lae kabot čhalačhon nai samai prachathipathai haeng prathet thai* ("Revolution, *Coup d'Etat*, and Rebellion in Thailand during the Democratic Period"; Bangkok, 1949), pp. 243–244.

stitutional groups such as the army or the national assembly which they dominate lies in the characteristics of being exclusive and fraternal in nature. It would be an exaggeration to say that these groups are secret societies, and yet they clearly partake of some of the qualities of a secret society. In Thai politics since 1932 they have been the supreme in-group and virtually the sovereign power. For that reason they are, or more precisely their leaders are, the ruling group.

In the usual pattern for the formation of these groups preparatory to a *coup d'état* a number of persons come together as leaders of cliques to combine their forces. In Phraya Phahon's account of the planning for the coup of 1932 he described his coming together with Phraya Song and Phra Prasad at first. They later discovered by way of Prayun Phamonmontri that there were other groups in sympathy including

Major Phibunsongkhram with a group of officers who were connected with the general staff and officers in the artillery. There was also Captain Luang Thatmai Niyomsuk with a group of cavalry officers in the armored department. On the navy side there was Lieutenant Commander Luang Sinthusongkhramchai with a group of naval officers. On the civil side there was Luang Pradit Manutham with a big group. There were also Nai Tua Planukrom and Luang Naru Betsamanit with two more groups of civil officials.[24]

A similar process of bringing together various leaders of cliques to combine forces was followed in 1947.[25]

Therefore *khana* are not cliques, properly so called, but

[24] Kulab Saipradit, *Büanglang kan pathiwat, 2475* ("Behind the Revolution of 1932"; Bangkok: Čhamlǫngsan Press, 1947), pp. 153–154.

[25] See W. Čh. Prasangsit, pp. 153–186, for a detailed account of the recruitment of the Coup d'Etat Group and the planning of the coup.

rather clusters of cliques. The clique leaders form the leadership of the group. From among themselves they chose their
leader according to a subtle calculus of qualifications. Evidently Phraya Phahon was designated leader among the top
military officers of the 1932 group because he was senior in
age and rank. In 1947 Phibunsongkhram was designated leader.
The background of this choice is somewhat obscure in detail
because it is still maintained to this day that he personally was
not active in organizing the group. Although this may be
literally true in that he may not have taken part in the gathering of the group and planning of the coup, his fate was so
inextricably linked with the army's at that moment that his
approval of the idea was the equivalent of promoting the
attempt.

His qualifications for the position of leader have been outlined as follows:

There was no one better suited to lead the *coup d'état* than
Field Marshal Phibunsongkhram for the following reasons:

Field Marshal P. Phibunsongkhram is a man who loves the nation, the religion, the king, and the constitution very firmly.
Every soldier knows him, and he is respected by all soldiers.
When Field Marshal P. Phibunsongkhram left the positions of
Prime Minister and supreme commander, all the soldiers were
depressed and sorry. Field Marshal P. Phibunsongkhram has a
cool, shrewd, and skillful character and is endowed with broad
intelligence in politics, having held a high position in government
already. He has also conducted *coups d'état* successfully several
times [*sic*] without bloodshed.[26]

In 1957 Field Marshal Sarit's position as commander in chief
of the army was sufficient to qualify him as leader of the
Military Group.

By the nature of their origins *khana* are beyond the orderly

[26] *Ibid.*, pp. 171–172.

procedure of the law and insofar as they are successful, constitute the ultimate sovereign power. In this respect their role is analogous to that of the king and his supporting princes or ministers before the constitutional period. The public pronouncements of these groups do not explicitly claim this power, but the rationale of their actions implies it. They proclaim themselves the protectors of values higher than the working of the government. For example, in 1933 upon the overthrow of the government of Phraya Mano, it was announced that "as the action of the State Councilors in charge of the administration of the country is contrary to the provisions of the Constitution . . . the Army, Navy, and Civil services therefore find it necessary to take over control of the government.[27]

In November, 1947, on the morning after the overthrow of the government of Luang Thamrong, it was announced by the Coup d'Etat Group:

Whereas the soldiers, the officials, the civilians, the police, and the people of the Thai nation are of the unanimous opinion that in the circumstance in which the Thai nation finds itself these days the present government is not able to correct things in such a manner as to continue in a good way . . . so it is necessary to seize power and force the government to resign and set up a new government in accordance with the constitution [sic] in order to aid in cleaning up the dishonesty and evil of various kinds in the government circle.[28]

And in November, 1951, it was announced that

owing to the present state of emergency in world conditions serious Communist danger is pressing. The present Council of Ministers as well as Parliament have been unable to solve the Com-

[27] *Bangkok Times Weekly Mail*, June 20, 1933, p. 6.
[28] Bunchuai, pp. 477–478.

munist problem. Nor has it been able to stamp out the so called corruption as has been its intention. Disintegration has spread so deeply as to cause grave anxiety for the continued existence of the nation in its present political danger.

Wherefore the Army, Navy, Air Force, Police, members of the Coup d'Etat BE 2475 [1932] as well as loyal citizens, with a steadfast purpose to ensure the continuity of the nation, the Faith, and the Čhakri Dynasty as well as the constitutional regime act in complete accord and unanimity to revive the Constitution dated 10th of December 2475 [1932] for the safety and prosperity of the nation.[29]

In September, 1957, it was announced by Field Marshal Sarit that

at this time the country is in a difficult situation. If this government of Field Marshal P. Phibunsongkhram had been allowed to continue its administration of the country, there would have been only a daily increasing of difficulty for the people. The Military Group then felt that it would have been an unbearable situation if the conduct of affairs by peaceful means such as those by which they have been conducted had been continued to correct the situation. So it was unavoidably necessary to use the force of the three services to seize power from the government and to present it to the King in order that he may appoint a new government.

As for myself I have announced and demonstrated my purity to let it be seen that I hold the peace and happiness of the people to be first. Therefore when the people have suffered hardship and have called on me to correct the situation, I together with my military comrades of the three services have returned to serve you another time.[30]

[29] *Royal Thai Government Gazette* (*from the Thai Version*) (Bangkok: International Translation Service, 1951), p. 533.
[30] *Rathasapha san* ("Journal of the National Assembly"), VI, no. 37 (Sept. 21, 1957), 50–51.

In October, 1958, the following statements suggesting the attitude which justifies the action of this kind of organization are to found among others in an announcement of the Revolutionary Group:

The government had neither the time nor opportunity to gather together its thoughts and strength for the work of sustaining the country. . . . All the obstructions and dangers did not arise from having an incorrect assembly or an incorrect government. Rather they arose from undisciplined behavior which the assembly or the government could not correct with its present tools. It is necessary to construct new tools to make a way to sustain the nation according to our intentions.[31]

It is the need to set things right which is the core of the justification of the existence of these *khana.* The validity of this justification as a conscious personal motive cannot be denied out of hand in favor of more crude and hypocritical motives of self-interest. That is to say, the implementation of apparently willful and arbitrary decisions on the course of political events by sudden and forceful methods is consistent with the ultimate view of the nature of the world and politics which appears to be shared by the Thai.[32] If the world of politics has gone askew, it may be attributed to the bad will, the indiscipline, of some. Therefore a counterwill of a more forceful nature can right it and set it on a wholesome course again.

[31] "The Revolutionary Group Announces the Reasons for the Revolution," *Rathasapha san,* VII, no. 6 (Feb., 1959), 73–74.
[32] See above, Chapter III, pp. 80–81.

IX

COUPS AND CONSTITUTIONS

THE ruling class is small in Thailand. Therefore, political conflict is intimate. Moreover, it appears to have certain unspecified limits. The groups which have successively replaced each other from 1932 to 1959 have not been socially revolutionary. In fact, each succeeding group has emerged from a preceding one. The dominant group at any single time is more or less a coalition of segments of the ruling class, each of which tends to have an institutional base. It is the army-based segment which has been most successful in this political interaction. At the same time the army has not yet destroyed the bases of nonarmy segments of the ruling class although from time to time certain leaders have been eliminated from the political scene either by exile or by death.

Over the quarter century during which the political system of the kingdom has ostensibly been a constitutional monarchy, a distinguishable pattern has emerged in the interplay of the segments of the ruling class struggling to attain a dominant position. This pattern takes into account the numerous occasions of civil strife in the constitutional period; it turns upon a hypothetical psychic drive for status which provides motive power. The forms or styles of action by which this drive is realized are related to base institutions, e.g., the national assembly, the army, and so on.

Since Thai political life is organized by cliques, the motive to gain status tends to be manifested in conflicts between cliques as well as competition among individuals. Moreover, because the political system is no longer ordered by a set of traditional offices and lines of progress but under the constitutional regime has become much more complex, the stability of status has been affected. The appearance of new institutions, notably the national assembly; the introduction of new ranking systems, e.g., educational degrees; and an increased complexity of the government and urban society—these have opened a variety of paths to higher status. But no fully legitimate and successful procedure for deciding conflicting claims at the highest level has been established. The result is much tension, which often breaks out in a show of force and violence.

Force and Violence

In the process of political struggle, there have been four kinds of overt actions. Their differences lie in the effect they have upon the relationships among segments of the ruling group. These actions are (1) a shift of power,[1] (2) the at-

---

[1] The Thai term for this has been either revolution (*kan pathiwat*) or *coup d'état* (*kan rathaprahan*).

tempted coup (*kabot*), (3) the suppression of a rebellion (also *kabot*), and (4) the seizure of power (*yüt amnat*).

The shift of power involves a substantial change of ruling group including a large number of "permanent" government officials. Such shifts are climactic events. There have been four such shifts in modern times—the coups of 1932, 1947, and 1957 and the overthrow of the Phibun government in 1944. On each of these occasions there was a dramatic shift from one ruling group to another as well as a major shake-up in the top positions of the bureaucracy.[2]

The shift of power requires the active or tacit cooperation of a number of segments of the ruling group in the effort to overthrow the existing regime. Such cooperation depends upon the mobilization of public opinion against the ruling regime in terms of a number of real or imagined complaints. Public opinion is moved and stimulated by every means of communication open to the opposition groups, including newspapers, parliamentary debate, public speeches, rumor, and private communication. The points of attack upon the ruling regime may range from the magical (e.g., the rumor current in 1932 that the Čhakkri dynasty was destined to rule for only 150 years), through political (e.g., the high cost of living in 1947), to personal (e.g., the reports in 1957 that General Phao was a drunkard and Phibun an old lecher). The sum effect of this effort at public opinion molding is to undermine the prestige of the ruling regime, to break the spell of its power, and to create an atmosphere of crisis, uneasiness, and expectation.

In such an atmosphere conspirators come together to plan a coup. It may be imagined that there are always some such adventurous souls, particularly in the military, prepared to

[2] See Net Khemayothin, *Chiwit nai phon* ("Life of a General"; Bangkok: Phadung Süksa Press, 1956), p. 14.

risk all to seize the main chance. There is no way of estimating the number of cabals which have discussed these possibilities. As has been mentioned above, since 1932 there have been four which tried and succeeded and four which tried and failed. On the basis of the four successful coups, it would appear that sufficient influence in the army units in Bangkok is normally the *sine qua non* of success. In the case of the overthrow of the Phibunsongkhram government in 1944 the peculiarities of the situation, in particular the presence of Japanese troops in the country and the recognition by both the Pridi and Phibun sides that the Japanese were losing the war, inhibited the army. Rather than risk further commitment to the Japanese or, alternatively, Japanese intervention, the army was willing to bide its time.

The conspiratorial group, which in case of success will become the *khana*, does not include all those segments of the ruling group which are opposed to the regime. The coalition of segments which participate in the mobilization of public opinion does not correspond completely to the *khana* which emerges from the coup. For example, in both 1947 and 1957 the Democrat Party group attacked the government in newspapers and in the assembly, but neither the Coup d'Etat Group of 1947 nor the Military Group of 1957 included the Democrats.

When the conspirators feel themselves ready, they make their move to take power. The taking of power is accompanied by the dissolution of the displaced regime. This process often involves the exiling of the top leaders (e.g., Prince of Nakhọn Sawan in 1932, Pridi Phanomyong in 1947, and Phibunsongkhram and Phao Siyanon in 1957; in 1944, again because of the special circumstances, there were no exiles). A number of second-level followers of these top leaders are retired from office while the lines of influence of the displaced regime are destroyed by the transfer of other loyal followers in the government service to less influential positions.

A successful shift of power is followed by a period of conciliation of various important groups, the bureaucracy as a whole, the foreign community, and the public at large. The formation of postcoup governments under the prime ministership of men outside of the *khana* itself is the outstanding indication of such conciliation. In 1932 Phraya Mano, in 1944 and in 1947 Khuang, and in 1957 Phot were all invited to rule by the group which put over the coup. This practice demonstrates to the sensitive public that the coup was not motivated by crass seeking for advantage. In addition to the formation of an ostensibly disinterested government, the incoming group invariably makes public and private assurances to the bureaucracy and to the foreign embassies that the change in government represents no threat to their interests. The elaborate ceremony of apology and reconciliation between King Rama VI and the Promoters of the Coup of 1932 which took place on December 7, 1932, is an outstanding example of conciliation.[3] Moreover, it is characteristic that the incoming group always seeks and receives an amnesty from the throne and legal enactments authorizing ex post facto their actions.

In effect the period of conciliation is a repetition in reverse of the period of arousing public opinion which precedes the actual coup. The people and the specially concerned groups are calmed, and the new group seeks to establish an impression that it is well in control. By means of the activities which take place in this period, the incoming group legalizes and legitimates itself. It is at this time that it fulfills the requirements of a decision of the Supreme Court of Appeals on the appeal of defendants convicted of attempting the overthrow of the government: "The overthrow of a previous government

[3] *Bangkok Times Weekly Mail,* Dec. 12, 1932, p. 24.

and establishment of a new government by the use of force are perhaps illegal in the beginning until the people are willing to accept and respect it." [4] The receptivity of the public to this process of reconciliation is an extraordinary element in the Thai political system. It would appear that such receptivity is not merely resignation in the face of the inevitable but rather the belief that coups are right and proper. There may be incidental complaints as to methods, but ultimately even those most committed to law and order incline to accept coups as the proper way to right the world's wrongs.[5] Such an attitude must be related to the conception of the world as a structure of beings with their proper orders of virtue and power which are controlled by their wills. It is conceivable that such a world can get out of its proper order and that it can be righted by the act of a superior will. In some way the place of these sudden political strokes can be explained in these terms, for after a coup it is as if a sigh of relief passed through the political community.

During this phase of the shift of power, cooperation reigns among segments of the ruling class. At times of a crisis the pressure is strong for all segments to submerge their differences and to commit themselves to one side or the other. Thus in 1957 there was a tacit coalition among Khuang and his Democrat followers, the Socialist Front, the army, and the Sarit fac-

[4] *Decisions of the Dika, BE 2495* (AD 1952) 1153–1154/95 (Bangkok: Ministry of Justice, 1953), p. 1.

[5] Perhaps the most extraordinary revelation of Thai thinking on this matter, as well as on constitutionalism and the place of the national assembly, was contained in a draft amendment to the constitution offered in Feb., 1958. The draft to amend the section on termination of membership in the assembly said that "a coup or any other action which results in changing and overthrowing of the Government and/or proclamation of a new constitution resulting in changing and overthrowing of the Government does not terminate membership in the Assembly" (*Bangkok Post*, Feb. 21, 1958).

tion to overthrow the Phibun-Phao leadership. This coopera-
tive relationship rapidly falls away after a successful coup.

It is replaced by conflict and competition for the rewards
of political status—position, fame, and money. Within the
group in power there is competition for these rewards. After
a coup the incoming group must move to consolidate its position by taking control of key bureaucratic positions, which
in addition to the cabinet and other "political" posts would
include military commands and police and other control departments. Loyal members of the group are put in these positions. A parliamentary group must be organized along the
lines discussed in Chapter VIII. The incoming regime in general appears to tie to itself as many bureaucrats, parliamentary
politicians, and persons of influence as it can. This is accomplished by the distribution of rewards or promises of rewards
in the form of position, money, or opportunity to enhance
one's position or fortune. The need to provide financial and
status rewards creates a pressure for new sources of money
and new offices.

This pressure is at the root of much of the high-level corruption and bureaucratic capitalism. In the past decade there
has been an extraordinary infiltration of political power into
the business world along with a number of practices such as
the granting of certain monopolies and the formation of public
enterprises which can be lumped together under the term
bureaucratic capitalism. Thai politicians—like human beings
everywhere—have an understandable desire to be rich. In
part, however, the motive for promoting such activities may
lie in the special problems of political organization which
demand almost endless supplies of rewards.

It is during this period of the consolidation of power that
the incoming group is likely to be challenged most seriously
by alternative ruling groups. The attempted coup needs little

explanation—it is a concerted effort to overthrow the existing ruling group by force and replace it with another group. The first of these attempted coups was the Bǫwǫradet rebellion in 1933 which was suppressed by a combined force under the command of Phibunsongkhram. Between 1948 and 1951 there were three attempts. The first in October, 1948, was nipped in the bud by the police under the command of Phao Siyanon.[6] The second, in February, 1949, involved brief but sharp fighting in Bangkok and was suppressed by the army under the command of Sarit Thanarat.[7] The third took place in June, 1951, and there was hard fighting for three days between the army and air forces on the one hand and naval ground forces on the other before the navy's attempt to take power was suppressed.[8] During the period from 1944 to 1947, there were no outbreaks of fighting, although plans were rumored.[9] In effect the coup of 1947 revealed the impotence of the ruling group to suppress a determined attempt to overthrow it.

In contrast to serious attempts to overthrow the ruling group, there have also been a number of "rebellions" which were suppressed with a flourish and are of a different nature. These incidents appear to have been initiated by the ruling group or its dominant element for the purpose of suppressing other troublesome or rival elements. It is, of course, difficult

[6] Udom Utraphonlin, in *Kabot 1 tula 91* ("Rebellion of October 1, 1948"; Bangkok: Odeon Store Press, 1950), gives documents and details of this affair.

[7] W. Čh. Prasangsit, *Pathiwat rathaprahan lae kabot čhalačhon nai samai prachathipathai haeng prathet thai* ("Revolution, *Coup d'Etat*, and Rebellion in Thailand during the Democratic Period"; Bangkok, 1949), pp. 298–369.

[8] Thai Noi, in *Kabot 29 mithunayon* ("Rebellion of June 29"; Bangkok: Odeon Store Press, 1955), gives documents and details.

[9] "Kiat," pseud., *Phongsawadan kan müang* ("Political Chronicles"; Bangkok: Kiatthisak Press, 1950), pp. 46–48.

to be sure in some cases, but clear-cut examples are the Phraya Song rebellion of 1938,[10] the Luang Kat rebellion of 1950,[11] and the Peace Rebellion of 1952.[12] In the first example a number of military officers and civilians, including Phraya Song Suradet, who had been one of the four top leaders of the 1932 coup, were arrested, tried, and convicted. The initiative for this action seems to have come from Phibunsongkhram, who was by then Prime Minister and wished to root out remnants of antagonistic cliques in the army. The result was the execution, imprisonment, or exile of the defendants. In 1950, Luang Kat Katsongkhram, a leading figure in the 1947 coup, was suddenly arrested by General Phao Siyanon and hustled out of the country. The explanation was that Luang Kat was plotting rebellion. In late 1952 a number of persons, mainly newspapermen and prominent Chinese, were arrested and charged with rebellion. The distinction between this type of incident and the attempted coup does not concern the innocence of those who are opposed to the government either as aggressor or victims. Rather it is a matter of which side takes the initiative. The effect of these challenges, insofar as they are unsuccessful, is to expedite the process of consolidation of power. Thus the potential countercoup from the direction of substantial opponents is an incalculable factor. But after the showdown of strength, as in the Bǫwǫradet rebellion and the incidents of February, 1949, and June, 1951, the successful suppression of the challenging side at one and the same time eliminates a threat and confirms the psychological effect of success.

The seizure of power seems to be the effort by which the

[10] *Bangkok Times Weekly Mail*, Feb. 6, 1939, p. 23.
[11] John Coast, *Some Aspects of Siamese Politics* (New York: Institute of Pacific Relations, 1953), pp. 54–55.
[12] *Bangkok Post*, Nov. 10, 1952, and following issues.

new ruling group seals the consolidation of its position and moves to change the rules. The most clear-cut instances of this kind of seizure of power were in the amendment of the constitution and election of the upper house in 1946, the "silent" coup in 1951 which reinstated the 1932 constitution, and the establishment of the military dictatorship and the interim constitution in late 1958 and early 1959. In incidents of the 1930's, the process was not so clear-cut because it was the Mano government which tried to change the rules by closing the assembly in April, 1933. The overthrow of Phraya Mano in June, 1933, and the assumption of the Prime Minister's office by Phraya Phahon was a declaration by the Promoters of the Coup that it was their interpretation of the rules which would prevail.

The Constitutions

Periodically in the process of shifting factions and cliques new written constitutions have been introduced. Evanescence has been the most notable quality of the constitutions of Thailand, and as a result it is almost impossible to take these documents very seriously. The basis of this legal kaleidoscope must be sought in the interplay of factions and alternative regimes and the difficulties arising from changing regimes. It is clear that Thailand has in its 30 years of constitutional government fallen into a very curious practice which might be called *faction* constitutionalism. The outstanding feature of this is the drafting of a new constitution to match and protect each major shift in factional dominance.

With the advantage of some historical perspective, it is

possible to see that the course of Thai politics since 1932 (perhaps since the succession to the throne of Rama VII) has involved the manipulation of the public law to protect the regime in power from that which has been ousted. The *coup d'état* of 1932 was the action of one group of government officials (mainly nonroyal) against another group of officials (mainly royal). The constitution of December, 1932, made provisions both to bar royalty from any attempt to gain popular support (Section 11 said that princes were to remain "above politics") and to ensure the complete control of the parliament and cabinet by the People's Party (in the provision for appointing half the members of the parliament for a decade).

There is no intent in this analysis to suggest conscious duplicity in the explanations given at the time for these two provisions, for there is unquestionably merit both in the idea that the dignity of the royal family should be preserved and in the idea that the revolutionary regime could with justice claim a decade to establish itself and to manage the precedent-setting elected assembly. On the other hand, it is too much to believe that in a nation where politicians are so sensitive to the nuances of power relationships the authors of these provisions were not fully aware of the protection for their tenure implied therein.

By the end of World War II the group which promoted the 1932 coup had fallen to pieces and the parade of shifting factions began in earnest. Pridi Phanomyong, whose sources of strength appear to have been largely oratorical and parliamentary, sought to shift more power into the hands of elected officials in the assembly. His establishment of an elected Senate was planned to provide a place of honorable retirement for the formerly appointed members of the assembly. In the course of events, however, the fact that he packed the Senate with his own loyal followers through his overwhelming majority in the newly elected assembly was unquestionably a source of consternation to his rivals.[13]

When Pridi's power was overthrown by the *coup d'état* of 1947, it was not feasible for the Coup Group to continue the old Senate filled with Pridi's supporters. The leaders of the coup therefore had no alternative but to overthrow the constitution even though this in effect gave the final mortal blow to the ideal that the constitution was the framework of politics and could be changed only by orderly procedures. It was set aside by decree, and a hastily drafted provisional document was put in its place.

The constitutional assembly which drafted the constitution of 1948 was heavily weighted with those favoring the Democrat Party of Khuang Aphaiwong. It is not surprising, then, that in the form of national assembly provided for in the 1948 constitution the interests of that group were protected although not made dominant. The Democrat Party had more influence in the royal court than any other group was likely to have, and its interests were well represented in the royally appointed upper house. At the same time the Democrats had proved quite successful at the polls and could expect to hold a substantial number of seats in the lower house as well.

The group then in power, based mainly in the army and police, had come to be dominant among the military by the middle of 1951 while at the same time it was having difficulty managing its affairs in the assembly. It evidently appeared to them much more convenient to return to the system of appointing half of a single house rather than continue with the existing system. The change of constitution took place by a mere announcement over the radio. Since the change was designed to protect the ruling group from the need to satisfy

[13] "Kiat," pp. 98–101.

some of its supporters and was not occasioned by any major change in the power situation, this may well be the most extreme example of faction constitutionalism. By this time the bitter factional fighting of the postwar years had subverted the constitution to the exigencies of the moment and the expedient interests of the dominant group.

In September, 1957, when the Sarit Military Group overthrew the government of Field Marshal Phibunsongkhram, the constitution was momentarily suspended and then reestablished. The effect of this was to remove the members of the assembly appointed by the ousted government and permit the appointment of a new group. The elected portion was, of course, also dissolved.

The seizure of power in October, 1958, culminated in another constitution (provisional) which legislated a configuration of institutions adapted to the intentions of the Sarit group. The assembly of this constitution was concurrently charged with the functions of general legislation and of drafting a new constitution.[14]

It is clear from a summary of constitutional history (see Table 2) that written constitutions are not venerated in themselves. The idea of a constitution was introduced into a prior and vital political system with a fully developed body of legislation, a powerful structure of government, and a vigorous bureaucratic tradition. The process of the introduction of the constitution was itself revolutionary and contrary to the concept of orderly constitutional procedures. In such a setting, it is to be expected, perhaps, that the force of the documents is not dominant.

Moreover, because of these prior conditions, constitutional instability in certain respects is more apparent than real. The kingdom may in fact be said to have had at any given moment

[14] See Appendix B.

Table 2. Summary of constitutional history, 1932–1961

Constitution	Date of promulgation	Circumstances of introduction	Circumstances of drafting
Provisional constitution	June 27, 1932	Revolution of June 24, 1932	Said to have been drafted by Pridi Phanomyong
Constitution of the Kingdom of Siam (B.E. 2475)	Dec. 10, 1932	Promulgated by the king on an auspicious day	Drafted by a committee of the provisional national assembly
Constitution of the Kingdom of Siam (B.E. 2489)	May 9, 1946	Revision of the constitution under the direction of Pridi Phanomyong in order to abolish the appointed members and create a second chamber	Drafted by various committees under Pridi Phanomyong's supervision
Provisional constitution	Nov. 9, 1947	*Coup d'état* over throwing Pridi Phanomyong's power	Drafted by Luang Kat Katsongkhram, leader of the coup

Constitution of the Kingdom of Siam (B.E. 2491)	March 23, 1949	The Coup Group had promised a new constitution as part of its effort to gain legitimacy and support	Drafted by a constitutional commission of 40 persons chosen by the national assembly elected in 1948; the commission was strongly conservative
Constitution of the Kingdom of Thailand (B.E. 2475; as revised 2495)	Feb. 26, 1952	After the "silent" coup in Nov., 1951, the Coup d'Etat Group sought to reinstitute the 1932 permanent constitution; after royal objection various revisions were made	Revisions drafted by a cabinet committee in consultation with the king and discussed and approved by members of the national assembly appointed in Nov., 1951, by the Coup d'Etat Group

Table 2. Summary of constitutional history (*cont.*)

Same	Sept. 16, 1957	Constitution suspended and reestablished with a new slate of appointed members	Reestablishment of existing constitution after the coup of the Military Group against the Phibunsongkhram regime
Constitution (Interim) of the Kingdom of Thailand (B.E. 2502)	Jan. 29, 1959	After the *coup d'état* of Oct., 1958, the military regime proclaimed a provisional constitution of which one element was an appointed constitutional commission	Drafted by the Military Group's adviser

in the past quarter century two constitutions. In addition to the ephemeral written one, there has been a substantial structure of law and custom which has remained as the foundation upon which government rests. The monarchy, the bureaucracy, the courts of law, and the law codes have traditional roots and genuine substance and continuity which make them institutions of considerable stability. Besides the institutions there is a broad consensus that there is in fact a nation of Thailand, united by language and aspiration, that the state is a proper organic part of the nation, and that the state shall seek the people's well-being and happiness.

Beyond this broad consensus there is also agreement that the government is sovereign. It has the legitimate authority to rule. A most remarkable demonstration of this simple fact of Thailand's politics was the decision of the Supreme Court of Appeals (already quoted in part):

The overthrow of a previous government and establishment of a new government by the use of force is perhaps illegal in the beginning until the people are willing to accept and respect it. When it is a government in fact, which means that the people have been willing to accept and respect it, any person who attempts by rebellion to overthrow that government violates the criminal law.[15]

This decision is remarkable, of course, in that in appearance it legalizes successful *coups d'état*. To read such meaning into the decision, however, would reduce the law to nonsense. A more fruitful inference may be to see this as a recognition of the real fact that the government as an institution is sovereign and he who controls it is legitimate.

Why is it, since particular constitutions have been so unstable, that there is continued adherence to the idea of a written

[15] *Decisions of the Dika,* p. 1.

constitution? The answer has two parts. First of all, after 30 years the institutions created by the constitutions, in whatever form, have become so much a part of the lives of the stable ruling group that it is unlikely that they can imagine any alternative. Thus the national assembly, the cabinet, and the nonpolitical throne have taken on a vitality even though their precise forms and interrelations may be in dispute. The second part of the answer is closely related to the first. Constitutionalism in the historical context of Thailand is associated with, even though it may not be the root cause of, certain real political accomplishments. The most conspicuous of these is the maintenance of the throne as a point of stability, at least symbolically, among the shifting factions. This could not be done if the throne were not constitutionally as well as effectively excluded from politics. Moreover, the maintenance of the assembly as an outlet for political expression must be counted an accomplishment.

Uses of Elections

Elections have been a necessary concomitant of maintaining the national assembly. The first general election for the national assembly was held in 1933 after the constitutional revolution. In the succeeding years there have been eight general elections, and Thailand has accumulated considerable experience in electoral machinery. The fact of the matter is that in the mechanics of polling, the experience has been quite successful. A fairly simple balloting procedure has been developed which the public is able to grasp.

On any level but the mechanical, however, considerable confusion and no small degree of dissatisfaction have surrounded the election experience as a whole. In the quarter century of constitutionalism, the country has been governed under not only seven constitutions but six electoral laws as well. Interrelated with this profusion of legalism and the eight general elections have been the various *coups d'état* and unsuccessful rebellions. These facts indicate that the period has been characterized by a groping for political forms and stability. In the search the technique of election is only one of several alternative methods for selecting and stabilizing political leadership. So far it has had little success in this role. The drama and flamboyance of the military coup and the armed rebellion should not, however, be misunderstood. Thailand does take its elections seriously. But like so many borrowed forms in use there, the content and meaning are *sui generis*.

The political atmosphere and situation which condition the holding of campaigns and elections are important, particularly because elections are not by any means a matter of routine. For example, in the postwar years three out of five general elections have been held in the shadow of, and in a direct relationship with, a *coup d'état*. The election of 1948 was held immediately following the coup of November 8, 1947, and was one of the promises that the Coup Group made to the public. It was held under a provisional constitution and under a provisional government headed by Khuang, and no one was sure whether he could control the military. As it turned out, he could not. Even though he won a majority in parliament, he was turned out at gun's point two months after the election.

The election of 1952 was held immediately after the "silent" coup of November, 1951. The coup, which reestablished a half-appointed assembly, was directed against the elected members of the House and is assumed to have been motivated by the frightening thought that another election might so strengthen the assembly that military control could be threatened.

The election of December, 1957, was required as a result of the coup of September, 1957. It was held under the administration of a provisional government which did not put itself up for election and under the benign eye of Field Marshal Sarit who also stood aside from the hurly-burly of the campaign. In the other two elections of the postwar years—1946 and February, 1957—a strong government ostensibly had its head on the block. As was suggested before, a government in that position is inclined, in the face of possible defeat, to utilize without inhibition or restraint the organizational and fiscal opportunities that incumbency offers. In 1957 this helped to precipitate the disaster that was already in the making.

Elections have a variety of functions the world over, of course. What uses may they be said to have in Thailand? If the standard of excellence of a national election is to present to the electorate a clear-cut and meaningful set of alternatives on some political issue, then Thailand does not come up to standard. A choice of leadership would be the only meaningful issue in Thailand at present, and no election has ever presented the possibility of altering leadership.

Elections may have other uses, however. Perhaps the most tangible of these is the opportunity to drain off excess political energy, of which Thailand has its share. This energy is being directed more and more to the national level by a broader educational system and a loosening of social barriers. Elections provide an outlet for ambition and a real, if limited, opportunity to rise in the scheme of things. The binding of the nation into a closer system will continue to be a function of elections.

But there is a more direct effect of the electoral process upon political leadership at the present time. Although leadership is determined by other means, and policies and government actions are decided in other quarters, elections are not unimportant. They are one of the principal forms of legitimation of the ruling group. Many segments of the Thai nation, and particularly the Thai bureaucracy, feel the need for legitimacy in their leaders. The Thai appear to conceive of the state of political nature as a Hobbesian jungle in which hungry men struggle for power. With such a conception, it is not surprising that there is also a strong need for law and legitimacy. The present political system is a legal and spiritual heir of the absolute monarchy which was legitimated by magico-religious conceptions manifested and sustained ceremonially. In the present system, popular sovereignty legitimates and this conception is sustained by constitutional trappings of which the ceremony of elections is an indispensable part.[16] Therefore the fact that there is little effort to read any political meaning into election results is of no consequence to any but the few most politically sophisticated.

[16] See Herbert P. Phillips, "The Election Ritual in a Thai Village," *Journal of Social Issues*, XIV, no. 4 (Dec., 1958), 38–50, for the story of elections in the countryside.

X

CONCLUSION

THE alarums and excursions of Thai political life, the coups and countercoups, the constitutional shuffling, and the madcap elections suggest chaos wrapped in confusion. At the same time a slightly more penetrating observation reveals the persistence of the same leaders, much of the same law, and most of the same institutions year after year. The most extreme *coups d'état* have brought to power not the same people but their protégés or former associates. New constitutions have repeated much of the old, word for word. The state of affairs appears to be a paradoxical stable instability, an inconstant constancy.

What, then, are the impulses for movement? What are the forces for change? What is the shape of stability? The stability of Thai society—which is the bedrock of Thai politics—is to be explained by its simple structure, consisting of an extremely large agrarian segment and a small ruling segment. These two groups interact in a tenuous manner so that the smaller does not irritate the larger. The character of the relationship between the two must be fully appreciated in order to understand the stability of the arrangement. The rural agrarian segment is separated geographically from the urban ruling segment. The agrarian segment is, in the main, land-owning and survives by a quasi-subsistence economy. The ruling segment is salaried (when its members own property, this is usually urban or suburban) and lives on a cash economy. The cash for government comes from levies on rice exports and transaction taxes on imported goods which fall indirectly on the agrarian segment. The agrarian segment is uneducated (though not illiterate), and the ruling group is educated. This general social arrangement is explained by an ideology which is based on the principle of differential moral worth manifest-ing itself in differential status and experience. Thus the society of the Thai is characterized by a gross two-class structure, in which the classes are physically as well as economically sepa-rated and differential status is satisfactorily justified. The effect of this is a paucity of interests in the socioeconomic sense impinging on the political process. Direct relationships be-tween these two social segments are maintained through the district office, which is highly formal and socially (and often geographically) distant. The more intimate economic rela-tionship concerned in transfer of goods and services between town and county takes place through Chinese traders. These people as aliens are easily contained politically and at the same time serve the ruling group as a scapegoat for whatever hostilities the condition of the market may arouse in the rural segment.

There are forces for change present in Thailand. Agricul-ture has been tending for a century to become more com-mercialized. Mass education is providing a medium for under-mining the traditional ideology. Business grows in importance and becomes more assimilated to a national economy. Embryo industry with its working class is developing. But up to the present the slow pace of these tendencies and the assimilative capacities of the ruling group have kept these forces—which are, indeed, fundamental—from getting out of control.

Life does not stand still. There must be movement. The political man—he who would maximize his political status—is at the center of political movement. His judgments about the political situation and his efforts to change it provide the dynamic conflict which can result in movement. This political man is a hypothetical figure here because this work is not a psychological study. Yet because of the explicit importance of status in the Thai social structure and the reinforcing effect of the high ethical value of freedom from the dominations of other wills, political man may be partially realized in the Thai political system.

Political status in Thailand is not conceived of as merely power to dominate others, however. Rather it is a complex of position, fame, and money which combine to mark clearly the high position of the individual. Into the calculation of status may go the number of a man's subordinates, the extent to which his name is known and respected, the amount of goods and rewards he can distribute to followers. Judgment of status is ultimately subjective for all concerned.

Because his status is the mark of his moral worth and the symbol of his spiritual development, it is reasonable to hypothesize a psychological inclination to maximize these social and political attributes. Two circumstances may be set forth as most conducive to dissatisfaction and to stimulation of struggle—a clear opportunity to rise and a possibility of being surpassed by a manifestly "unworthy" equal.

The structure of this process is comprised of the associations of agencies of the government. The interests of these agencies are only marginally divergent, and therefore the changes brought about by their clashes are in the main personal.

Underlying political conflict in the past three decades is a pattern of recurrent tensions. These tensions, which are inter-related, must be looked at from different viewpoints to distinguish their various elements. Some 30 years ago the bu-reaucracy—much strengthened by the reorganization and de-velopment of the previous 40 years and by the new techniques of communication and control imported from the West—was cut free of the restraints of absolutism. This operation was carried out by the bureaucracy itself. As much as the leader-ship of the Thai revolution might have wished things to be otherwise, it was not able to muster much popular interest outside the bureaucracy upon which to base itself. As a result, politics has become a matter of competition between bureau-cratic cliques for the benefits of government. In this compe-tition the army—the best organized, most concentrated, and most powerful of the branches of the bureaucracy—has come out on top. When the monarchy faltered and royal authority was overthrown, the focus of the ideological framework from which moral purpose and direction were drawn was thrown over as well. The rather alien idea of popular control of the state was substituted for the ancient and admittedly limited and outworn monarchism. But parliamentary democracy, as a process wherein diverse aroused social interests are expressed through organizations outside the government and are syn-thesized by representative institutions into a statement of the public power, has not emerged in Thailand. Interest groups, such as they are, remain weak because Thailand rests firmly on a traditional agrarian socioeconomic base. Because the tra-ditional Thai rulers retained their autonomy in the face of Western imperialism and because a plenitude of land per-mitted an adjustment to the world of exchange by the expansion of rice culture, they had the opportunity as well as the ability to moderate the effect of an intrusive world of commerce and industry. Since the society remains relatively undifferentiated in this way, interest groups, public corporations, and free institutions are effectively lacking.

Thus the ideal of popular sovereignty and representative government failed to take life, and politics was without a moral focus. The government—ruling in an ambiguous moral position—has become a kind of bureaucratized anarchy. The various departments of the government seek to expand their activities and compete for the resources of the state. But the allocations of these resources, not by a hierarchy of values but rather by the relative power of the units, inevitably result in compromise and efforts are spread thin. Direction and purpose have been lost.

Moreover, the removal of the throne from politics in 1932 by no means ended traditional attitudes toward authority. As has been indicated elsewhere in this study, these attitudes persist in the psychological context of social relations. Because the ruling group has its origins in the traditional bureaucracy, it relies on these attitudes, bolstered by the manipulation of loyalty with rewards and punishments, to control the government.

The loss of direction and purpose, the moral ambiguity of authority, and the imperatives of strengthening and extending loyalties have all tended to corruption. By current standards ancient government, since it used its power primarily to maintain itself, was a kind of "corruption." Its two activities, war and ceremonial, were to a large extent private matters. But the extent of this "corruption" was limited by the static nature of society and the difficulties of making power effective over distance. Ideology was, of course, also a limitation. In the more dynamic society of commerce the opportunities for state activity and regulation are vast. With the breakdown of discipline and the pressure of inflation, the bureaucracy of Thailand seized these opportunities for personal enrichment. In the past 10 years, the use of public power for personal benefit has become both widespread and institutionalized.

But the breakdown of morale has not been complete by any means. One should not imagine that the ruling class is unusually deficient in public spirit. There is considerable revulsion against corruption even as it is going on. The wish for stability and the will to do good are strong. These sentiments have slowed down corruption to a large extent. The Thai ruling class may also be aware of the possible death of the goose that lays the golden egg.

Furthermore, the ideal of popular sovereignty and egalitarian representative government—whether genuinely or opportunistically adhered to—lies behind the constitution and thereby justifies the rule of bureaucrats rather than of the king. But this ideal is at odds with the traditional psychology. The national assembly, the institutionalization of the egalitarian ideas, is therefore a convenient base for challenging the bureaucratic rulers. A national assembly, insofar as it is elected, can resist the less subtle forms of authority. The members rest on their own bases of power; they show a tendency toward insubordination and are a source of trouble to the rulers. In recent years their stentorian demands have been calmed only at a high price in offices, privileges, or bribes. Moreover, the control of this undisciplined element has been sufficiently difficult to warrant closing the assembly periodically.

But up to the present the ruling bureaucrats have not dared abolish the national assembly. Their path to power by means of *coups d'état* is irregular, and their legitimacy is open to question. In order to gain legitimacy, the trappings of constitutional government must be maintained. Nevertheless, the constitutions have not successfully conformed to the fundamental configurations of the Thai political system. No recognition has ever been given the fundamental fact that governments are based in the bureaucracy rather than outside the government. Not institutionalizing this bureaucratic source of power, the constitutions have failed to provide for orderly succession from one group to another.

The court's reservation that the "establishment of a new government by the use of force is perhaps illegal *in the beginning*" (italics supplied) points to this area of difficulty which lies behind Thailand's constitutional instability. At issue is the question, how is the sovereign power to be gained by an individual or group and under what conditions is it to be held and used?

The irregularity of modes of gaining power contributes to a tension over succession. Thus a displaced leader such as Field Marshal Phibun in 1944 or Dr. Pridi in 1947 is not inclined to accept his irregular loss of power with equanimity. By the same token emergent leaders approaching the moment of decision, such as Field Marshal Sarit and General Phao in 1957, are likely in their anxiety to precipitate a crisis. The problem of the transfer of power from one individual or group to another is a matter of struggle and difficulty in any political system. One of the great values of a constitutional system is its solution of this problem. In an authoritarian system, because the establishment of personal authority is a delicate process, succession is most trying. But the Thai combination of irregular authority and ineffectual constitutionalism takes the worst of two worlds.

The problem still remains a matter of bringing the state machinery under some disciplining power to give it again a firm and directed purpose. Thailand has fallen between absolutism and popular democracy. There is no clear road backward or forward. Thai political analysts conceive of the problem as one of transition. They tend to see it as a matter of time, good will, and good men and not in terms of building bases of power and expressions of will outside the state machinery. Yet the self-control of bureaucracy appears to be declining rather than otherwise. It is difficult, indeed, to see a way out of the cliquism and corruption until some such extragovernmental power appears.

Whether or not a sense of legitimation and a constitution could be devised to give order and legality to this process is another matter. Under the temporary constitution of 1959 Marshal Sarit Thanarat has attempted to shift that burden of justification for his rule from constitutionalism to national peril—in the not-unconvincing guise of Hanoi, the Pathet Lao, and Prince Norodom Sihanouk—and to national economic development. Nevertheless, those groups in the ruling class, particularly elected politicians, who represent a challenge to bureaucratic rule have again been raising questions about a permanent constitution and a return to some form of elections. These expressions indicate that a return to absolutism even with a fairly high degree of royal support will not satisfy the political public.

Pressures that countervail the tightening of control by the bureaucrats, under Marshal Sarit's leadership, may be expected to develop along one of two lines. Plans for economic development may be implemented sufficiently fast to bring about a gradual mobilization of people into institutions other than governmental and thereby broaden the base of the political public. Such a development could add the discipline of manifest and explicit interest to the political process and solidify the function of representative institutions. On the other hand, a sudden revolutionary collapse of the traditional attitudes blocking massive popular participation in politics is not impossible. The generation of constitutional government since 1932 has created within the groups of parliamentary politicians, journalists, and intelligentsia a cadre of potential popular leadership which, under sufficient inducement, perhaps could and would disrupt the consensus which sustains the ruling class and move to arouse the peasants. Political science is incapable of predicting the circumstances under which such a change in structure will take place. Nevertheless, there are signs of incipient demands among the rural population; and increasing penetration of education into the lives of these people, along with improved transport, communications, and irrigation facilities, may, indeed, be weakening the hold of tradition.

Appendix A

POLITICAL CHRONOLOGY,

1932-1959

June 24, 1932	Revolution
June 27, 1932	Government of Phraya Mano
April 1, 1933	Mano *coup de main*
June 20, 1933	People's Party countercoup
June 22, 1933	Government of Phraya Phahon
Oct. 12–27, 1933	Bǫwǫradet attempted coup
Nov.–Dec., 1933	General election
April 5, 1934	Roundup of alleged rebels
March 6, 1935	Abdication of Prachathipok; Ananda succeeds
Nov. 7, 1937	General election
Nov. 12, 1938	General election
Dec. 10, 1938	Government of Luang Phibunsongkhram
Jan. 29, 1939	Phraya Song Suradet rebellion
Dec. 8, 1941	Japanese invasion
July 26, 1944	Phibunsongkhram resigns
Aug. 1, 1944	Government of Khuang Aphaiwong

Aug., 1945	Government of Tawi Bunyakhet
Sept. 7, 1945	Government of Seni Pramoj
Jan. 6, 1946	General election
Jan., 1946	2d government of Khuang Aphaiwong
March 24, 1946	Government of Dr. Pridi Phanomyong
June 9, 1946	Death of Ananda; Phumiphon succeeds
Aug. 24, 1946	Government of Admiral Thamrong Nawasawat
Nov. 8, 1947	*Coup d'état*
Nov. 11, 1947	3d government of Khuang Aphaiwong
Jan. 29, 1948	General election
April 6–7, 1948	*Coup de main* against Khuang
April 8, 1948	Return to office of Prime Minister by Field Marshal Phibunsongkhram
Oct. 1, 1948	General staff attempted coup
Feb. 26, 1949	Pridi Phanomyong attempted coup
June 26, 1951	"Manhattan" attempted coup
Nov. 29, 1951	"Radio" or "silent" coup
Feb. 26, 1952	General election
Oct., 1952	Roundup of Peace Committee or Peace Rebellion
Feb. 26, 1957	General election
Sept. 16, 1957	Military Group *coup d'état*
Sept. 28, 1957	Government of Phot Sarasin
Dec. 15, 1957	General election
Jan. 9, 1958	Government of General Thanom Kitthikhačhon
Oct. 21, 1958	Revolutionary group coup
Feb. 9, 1959	Government of Field Marshal Sarit Thanarat

Appendix B

CONSTITUTION (INTERIM) OF THE KINGDOM OF THAILAND, 1959

HIS Majesty King Phumiphon Adunyadet is graciously pleased to make known that

WHEREAS the Leader of the Revolutionary Party, after the successful seizure of power on October 20, B.E. 2501, has represented to him that the abrogation of the Constitution of the Kingdom of Thailand, B.E. 2475 as amended in B.E. 2495, was actuated by the desire to acquire an appropriate Constitution and to achieve greater improvements in the national administration than would have been feasible under the former Constitution:

AND WHEREAS to attain this end, it is deemed expedient to set up a Constituent Assembly composed of qualified members to draft a new Constitution; but pending the promulgation of such a Constitution it is deemed appropriate to enact an interim Constitution to meet the present needs and conditions:

His Majesty the King, approving these resolves and in order to give effect to the proposals of the Leader of the Revolutionary Party, hereby graciously commands that the following provisions be promulgated and enforced as the Constitution of the Kingdom of Thailand pending the Constitution to be drafted by the Constituent Assembly:—

Article 1. The sovereign power emanates from the Thai people.

Article 2. Thailand is a Kingdom, one and indivisible, with the King as Head of State and Commander in Chief of the Armed Forces of the Kingdom.

Article 3. The person of the King is sacred and inviolable.

Article 4. There shall be a Privy Council consisting of not more than nine persons who shall be appointed and relieved of their duties at the King's pleasure.

Article 5. The King shall enact laws by and with the advice and consent of the National Assembly.

The Council of Ministers exercises the executive power, and the Courts of Law exercise the judicial power in the name of the King.

Article 6. A Constituent Assembly, which has the function of drafting a constitution, shall be constituted and shall concurrently act as the National Assembly vested with the legislative power.

Article 7. The Constituent Assembly consists of 240 members appointed by the King.

Upon a vacancy of membership the King shall appoint a person to fill the vacancy.

Article 8. In accordance with the resolution of the Constituent Assembly, the King appoints from among its members a President and one or more Vice-Presidents.

Article 9. Subject to the provisions of Articles 10 and 11, the Constituent Assembly has the power to set up rules of procedure on the presentation of bills and motions, its sittings and deliberations, and other matters.

Article 10. On the completion of the drafting of the Constitution by the Constituent Assembly it shall sit as the National Assembly to resolve whether the draft Constitution can be submitted to the King for the Royal Signature prior to being promulgated. At such a sitting the Constituent Assembly shall not make any amendment to the draft Constitution.

At such a sitting as mentioned in the foregoing paragraph, not less than three-fourths of the total number of members is required to constitute a quorum.

The promulgation of the Constitution shall be countersigned by the President of the Assembly.

Article 11. In the case of failure to obtain a majority vote of more than half the total number of members of the Constituent Assembly in favor of submitting the draft Constitution to the King for the Royal Signature, in accordance with Article 10, the Constituent Assembly shall redraft the Constitution in accordance with the provisions of the present Constitution.

Article 12. At any sitting of the Constituent Assembly words uttered by members whether in making a statement of facts, expressing an opinion, or casting a vote are absolutely privileged. No action or charge whatsoever can be brought against them for such utterances.

This privilege extends to the printing and publication of the minutes of the sittings of the Assembly by its express order.

Article 13. In the case of a member of the Constituent Assembly being imprisoned or placed under detention or having a criminal charge brought against him, he shall be released or the trial shall be suspended upon the request of the President of the Constituent Assembly.

Article 14. The King appoints a Prime Minister and an

appropriate number of Ministers forming the Council of Ministers responsible for the national administration.

The Prime Minister and Ministers shall be excluded from membership of the Assembly.

The Prime Minister and Ministers have the right to attend a sitting of the Assembly to make statements of facts or express opinions, but they have no right to cast votes.

Article 15. The King holds the prerogative of relieving Ministers of their posts.

Article 16. Before the Council of Ministers is formed, the Leader of the Revolutionary Party shall discharge the duties of the Council of Ministers and the Prime Minister.

Article 17. During the enforcement of the present Constitution, whenever the Prime Minister deems it appropriate for the purpose of repressing or suppressing actions whether of internal or external origin which jeopardize the national security or the Throne or subvert or threaten law and order, the Prime Minister, by resolution of the Council of Ministers, is empowered to issue orders or take steps accordingly. Such orders or steps shall be considered legal.

All orders issued and steps taken by the Prime Minister in accordance with the provisions of the foregoing paragraph shall be made known to the National Assembly.

Article 18. Every law, Royal Rescript, and Royal Command relating to affairs of state shall be countersigned by the Prime Minister or a Minister.

The appointment of the Prime Minister shall be countersigned by the President of the Assembly.

Article 19. Judges are independent in conducting trials and giving judgments in accordance with the law.

Article 20. In the case where no specific provisions of the present Constitution are applicable, decision shall be based on Thai constitutional practices.

In cases where decisions in accordance with the previous paragraph are controversial and pertain to the affairs of the Assembly or where the Council of Ministers refers matters to the Assembly for decision, the Assembly shall decide the questions.

Countersigned by

FIELD MARSHAL SARIT THANARAT

Leader of the Revolutionary Party

BIBLIOGRAPHY

Newspapers and Periodicals

Bangkok Post
Bangkok Times Weekly Mail
Bangkok World
New York Times
Rathasapha san ("Journal of the National Assembly")
Thai raiwan ("Daily Thai")
USIS Press Section Summary of Editorials and Special Articles from the Thai Language Daily Newspapers, Bangkok (mimeographed)

Laws and Documents

"Act on the Organization of the Office of the President of the Council of Ministers, B.E. 2502 (1959)," *Royal Thai Government Gazette (from the Thai Version)*, LXXVI, pts. 24–25 (Feb. 28, 1959), 123–128.

"Act on the Organization of the Office of the President of the Council of Ministers (no. 7), B.E. 2503," *Royal Thai Government Gazette (from the Thai Version)*, LXXVII, pts. 30–31 (May 14, 1960), 226–232.

Constitution of the Kingdom of Thailand 2475 (1932) as amended 2495 (1952).

Decisions of the Dika, BE 2495 (AD 1952), 1153–1154/95. Bangkok: Ministry of Justice, 1953.

Final Report of the Demographic and Economic Survey, 1954. Vol. I. Bangkok: Central Statistical Office, Office of the National Economic Development Board, 1959.

Manual of Organization of the Government of Thailand. Bangkok: Institute of Public Administration. (In draft.)

Raingan kan prachum sapha phuthaen ratsadǫn ("Reports of the Meetings of the House of People's Representatives").

Royal Thai Government Gazette (from the Thai Version). Bangkok: International Translation Service, 1951.

Sathian Lailak *et al.*, compilers. *Prachum kotmai pračham sok* ("Collection of the Laws Arranged by Year"). Bangkok: Daily Mail Press, 1935 and occasionally thereafter. (Cited as *PKPS*.)

"Phrarachabanyat ken thahan, R.S. 124" ("Act on Drafting Soldiers, 1905"), *PKPS*, XX, 302–314.

"Phrarachabanyat kep ngoen kharachakan, R.S. 120" ("Act on Collecting Money for Government Service, 1901"), *PKPS*, XVIII, 224–230.

"Phrarachabanyat laksana ken čhang, R.S. 119" ("Act on the Forms of Draft and Hire, 1900"), *PKPS*, XVII, 528–531.

"Phrarachabanyat rathamontri, R.S. 113" ("Act on the Council of State"), sec. 1, *PKPS*, XIV, 214.

"Phrarachabanyat that" ("Slavery Act"), *PKPS*, XX, 24–26.

"Prakat kan nai thi prüksa rachakan phaen din" ("Announcement on Affairs of Advising the Government"), *PKPS*, VIII, 169–170.

"Prakat phoemdoem phrarachabanyat laksana ken čhang" ("Announcement of an Amendment to the Act on Forms of Draft and Hire"), *PKPS*, VIII, 230–231.

"Prakat plian thamniam mai" ("Announcement of a Change of Rules"), *PKPS*, VIII, 114–117.

"Prakat tang tamnaeng senabodi" ("Announcement of Appointment to Positions of *Senabodi*"), April 1, 1892, *PKPS*, XIII, pt. 2, 93–98.

"Prakat wa duay tang khaosin lae phrarachabanyat" ("Announcement about Establishing a Council and an Act"), *PKPS*, VIII, 115.

Thailand, Ministry of Finance, Economic Survey Group. *Report on Economic Development Plans*. Bangkok, 1957. (Mimeographed.)

Thailand, National Economic Council. *Statistical Year Book of Thailand*. Bangkok, 1952.

"Thalaengkan" ("Announcement"), *Royal Thai Government Gazette (from the Thai Version)*, Special Edition, vol LXVIII, pt. 71, Nov. 30, 1951.

Thalaengkan rüang phrabat somdet phraboromintramahaprachathipok phra pokklaočhaoyuhua song sala rachasombat ("Announcement concerning the Abdication of King Phrapokklao"). Bangkok, 1935.

General

Asawaphahu (Rama VI). *Kan phai nai müang čhin* ("Affairs in China"). In *Pramuan bot phrarachaniphon nai phrabat somdet phramongkut klao čhaoyuhua* ("Collection of Royal Writings of Rama VI"). Bangkok: Fine Arts Department, 1955.

Asawaphahu (Rama VI). *Khlon titlǫ* ("Mud on the Wheels"). In *ibid*.

Asawaphahu (Rama VI). "Khwam khaochai phit" ("A Misunderstanding"). A letter dated 1915.

Asawaphahu (Rama VI). *Mai chop thai* ("Don't Like Thai"). In *Pramuan bot phrarachaniphon nai phrabat somdet phramongkut klao čhaoyuhua* ("Collection of Royal Writings of Rama VI"). Bangkok: Fine Arts Department, 1955.

Asawaphahu (Rama VI). *Thukbangkhap hai pen čhin* ("Forced to Be Chinese"). In *ibid*.

Bowring, Sir John. *The Kingdom and People of Siam*. 2 vols. London: J. W. Parker and Son, 1857.

Bunchuai Sisawat. *Phantri khuang aphaiwong* ("Major Khuang Aphaiwong"). Bangkok: Rapphim Press, n.d.

Čhaofa prachathipok ("Prince Prachathipok"). Bangkok: Surirat Press, 1949.

Charoen Chaiyachana. *Sangkhom Süksa* ("Social Studies"). Bangkok: Thai Wathana Phanit, 1952.

Čharun Kuwanon. *Chiwit kan tǫsu khǫng bukkhon samkhan* ("Lives of Important People"). Bangkok: Aksǫn Čharoen That Press, 1953.

Čharun Kuwanon. *Chiwit kan tǫsu khǫng bukkhon samkhan songkhram* ("The Life and Struggle of Field Marshal P. Phibunsongkhram"). Bangkok: Aksǫn Čharoen That Press, 1953.

Christian, John L., and Ike, Nobutaka. "Thailand in Japan's Foreign Relations," *Pacific Affairs*, XV (1942), 195–221.

Čhulalongkǫn, King (Rama V). *Phraboromarachathibai rüang samakhi* ("Royal Lecture on Unity"). Bangkok: Fine Arts Department, 1946. First delivered about 1903.

Čhulalongkǫn, King (Rama V). *Phrarachadamrat nai phrabat somdet phračhulačhomklao čhaoyuhua song thalaeng phraboromrachathibai kaekhai kanpokkhrǫng phaen din* ("Royal Address of His Majesty King Čhulačhomklao Explaining Changes in the Government"). Bangkok: Fine Arts Department, 1950.

Coast, John. *Some Aspects of Siamese Politics*. New York: Institute of Pacific Relations, 1953.

Damri Pathamasiri. *Samkhan thi phu nam* ("Mark of the Leader"). Bangkok: Bangkok Municipality Press, 1939.

Damrong Rachanuphap, Prince. "The Introduction of Western Culture in Siam," *Journal of the Siam Society*, XX (Oct., 1926), 89–100.

Damrong Rachanuphap, Prince. *Khwam songčham* ("Memoirs"). Bangkok: Klang Witthaya Press, 1951.

Damrong Rachanuphap, Prince. "Laksana kan pokkhrǫng prathet sayam dae boran" ("Ancient Forms of Government in Siam"). In *Chumnum phraniphon (bang rüang) khǫng somdet krom phraya damrongrachanuphap* ("Collection of the Writings

[Some Selections] of Prince Damrong Rachanuphap"). Bangkok: Government Lottery, 1957.

Damrong Rachanuphap, Prince. *Phrarachaphongsawadan krung rathanakosin rachakan thi 5* ("Royal Chronicles of the Bangkok Dynasty, Fifth Reign"). Bangkok: privately printed by Samosan Sahamit, 1951.

Damrong Rachanuphap, Prince. *Prawat bukkhon samkhan* ("Biographies of Important People"). Bangkok: Phrae Bhithaya Co., 1953.

Damrong Rachanuphap, Prince. *Thesaphiban* ("Administration"). Bangkok: Klang Witthaya Press, 1952.

Detchard Vongkomolshet. "The Administrative, Judicial and Financial Reforms of King Chulalongkorn, 1868–1910." M.A. thesis, Cornell University, 1958.

Dhani Niwat, Prince. "The Old Siamese Conception of the Monarchy." In *The Siam Society Fiftieth Anniversary Commemorative Publication—Selected Articles from the Siam Society Journal.* 2 vols. Bangkok: Siam Society, 1954.

Dhani Niwat, Prince. "The Reconstruction of Rama I of the Čhakkri Dynasty." In *Rüang phrabat somdet phraphuttha yotfa čhulalok song fünfu wathanatham* ("On the Cultural Reconstruction of Rama I"). Bangkok: printed by Sana Bunyasiriphan, 1957.

Düan Bunnak. *Than pridi rathaburut awuso* (Mr. Pridi, Elder Statesman). Bangkok: Soemwithaya Banakhan, 1957.

Düan Bunnak and Phairot Chaiyanam. *Kham athibai kotmai ratthathammanun kap kotmai lüak tang* ("Lectures on the Constitution and the Election Law"). Bangkok: Thammasat University, 1935.

Embree, John F. "Thailand—A Loosely-structured Social System," *American Anthropologist,* LII (1950), 181–193.

Fifield, Russell H. *The Diplomacy of Southeast Asia, 1945–1958.* New York: Harper and Brothers, 1958.

Graham, Walter A. *Siam.* 2 vols., 2d ed. London: Alexander Moring, Ltd., 1924.

Griswold, A. B. *King Mongkut of Siam.* New York: The Asia Society, 1961.

Guyon, René. *The Work of Codification in Siam.* Paris: Imprimerie Nationale, 1919.

Haas, Mary Rosamond. "The Declining Descent Rule for Rank in Thailand: A Correction," *American Anthropologist,* XXIII (Oct.–Dec., 1951), 585–587.

Hall, D. G. E. *A History of South-East Asia.* London: Macmillan and Co., 1955.

Hanks, Lucien M., Jr. "The Cosmic View of Bang Chan Villagers." Paper presented to the Pacific Science Conference, Bangkok, Dec., 1957.

Hanks, Lucien M., Jr., and Phillips, Herbert P. "A Young Thai from the Countryside." In B. Kaplan, ed., *Studying Personality Crossculturally.* Evanston, Ill.: Row, Peterson and Co., 1961. Pages 637–656.

Heine-Geldern, Robert. *Conceptions of State and Kingship in Southeast Asia.* (Southeast Asia Program, Cornell University, Data Paper no. 18). Ithaca, N.Y., 1956.

Ingram, James C. *Economic Change in Thailand since 1850.* Stanford, Calif.: Stanford University Press, 1955.

International Bank for Reconstruction and Development. *A Public Development Program for Thailand.* Baltimore: Johns Hopkins Press, 1959.

Janlekha, Kamol Odd. *A Study of the Economy of a Rice Growing Village in Central Thailand.* Bangkok: Ministry of Agriculture, 1955.

Kasem Udyanin and Smith, Rufus D. *The Public Service in Thailand.* Brussels: International Institute of Administrative Sciences, 1954.

Kassebaum, John C. *Economic Farm Survey, 1953.* Bangkok: Ministry of Agriculture, 1955.

"Khon Khaw Itsara," pseud. *Büang lang khadi lüat yuk asawin phayǫng* ("Behind the Bloody Affair of the Period of the Bullying Knights"). Bangkok: Sombun Woraphong at Aksǫrabǫrikan Press, 1957.

Khuang Aphaiwong. *Kan tǫsu khǫng khaphačhao* ("My Struggle"). Bangkok: Pramuansan, 1958.

Khükrit Pramoj, M. R. "The Social Order of Ancient Thailand (II)," *Thought and Word*, I (March, 1955), 10–18.

Khükrit Pramoj, M. R., *et al. Čhomphon nai thatsana khǫng khaphačhao* ("My Opinion of the Field Marshal"). Bangkok: Wibunkit Press, 1949.

"Kiat," pseud. *Phongsawadan kan müang* ("Political Chronicles"). Bangkok: Kiatthisak Press, 1950.

Kiat Thanakhum, "Naew kan borikan rachakan phaendin nai yuk pathiwat" ("Methods of Administration in the Revolutionary Period"), *Rathasapha san* ("Journal of the National Assembly"), March, 1960, pp. 10–23; April, 1960, pp. 34–44.

Kulab Saipradit. *Büanglang kan pathiwat, 2475* ("Behind the Revolution of 1932"). Bangkok: Čhamlǫngsan Press, 1947.

Kumut Chandruang. *My Boyhood in Siam*. New York: John Day Co., 1940.

Landon, Kenneth P. *Siam in Transition*. Chicago: University of Chicago Press, 1939.

Lapomarède, Baron de. "The Setting of the Siamese Revolution," *Pacific Affairs*, VII (Sept., 1934), 251–259.

LeMay, Reginald Stuart. *An Asian Arcady*. Cambridge, Eng.: W. Heffer and Sons, Ltd., 1926.

Luang Nathabanja. *Extra-Territoriality in Siam*. Bangkok: Bangkok Daily Mail, 1924.

Luang Vichitr Vadakarn. *Thailand's Case*. Bangkok: Thammasat University, 1941.

McFarland, George Bradley. *Thai-English Dictionary*. 1st American ed. Stanford, Calif.: Stanford University Press, 1944.

Madge, Charles. *Village Communities in Northeast Thailand*. New York: UNTAA, 1956.

Maha-ammattayathibodi, Phraya. "Rüang Mahatthai" ("On Interior"). In *Anusǫn nüang nai ngan chalong wan thi ralük sathappana krasuang mahatthai khroprop 60 pi bǫribun* ("Memorial Volume on the Occasion of the Sixtieth Anniversary of the Ministry of the Interior"). Bangkok: Ministry of the Interior, 1952.

Manich Jumsai. *Compulsory Education in Thailand.* (UNESCO Studies in Compulsory Education, VIII). Paris: UNESCO, 1951.

Moffat, Abbot Low. *Mongkut, the King of Siam.* Ithaca, N.Y.: Cornell University Press, 1961.

Mosel, James. "Thai Administrative Behavior." In William Siffen, *Toward the Comparative Study of Public Administration.* Bloomington, Ind.: Indiana University, Department of Government, 1957.

Nathawut Suthisongkhram. "Sapha kanphaendin nai müang thai" ("Government Councils in Thailand"), *Rathasapha san* ("Journal of the National Assembly"), vol. VI, nos. 25–31 and 34–43 (June–Oct., 1958).

Net Khemayothin. *Chiwit nai phon* ("Life of a General"). Bangkok: Phadung Süksa Press, 1956.

Net Khemayothin. *Ngan tai din khọng phan-ek yothi* ("The Underground Work of Colonel Yothi"). Bangkok: Thanakan, 1957.

Phairot Chaiyanam. *Khamathibai kotmai rathathammanun priap thiap* ("Lectures on Comparative Constitutional Law"). 2 vols. Bangkok: Thammasat University, 1952.

Phibunsongkhram, Field Marshal. Message. In Thailand, Ministry of Defense, *Wan kọng thap bok, 2498* ("Army Day, 1955"). Bangkok: Ministry of Defense, 1955. Unpaged.

Phillips, Herbert P. "The Election Ritual in a Thai Village," *Journal of Social Issues,* XIV, no. 4 (Dec., 1958), 38–50.

Phin Chunhawan, Field Marshal. Message. In Thailand, Ministry of Defense, *Wan kọng thap bok, 2498* ("Army Day, 1955"). Bangkok: Ministry of Defense, 1955. Unpaged.

"Phrarachadamrat" ("Proclamation"), 1911. Quoted in S. Wathanaset, *Kiatthikhun phramongkut klao* ("The Virtue of Rama VI"). Bangkok: Watthana Phanit, 1957.

Phumiphon, King. Message. In Thailand, Ministry of Defense,

Wan kǫng thap bok, 2498 ("Army Day, 1955"). Bangkok: Ministry of Defense, 1955. Unpaged.

Pickerell, Albert G. "The Press of Thailand," *Journalism Quarterly*, XXXVII, no. 1 (Winter, 1960), 83–96.

Prachuap Thǫngurai. *Sin yuk müt* ("End of Darkness"). Bangkok: Phrayun Phitsanakha, 1957.

Prasangsit, W. Čh. *Pathiwat rathaprahan lae kabot čhalačhon nai samai prachathipathai haeng prathet thai* ("Revolution, *Coup d'Etat*, and Rebellion in Thailand during the Democratic Period"). Bangkok, 1949.

Prasoet Suphamatin. *Kotmai pokkhrǫng* ("Administrative Law"). Bangkok: Thammasat University, 1937.

Pridi Phanomyong. *Khao khrongkan sethakit khǫng luang pradit manutham lae phraborom rachawinitchai* ("The Economic Plan of Luang Pradit Manutham and the Royal Criticisms"). Bangkok: Samnak phim S. Silapanon, 1956.

Reeve, W. D. *Public Administration in Siam*. London and New York: Royal Institute of International Affairs, 1951.

"The Revolutionary Group Announces the Reasons for the Revolution," *Rathasapha san* ("Journal of the National Assembly"), vol. VII, no. 6 (Feb., 1959).

Sanguan Tularak. Speech. *Bangkok Times Weekly Mail*, June 28, 1932.

Sathian Phantharangsi. *Phramongkutklao lae čhaofa Phecharat* ("King Rama VI and Princess Phecharat"). Bangkok: Phrae Phitthaya Press, 1939.

Sawai Sutthiphithak. *Dr. pridi phanomyong kap kan pathiwat* (Dr. Pridi Phanomyong and the Revolution"). Bangkok: Sirithamnakhǫn, n.d.

Sayre, Francis B. "Siam's Fight for Sovereignty," *Atlantic Monthly*, CXL (Nov., 1927), 674–689.

Seni Pramoj, M. R. "King Mongkut as a Legislator," *Journal of the Siam Society*, vol. XXXVIII, no. 1 (Jan., 1950).

Sharp, Lauriston, ed. *Thailand*. New Haven: Human Relations Area Files, Inc., 1956.

300 *Bibliography*

Sharp, Lauriston, *et al. Siamese Rice Village.* Bangkok: Cornell Research Center, 1953.

Skinner, G. William. "Chinese Assimilation and Thai Politics," *Journal of Asian Studies,* XVI (Feb., 1957), 237–250.

Skinner, G. William. *Chinese Society in Thailand: An Analytical History.* Ithaca, N.Y.: Cornell University Press, 1957.

Skinner, G. William. *Leadership and Power in the Chinese Community of Thailand.* Ithaca, N.Y.: Cornell University Press, 1958.

Skinner, G. William. "Overseas Chinese in Southeast Asia," *Annals of the American Academy of Political and Social Science,* CXXI (Jan., 1959), 136–147.

Smith, Nicol, and Clark, Blake. *Into Siam.* New York: Bobbs-Merrill Co., 1946.

Suriyabongse, Dr. Luang. *Buddhism in Thailand.* Bangkok: Phrae Bhithaya Co., n.d.

Thai Noi. *Kabot 29 mithunayon* ("Rebellion of June 29"). Bangkok: Odeon Store Press, 1955.

Thai Noi. *Phraya phahon.* Bangkok: Phrae Phitaya and Odeon Store, 1954.

Thailand, Ministry of Defense. *Thi ralük wan sathapana krasuang kalahom 8 mesayon 2430—8 mesayon 2495* ("In Commemoration of the Anniversary of the Ministry of Defense, April 8, 1887—April 8, 1952"). Bangkok: Ministry of Defense, 1952.

Thailand, Ministry of Defense. *Wan kong thap bok* ("Army Day"). Bangkok: Ministry of Defense, 1955.

Udom Utraphonlin. *Kabot 1 tula 91* ("Rebellion of October 1, 1948"). Bangkok: Odeon Store Press, 1950.

Vella, Walter F. *The Impact of the West on Government in Thailand.* Berkeley and Los Angeles: University of California Press, 1955.

Wales, Horace G. Quaritch. *Ancient Siamese Government and Administration.* London: Bernard Quaritch, Ltd., 1934.

Wales, Horace G. Quaritch. *Siamese State Ceremonies.* London: Bernard Quaritch, Ltd., 1931.

Wan Waithayakǫn, Prince. "Pathǫkatha rüang kan lüaktang" ("Lecture on Elections"). In *Khumü rabop mai* ("Handbook on the New Regime"). Bangkok: compiled and printed by Bunthǫng Lekhakhun, 1934.

Wathanaset, S. *Kiatthikhun phramongkut klao* ("The Virtue of Rama VI"). Bangkok: Watthana Phanit Press, 1957.

Young, Ernest. *The Kingdom of the Yellow Robe*. Westminster: Archibald Constable, 1898.

INDEX